UNIX® Applications Programming:
Mastering the Shell

UNIX® Applications Programming: Mastering the Shell

Ray Swartz

SAMS

A Division of Macmillan Computer Publishing
11711 North College, Carmel, Indiana 46032 USA

International Standard Book Number: 0-672-22715-0
Library of Congress Catalog Card Number: 90-61476

Acquisitions Editor: *Scott Arant*
Development Editors: *C. Herbert Feltner and Linda Sanning*
Manuscript Editor: *Sara Black*
Production Editor: *Andy Saff*
Illustrator: *Don Clemons*
Cover Artist: *Tim Amrhein*
Production: *Jill D. Bomaster, Sally Copenhaver, Travia Davis,
Susan Hill, Tami Hughes, William Hurley, Diana Moore, and
Marybeth Wakefield*
Indexer: *Hilary Adams*
Technical Reviewer: *Rebecca Thomas, PhD*
Compositor: *Cromer Graphics*

Printed in the United States of America

*This book is dedicated to my wife, Rita,
who has inspired much of the work I've done
in the last ten years.*

Overview

Part 4   *Creating Applications with UNIX Tools*

Appendixes

Contents

Part 1
Getting Started

Part 2
Using UNIX Tools

3 UNIX Filters   41

4 The *grep* Command   47

5 Regular Expressions   57

Part 3

Bourne Shell Programming

Part 4
Creating Applications with UNIX Tools

19 The *awk* Programming Language   315

20 Mail Merge, UNIX Style   345

Foreword

by Rebecca Thomas, Ph.D.

The UNIX System comes equipped with many powerful features, including a hierarchical file system to organize data; compatible file, device, and interprocess I/O to streamline access to operating system facilities; user-selectable command interpreters (shells); hundreds of utility programs; and several language systems. All this power can be harnessed and directed to help you develop useful applications.

The ability to solve your problems using the supplied utility programs in conjunction with the shell has been touted as one important reason for using the UNIX System. However, there isn't much literature available on writing shell-level applications. Sure, several books on shell programming have been published, but they generally don't provide examples of the significant programs you might design in your everyday work.

Ray Swartz has helped fill this void for several years by teaching shell programming training seminars and in his writing. His most notable work on this subject includes the ''Doing Business with UNIX'' columns, which appeared in *UnixWorld* magazine (April 1986 through December 1988), and now this book, which teaches you shell programming while presenting several useful business-oriented applications.

Ray effectively shows you how to program with the shell and how to use UNIX system tools through a series of step-by-step examples designed to be entered at the terminal. As you read through the text, the examples evolve naturally—just like an experienced programmer might design and code them. This approach demonstrates programming techniques as the related concepts are covered in the book. As an extra bonus, the many exercises (with solutions) throughout the earlier chapters let you apply your understanding of the material and help you gain new insights. Enjoy.

Dr. Thomas is System Software/Tutorial Editor for UnixWorld *magazine and the author of several books on the UNIX System. Her most recent title, coauthored with Rik Farrow, is* UNIX Administration Guide for System V.

Preface

Since 1981, I have worked directly with computers, as a college instructor, consultant, programmer, seminar leader, magazine editor, newsletter publisher, and book author. Most of that time has been spent on, and occasionally fighting with, the UNIX System. As both a user and a teacher of the UNIX System, I have come to rely on and appreciate many of its features. This book is an attempt to share what I have learned and my enthusiasm for UNIX.

The book contains three parts. Part 1, "Getting Started," serves as an introduction and provides a look at the underlying design of the UNIX System. I discovered that once I understood why UNIX works the way it does, I was able to make more sense of it. The first chapter provides a look at how UNIX works. The second chapter delves into the interactive features of the UNIX Bourne shell.

Part 1 also focuses on several of the utility programs included in the UNIX System. Each major tool—`grep`, `sort`, `sed`, and `awk`—is discussed in its own individual chapter, and another chapter explains how to create meaningful applications by tying these tools together into pipelines. Because most UNIX tools process text, an entire chapter is set aside to cover regular expressions, a common text-based language used among the UNIX tools. Part 1 concludes with a brief discussion of several of the additional text tools.

Part 2, "Bourne Shell Programming," moves the focus from tools back to the shell, and covers shell programming in depth. Besides describing the shell's programming features, Part 2 also demonstrates techniques for creating useful applications. Part 2 ends with an abbreviated look at `awk`'s programming language.

Part 3, "Creating Applications with UNIX Tools," tries to answer the question, "Now that I know all this stuff, what do I do with it?" Each chapter in Part 3 describes a different application that is created using only the features covered in the book. The purpose of Part 3 is to demonstrate techniques for handling those everyday problems that deserve a computer solution but that are not so important as to warrant a lot of time to implement.

Among the important features of this book are the exercises that appear in Chapters 2 through 18. These exercises serve two purposes. First, they let you test your understanding of the material covered and see whether you can apply it. Second, they show you how different features of the UNIX System can be used effectively. The solution for every exercise is in Appendix D. To get the maximum benefit from this book, you should work as many of the exercises as you can.

Currently, three major UNIX shells are available, the Bourne, Korn, and C shells. This book only covers the Bourne shell. The reason for this is that, regardless of which shell you use, you have access to the Bourne shell. Thus, everyone who works on a UNIX System can use this book, and the information and techniques covered in this book will be useful to you regardless of which shell you decide to use.

This book is not intended as an introduction to UNIX. I wrote this book for people who are already experienced UNIX users. Therefore, I assume that readers know how to use `ls`, `rm`, `cp`, `mv`, `cd`, `vi` (or some other editor), `cat`, `date`, `more` or `pg`, `pwd`, `who`, `mkdir`, and `rmdir`. If you do not feel confident using these commands, you should read a more introductory text before attempting this one.

The UNIX System is undergoing a great deal of change as the marketplace and different standards organizations vie to create a single version of UNIX that is used worldwide. I believe that no matter how UNIX evolves, the information in this book will remain relevant. Undoubtedly, some of the minor points will change. But, by and large, I expect the UNIX System of tomorrow to look a great deal like the UNIX System of today.

No book is written only by the person whose name is on the cover. There are many people that help edit the rough drafts and encourage the author when the going gets tough. I would like to single out four people whose help made writing this book a good deal easier. Chuck Jaffee, a fellow trainer and friend, reviewed much of the book and provided many insightful thoughts that made this book much better. Thanks, Chuck. Also, my wife, Rita Risser, listened to my complaints with a smile, always urging me to continue on and do my best.

I would like to thank Dr. Rebecca Thomas, who provided a sounding board for many of the examples and ideas expressed here. She deserves thanks for another reason also. As the System Software and Tutorial editor of *UNIXWorld Magazine*, she has edited my monthly columns and steadily improved my writing skills, in both English and UNIX.

In the 12 months that it has taken to write this book, I also ran Berkeley Decision/Systems, a C and UNIX training company. In this year, I delivered approximately 100 full days of training. Between the book and the seminars, I haven't spent much time in the office. However, Richard Heintze has. I want to thank Rich for running everything so smoothly, which allowed me time to write and speak.

This book has had three editors. Scott Arant was the editor who accepted my proposal and saw the project through its early stages. Herb Feltner took over after Scott was promoted to a new job. Just as I was finishing the book, Linda Sanning took over. I want to thank all three of them for the professional manner in which I have been treated and for their support.

Last, I would like to thank the thousands of people who have attended my seminars and read my columns. I have had the good fortune to test my thoughts and explanations on you. This book contains the ones that worked. Many of you may still remember the ones that didn't.

Although these people helped me, I am responsible for what is written in this book. I have tried to make the explanations crisp and the examples complete. If I have failed, it is not for lack of trying.

However, books, like programs, are shipped with bugs. If you find one or would like to communicate with the author, please write to Ray Swartz, P.O. Box 2528, Santa Cruz, CA 95062.

## Part One

GETTING STARTED

The most important part of any book is introducing readers to what they need to know before they start. This is the purpose of the next two chapters. The first chapter provides an overview of the data processing model used by the UNIX System. The second chapter gives you a detailed look at how the UNIX shell works.

1

Computer Incompatibilities

Computers are known for being incompatible. It seems as if every machine has its own combination of connectors, cables, storage and display hardware, system commands, and software. Even though computers all do pretty much the same things, they all seem to do them in different ways.

As a consultant for several years, I've spent a good deal of time working with different computers. I've used IBM and Univac mainframes, UNIX minicomputers, and micros running UNIX, Apple, CP/M, and MS-DOS operating systems. It seemed that every time I needed to access another new machine, I had to relearn virtually everything I knew about computers. For example, almost every computer has its own way of listing files currently available to the user. Here are some of the ones I've encountered:

```
prt,t
ls
dir
listf
catalog
Dir,f1
```

Becoming fluent in the local dialect every time a new assignment came around wasted much of my time and other people's money. What's more, it is very frustrating to know what you want to do but not know how to do it. Thus, not only was I constantly being reeducated, but I was also not as productive as I should have been.

This problem came to an abrupt end when I started working with the UNIX System. Because UNIX has been ported to almost every machine, I suddenly found that no matter what machine I worked on, all the commands were virtually the same. It is gratifying to sit at a computer and bring 10 years of experience to bear on a problem without having to worry about how to issue the simplest commands.

A Portable Operating System

One of the main design objectives of the UNIX System was to create a computing environment that is consistent across different hardware configurations. In other words, the designers wanted to make UNIX a portable operating system. The first step in learning how to use the UNIX System is to understand its underlying design.

Before we continue, we should clarify what is meant by a *portable operating system*. The dictionary definition of *portable* is "capable of being carried or moved." When "portable" is applied to a computer program, it means that the application can be executed on (i.e., moved onto) different computers with little or no modification to the source code.

We must use a different standard when talking about operating systems. Because an operating system actually runs a computer, it must know a great deal about the computer hardware it controls. Given the differences between CPU chips, bus designs, and other computer hardware features, the chances are small that an operating system could be moved from one machine to another with "little or no modification." Operating system portability means that the software has been designed to minimize the changes required to transport it to a new computer.

Assumptions About Computers

To minimize porting requirements, UNIX insulates itself from any special features of a particular piece of hardware. In fact, the more "generic" UNIX is, the more portable it will be. Put another way, the fewer capabilities that UNIX requires from a computer, the less UNIX has to depend on any specific hardware characteristic.

The result is that UNIX assumes the hardware it runs on is a very simple computer. The UNIX System is then built on the few capabilities supplied by such a machine. The idea is that every computer providing a minimal number of features should be capable of supporting the UNIX System.

The first assumption UNIX makes is that a computer consists of two things: processes and data. A *process* is a currently executing program. *Data* is everything else.

Processes

UNIX is a multiprocessing operating system. This means that several processes can be executed simultaneously. Most computers have only one central processing unit (CPU), although some have several. A single CPU can execute only one process at a time. A computer with four CPUs can run four processes concurrently. The number of CPUs is of no concern to UNIX. This is because UNIX is a *time-sharing* operating system. That is, UNIX keeps track of all the processes *ready* to run and executes each one for a fraction of a second, sharing the available CPU time among the executing processes. If there are more CPUs, there is more CPU time to share.

The UNIX System defines a process as an instance of an executing program. If the same program is being executed twice, it requires two processes. Everything done on a UNIX System is done by a process.

For something to be called a computer, it must have the capability to execute processes. However, computers offer different hardware peripherals, such as disks (hard, floppy, CD), tapes (9-track, ¼-inch cartridge, and others), terminals, modems, mice, networks, and dozens of other input, output, and storage devices. How is UNIX able to handle each individual computer's devices and remain portable at the same time? UNIX does it by ignoring them.

Data

The designers of UNIX made a limiting assumption with regard to the data handled by the UNIX System. To generalize how data is handled, all data on the UNIX System is represented by a *stream of characters*. Thus, regardless of how the data is generated or stored, it moves through the UNIX System a character at a time.

Because all data looks alike, UNIX doesn't have to be concerned about the details of how the data is stored or retrieved. UNIX doesn't care which device generates the data, as long as the data still looks like a stream of characters. The same is true for output to a device. UNIX outputs a stream of characters regardless of which device receives it.

Devices

Further, UNIX also assumes that all sources and destinations of data (i.e., devices) are part of the computer's file system. That is, all devices connected to a UNIX System appear as files in the file system. Even though each hardware configuration is different, the UNIX System views all configurations the same way—as a set of files that can send and receive streams of characters to currently active processes.

Viewing all devices as files greatly enhances portability. Note the elegance of this design. Because all devices look like files and all files look like streams of characters, a program that can read one character stream can read any character stream. Put another way, if a program can read one file, it can read any other file or device on the system without modification*.

UNIX Processes

A UNIX process results when an executable file and the appropriate data streams are combined and then scheduled for execution, usually in response to a command entered by a user, although UNIX can also start processes on its own. A process is independent of the program it executes and the data it processes. Put another way, a process can execute any program connected to any data streams on the system.

It is important to emphasize that a process is not a program. A process is an environment within which a program executes. Part of a program's environment includes the data streams it is connected to. A process is dynamic, it exists only while it is being executed. Further, the actual connection of an executable program with data streams is done at *runtime*, when the process is created.

How does a process know which streams to connect to the executable program? There are two ways. First, a stream can be directly accessed by name from inside the process. Second, a process can use the default streams.

---

*Subject to the file's access permissions.

Default Streams

Every UNIX process, when created, is connected to three default streams: *standard input, standard output,* and *standard error* (see figure 1.1). Unless changed,* all three standard streams are connected to the process's terminal.

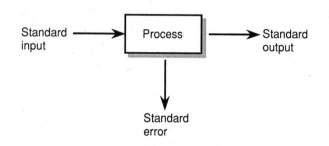

Fig. 1.1.   *Every process has three default streams.*

The standard input stream, often called *standard in* or *stdin,* is where a process will get characters if the program reads data without referring to a specific file. The standard output stream, often called *standard out* or *stdout,* is where a process will send characters if the program prints data without referring to a specific file. The standard error stream, often called *stderr,* is where a process writes error messages to the user when the program doesn't identify a specific error-logging file. The standard error stream is used to separate error messages from ordinary output.

By default, a UNIX command will read from that terminal's keyboard and write output and errors to that terminal's screen. As we shall see, the use of default input, output, and error streams connected to a program at runtime is a powerful construct.

Because a process is independent of the data streams it uses, the process doesn't care how the data it is using is generated (or consumed). This independence lets UNIX generate and consume character streams in yet a third way—from other processes.

---

*How to direct where the three defaults go is covered in detail in Chapter 2.

Pipelines

To make more efficient use of the UNIX System's multiprocessing resources, UNIX lets the output of one process be connected to the input of another. Such connections are called *pipelines*. Figure 1.2 illustrates a pipeline.

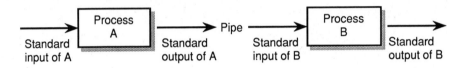

Fig. 1.2.   *Creating a pipeline from process A to process B.*

Anything done by a pipeline can also be done by storing the output of process A into a file and then using the same file as input for process B (see figure 1.3). However, a pipeline is more efficient because it doesn't require that the output from process A ever be stored in a file. It is directly consumed by process B. Pipelines play an important part in the creation of applications with UNIX tools.*

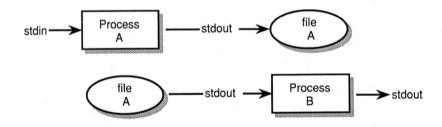

Fig. 1.3.   *Storing the output of process A and the input of process B in the same file.*

Summary

Much of the power of the UNIX System comes from these few simple ideas, and we will come back to them over and over again. To emphasize their importance, let's summarize the key points.

• UNIX is a portable operating system.

---

*Pipelines are covered in detail in Chapter 9.

- UNIX views computers as suppliers of two things: processes and data.

- A process is an instance of a currently executing program.

- All data is represented by streams of characters.

- All sources and destinations of data (i.e., devices) are seen as files in the file system.

- A UNIX process results when an executable file and the appropriate data streams are combined and executed.

- Every UNIX process, when created, is connected to three default streams: standard input, standard output, and standard error.

- Unless changed, all three standard streams are connected to the process's controlling terminal.

- UNIX lets the output stream of one process be connected to the input stream of another to form a pipeline.

2

The UNIX
Command Processor

Everything done on the UNIX System is done by a process, so how do you create a process? One way is to write programs that know how to create processes. However, this solution requires far too much effort to execute a single command.

Like virtually all operating systems, UNIX supplies a command processor to act as the interface between a command (entered by the user) and the actual execution of that command (done by the UNIX System). The UNIX command processor is called the *shell*. Several UNIX command processors are available. In fact, some of the command processors have been adapted to work with other operating systems, most notably MS-DOS-based PCs.

The three most common UNIX command processors are the Bourne, C, and Korn shells. This book focuses on the Bourne shell, the original UNIX command processor. Both the C and Korn shells were developed after the Bourne shell and should be considered extensions of it. Much of what is discussed in this chapter applies to all three shells; however, the specific examples are based on how the Bourne shell does things.

The whole purpose of the shell is to start processes running your commands. The shell prompts you for a command, using the familiar $ prompt. When you enter a command, the shell reads the input, interprets the command line, and then creates a process to execute it. Figure 2.1 shows the steps involved as a command becomes a process.

The shell sits between the user and UNIX. The command you enter is not *directly* executed by UNIX. Rather, the shell scans the entered command line to figure out how to create the process that executes your command. UNIX executed the process created by the shell.

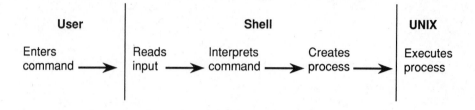

Fig. 2.1.   *How a command becomes a process.*

Initially, this process may seem counterintuitive. It appears that the system executes the commands you enter. For example, you enter the date command, and the system prints out the current time and date:

```
$ date
Fri May 19 08:45:24 PDT 1989
```

Let's take a closer look at how the date command is actually executed. Recall that every process is assigned three standard locations: one for input, one for output, and one for error messages. The output of the date command has been printed on this process's standard output, which has been connected to your computer terminal. Thus, although you entered only date, the shell interpreted the command to mean that you wanted the output to go to your terminal. The shell then created a process to execute the date command and connect its standard output to your terminal. Figure 2.2 shows how date is executed.

Shell Metacharacters

Like all data on the UNIX System, the output of date is a stream of characters. Thus, instead of printing date's output on the terminal, you can send it to any other file on the system. How do you create a process whose standard output is connected to a date file, not your terminal? The answer is to use special characters, called *shell meta-characters*, to tell the shell that the standard output of this process is to be connected to a specified file.

For example, suppose that you wanted to record when the current log-in session began using date. Instead of printing date's output to the terminal, you could save it in a file by telling the shell to connect the standard output of the process to that file. This is called

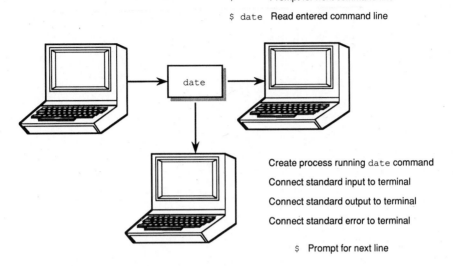

$ Prompt for next command line

$ date   Read entered command line

Create process running date command

Connect standard input to terminal

Connect standard output to terminal

Connect standard error to terminal

$ Prompt for next line

Fig. 2.2.   *Executing* date.

redirecting a command's output and is represented by the > character. To record the beginning of the current log-in session, you can use:

```
$ date > login.time
```

In English, this command says to put the current time and date (the output of date) into the file login.time. Note that > login.time is not part of the command to be executed. Instead, it describes how the process's output is to be handled. That is, > login.time says to connect the output of this process to the login.time file. Regardless of the program being executed (date in this case), > login.time says where to send the process's output. Incidentally, the shell will recognize a metacharacter even if it is not surrounded by spaces. The previous command can be entered date>login.time without problem. Figure 2.3 shows how standard output is redirected.

In reality, the command date > login.time contains two distinct pieces of information. One, represented by date, is the program to execute. The other is a message to the shell describing how the process's output is to be handled. Because a process is independent of the data it uses, the two parts of this command are not related. The date command does not know where its output is going, and login.time does not know where the characters it stores come from.

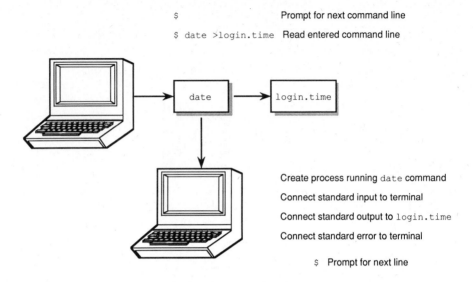

```
                              $                   Prompt for next command line

                              $ date >login.time  Read entered command line
```

```
                                            Create process running date command

                                            Connect standard input to terminal

                                            Connect standard output to login.time

                                            Connect standard error to terminal

                                            $  Prompt for next line
```

Fig. 2.3.   *Redirecting standard output.*

How is the command date > login.time actually accomplished? First, the shell interprets the command line by scanning it for shell metacharacters. The shell finds the >, which tells it that the following file name is to be connected to the process's output stream. Because > login.time is a directive to the shell, the shell removes the > login.time from the command line and then creates a process running date, whose output is connected to login.time.

All of this can be boiled down to one vitally important rule: *The shell scans every command line entered for metacharacters before that command is executed.* If the shell finds any metacharacters, they are interpreted and implemented before the process executing the command line is created.

There are no exceptions to this rule. Every command line executed by the shell is scanned for metacharacters. Further, the shell doesn't try to determine if the resulting command line makes sense. The shell's job is to execute it, if possible.

For example, suppose that you make a typing error while checking whether a file named chapter.1 is in the current directory. Instead of ls chapter.1 you type ls chapter>1. Even though the command line looks odd, the shell dutifully runs the ls command looking for a file named chapter, sending the output to the file 1. Many user errors are caused by users typing mistakes like this.

The > tells the shell to connect the standard output of a process to the specified file.* If the file doesn't exist, the > instructs the shell to

---

*Here, and throughout the rest of this book, the word *file* is used in a generic sense to mean anything that looks like a file to UNIX. That is, any device or file that is in the file system.

create it, assuming the user has permission to create the file (the command will fail otherwise). If the file does exist, the > tells the shell to erase all the characters in the file. Thus, when a command's output is redirected to a file with >, the file will contain only that command's output, regardless of whether the file existed before the command was executed.

The shell offers another output redirection that doesn't erase a file if it exists, >>. Note that this metacharacter consists of two >s without a space between them. The shell is highly sensitive to spaces. Putting a space between the >s will cause an error (the shell will think it's two > redirection commands). The >> acts just like > except when the named file already exists. Then, >> appends the standard output of the command to the end of the named file.

Earlier, the output of the `date` command was redirected into the `login.time` file to keep track of when you logged in. To record how long you were on the system, you can now run

```
$ date >> login.time
```

just before you log out. This will add the current time to the file.

```
$ cat login.time
Fri May 19 08:45:24 PDT 1989
Fri May 19 12:23:52 PDT 1989
```

Because you used the >> instead of >, the output of `date` is added to `login.time`. Incidentally, printing or storing the output of two `date` commands is a common UNIX technique for keeping track of elapsed time.

Hands-on Exercise 2.1

What happens if you now enter the command
    `date > login.time`

Redirecting Input

The shell also provides a way to redirect the input of a process. The input redirection metacharacter is <. When the input of a process is redirected, the shell connects the listed file to the process's standard input. As with > and >>, the < is a command to the shell, not UNIX, and both the metacharacter and the file name following it are removed from the command line.

Virtually all UNIX commands that read from a listed name on the command line will work the same if the command's input is redirected from that file. Thus, `cat file1` and `cat < file1` do exactly the same thing. You won't be able to determine from the output which of these two command lines was actually used.

The `cat` command copies its standard input to its standard output. Thus, both standard input and standard output can be redirected in the same command. The command `cat < file1 > file2` copies `file1` to `file2`. Commands that let both their standard input and standard output be redirected are called *filters*. Filters are discussed in detail in Chapter 3.

Although the output from the two commands lines (`cat file1` and `cat < file1`) is identical, the shell processes them differently (see figure 2.4). The command `cat file1` has both its standard input and output connected to the terminal, and `cat` is passed `file1` as an argument. The command `cat < file1` invokes the `cat` command in a process whose standard input has been connected to `file1`. Even though the input has been redirected, the standard output hasn't, so the contents of `file1` are listed on the terminal.

Ignoring Redirection

How does `cat` know whether to read `file1` or its standard input? If `cat` is passed to an argument, it assumes the argument is the name of the file (or files, if there are multiple arguments) to print. If `cat` receives no arguments, it reads the standard input. This means that the command `cat file1 < file2` displays only the contents of `file1`. The redirection occurs but is ignored because `cat` is passed an argument.

The command `cat file1 < file2` demonstrates an important point. Just because a command's standard input or output has been redirected doesn't guarantee that the redirection will be used. Further, the command doesn't know it's been redirected.*

Here's another example of ignored redirection:

```
$ date < login.time
Fri May 19 12:35:29 PDT 1989
```

---

*However, there are ways for a process to test the standard input and output to see if they are terminals, files, or something else.

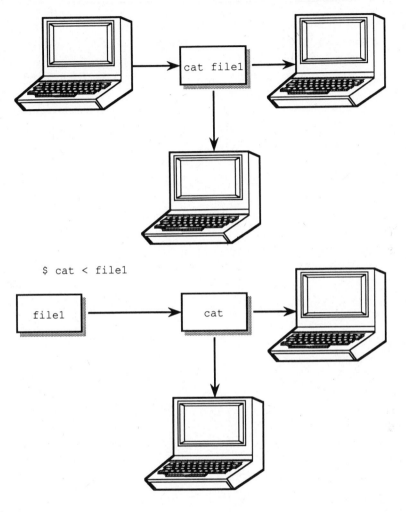

Fig. 2.4. *Two* cat *commands.*

Unlike cat, the date command doesn't check its standard input under any circumstance, and the redirection has no effect. Also, note (by the absence of an error message) that the shell is unaware that the redirection is useless; it simply does what you ask without question. Incidentally, the same would happen with any command that ignores its standard input, such as ls, cd, and mkdir.

Redirecting the Standard Error

We've talked about redirecting two of the three streams associated with a process. What about redirecting the standard error? The shell also provides the 2> metacharacter, which tells the shell to connect this process's standard error to the listed file. No spaces are allowed between the 2 and the >.

For example, the cat command prints an error if it can't find the file to print:

```
$ cat jkljsldkfj
cat: cannot open jkljsldkfj
```

The error message is sent to the standard error. To demonstrate this, redirect the output of the command and see if the error message still shows up on the terminal:

```
$ cat jkljsldkfj > outfile
cat: cannot open jkljsldkfj
```

As expected, the outcome is the same. Incidentally, the shell creates outfile before cat is executed. Thus, the outcome of this command is a bit different because you have added an empty file to the current directory.

The error message can be redirected to a file using 2>:

```
$ cat jkljsldkfj 2> errfile
$ cat errfile
cat: cannot open jkljsldkfj
```

The 2> overwrites the error file if it already exists; otherwise, the file gets created. As with output redirection, the shell also provides error redirection that adds to the end of an existing file: 2>>.

Hands-on Exercise 2.2

Assuming that badfile doesn't exist, explain this output:
```
$ cat < badfile 2> errfile
badfile: cannot open
```

In-Line Redirection

So far, all the redirections we've done have involved files. The shell has another input redirection, called *in-line redirection*, that allows you to list the input character stream as part of the command line. The in-line redirection metacharacter has two parts: the redirection, represented by <<, and a stream *marker*. Because the entire input stream is listed as part of the command line, a unique token must be used to show where the input stream ends.

As an example, this command prints the listed lines:

```
$ cat << EOF
> This is an example of
> "in-line" redirection
> EOF
This is an example of
"in-line" redirection
```

In this command, EOF is the beginning and ending token. You can use any set of characters to mark the input stream. In using in-line redirection, there are two things to remember. First, the same string that begins the stream must end it. Second, the ending token must appear at the beginning of the line. In-line redirection is a flexible way to create input and is quite useful in some applications.

You may have noticed the >s, under the $, at the beginning of each additional line. The > is the shell's *secondary prompt*. It is used when a command line spans more than one line. The > is the shell's way of telling you it expects more input.

The output from a command that has in-line redirection can also be redirected. For example, this command can be used to enhance the information in login.time:

```
$ cat << EOF
> Logged in
> EOF > login.time
$ date >> login.time
$ cat login.time
Logged in
Fri May 19 12:40:14 PDT 1989
```

Table 2.1 lists the redirection metacharacters discussed so far. The shell offers other redirection options. These additional metacharacters are discussed later in this book.

Table 2.1. *Shell redirection metacharacters.*

Metacharacters	Function
>	Output redirection (overwrite)
>>	Output redirection (append)
<	Input redirection
<< *word*	Input redirection (in-line)
2>	Error redirection (overwrite)
2>>	Error redirection (append)

Using the `cat` command with in-line and output redirection is one way to put information directly into a file. UNIX offers another command to do this, `echo`. The `echo` command is the UNIX System's version of a print command. `echo` puts its arguments on its standard output, which in the following example is your terminal:

```
$ echo Logged in
Logged in
```

You can use `echo` instead of `cat` to create the `login.time` file:

```
$ echo Logged in > login.time
$ date >> login.time
```

Process Control Metacharacters

In most cases, users execute commands interactively. That is, they enter a command which the shell then executes. When the program finishes, they enter another command. This is called *foreground* processing. Executing commands in the foreground means that you wait for the previous command to finish before entering another one.

Some commands take a long time to finish. For example, sorting a large file can take quite a while. Instead of waiting for a command to complete, you can tell the shell to execute a command in the *background*. If you execute a command using background processing, it is disconnected from your terminal and runs concurrently with any other commands you enter. Background processing lets you execute long-running commands while still working interactively.

Because a command run in the background was disconnected from your terminal, a background command cannot read input from your keyboard. A background process terminates with an *input read error* if the process attempts to read from the keyboard. However, unlike input, a background command's standard output is connected to the terminal unless it is redirected elsewhere. A common error is to put a command in the background but forget to redirect the command's output. This causes output from the background process to be displayed on your screen while you try to work interactively, which can be very confusing.

Ampersand, the Background Metacharacter

The UNIX kernel doesn't know anything about foreground or background processing. Instead, the shell controls how a process is executed. You can execute a command in the background by putting the background metacharacter, an ampersand (&), at the end of the command line. By default, command lines that don't end with & are run in the foreground. For example, the following command sorts huge.file, putting the sorted output into sorted.file:*

```
$ sort huge.file > sorted.file &
2387
```

Whenever you put a command into the background, the shell tells you the ID number of the background process. This number enables you to keep track of the process with ps.

```
$ ps
    PID  TTY       TIME COMMAND
    1845 console   0:03 sh          login shell
    2387 console   0:15 sort        background process
    2397 console   0:01 ps          foreground process
```

You also can use the process ID number to terminate the background process.

```
$ kill 2387
```

---

*Chapter 8 covers the sort command in detail.

The shell reports that the background command was terminated with the message `2387 Terminated`. It displays this message after you execute the next command. Note: Your shell may print a similar but not exactly identical message.

Semicolon

Sometimes it is easier to enter two commands at the same time. The sequential processing metacharacter, the semicolon (`;`), enables you to execute two commands, one after the other, from a single command line. For example, the following command line prints a file (`lp`) after editing it (`vi`):

```
$ vi chapter.2 ; lp chapter.2
request is laser-341 (1 file)
```

The `;` doesn't provide any special processing. It simply lets you specify two commands on one command line. The foregoing commands could also be performed separately:

```
$ vi chapter.2
edit screen
$ lp chapter.2
request is laser-342 (1 file)
```

Sequential processing is rarely used interactively, but it can come in handy when combined with other shell features which are discussed later in this chapter.

The semicolon is interpreted before most other metacharacters. This means commands to the left of the semicolon are separate from commands to the right, regardless of what metacharacters appear in each command. For example, in this command line

```
$ date ; sort huge.list > sorted.list &
Fri May 19 12:58:41 PDT 1989
2458
```

the `&` and `>` refer only to the `sort` command to the right of the semicolon. The `date` command's output is printed on the standard output, not redirected into `sorted.list`. Also, because `date`'s output is printed before the process ID of the background process, `date` must have been executed in the foreground. When `date` finishes, the shell runs the `sort` command in the background.

Parentheses

The shell lets you group commands together by using parentheses. The shell interprets parentheses before semicolons, which let you redirect the output of several commands with only one redirection. The following command

```
$ (date ; who) > system.status
$ cat system.status
Fri May 19 12:40:14 PDT 1989
ray          console      May 19 06:16
rich         /dev/tty4c   May 19 08:34
```

executes `date` and `who`* together, putting the output of both commands into the `system.status` file. Now, the `>` refers to all the commands inside the parentheses. The same would be true for any redirection or process control metacharacters placed outside the parentheses. Inside the parentheses, shell metacharacters are interpreted properly but only refer to what's inside the parentheses.

Your login shell's standard input, output, and error streams were determined when that shell was executed. Your login shell was created without redirection when you logged in, so it uses the terminal for its default streams. The parentheses work by creating a *subshell* that executes the command line listed inside the parentheses. The metacharacters appearing outside the parentheses set up the default conditions of that subshell.

In the command line `(date ; who) > system.status`, the standard output of the subshell is connected to `system.status`. This makes the standard output the file `system.status`, not the terminal. Because the commands inside the parentheses are not redirected, their output goes to the subshell's standard output.

Unlike other metacharacters, `()` must enclose an entire command line. As a result, the shell requires that a *command terminator* appear to the right of the closing parenthesis. A command terminator is a newline metacharacter that terminates a command, such as, `&`, `;`, `¦` (discussed in the "Pipeline" section), and others which are covered later.

---

*The `who` command lists the users currently logged onto the system.

Hands-on Exercise 2.3

Assuming the file `junk` existed before execution, explain this command's output:

```
$ ( who > junk ; cat ; date > junk ; cat junk ) < junk
ray      console    May 19 06:16
rich     /dev/tty4c May 19 08:34
Fri May 19 12:45:31 PDT 1989
```

Earlier, I combined the `echo` and `date` commands to create an annotated `login.time` file:

```
$ echo Logged in > login.time
$ date >> login.time
$ cat login.time
Logged in
Fri May 19 12:50:52 PDT 1989
```

To make this easier to read, you can put the message `Logged in` and the date on the same output line. One way to do this is to execute `date` and make its output part of `echo`'s arguments before `echo` is run.

Stated more generally, it often is useful to execute a command contained in a larger command line and then *replace the executed command with what gets sent to that command's standard output*. The result is that the output of one command becomes the arguments of another. For example, in the command `echo Logged in` *date*, you would want the `date` command executed and replaced by the current date and time (`date`'s output), which is made part of `echo`'s command line before it is executed.

Backquotes

The shell provides a *command substitution metacharacter*, represented by backquotes (` `` `). Any command appearing inside backquotes gets executed and replaced by its standard output before the resulting command line is run (see figure 2.5). The command

```
$ echo Logged in `date`> login.time
```

tells the shell to execute date first, to substitute what is inside the backquotes with the command's output, and then to execute the resulting echo command. Thus,

```
echo Logged in `date`> login.time
```

becomes

```
echo Logged in Fri May 19 12:52:25 PDT 1989 > login.time
```

which is the echo command finally executed by the shell:

```
$ echo Logged in `date` > login.time
$ cat login.time
Logged in Fri May 19 12:52:25 PDT 1989
```

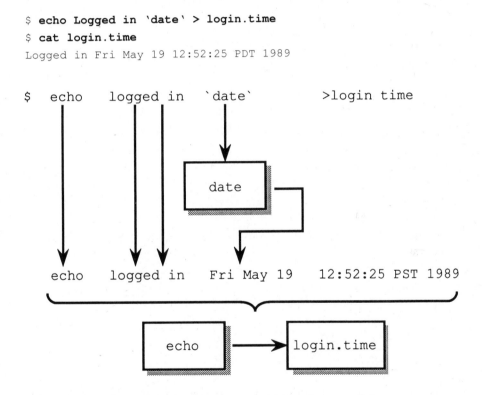

Fig. 2.5. *Command substitution is done before the rest of the command line is processed.*

Incidentally, command substitution can be used to insert a command's output into in-line redirection. Thus, the Logged in message and the date can be put on the same line with the following:

```
$ cat << EOF
> Logged in `date`
> EOF > login.time
$ cat login.time
Logged in Fri May 19 12:53:43 PDT 1989
```

Pipeline

If you want to print a list of users currently logged on the system, you can create a temporary file with `who` and then print that file with `lp`:

```
$ who > /tmp/temp.file
$ lp /tmp/temp.file
request is laser-343 (1 file)
```

This command works fine; however, it is inefficient for two reasons. First, you have to create a temporary file. Second, `lp` must read the temporary file.

Note that the temporary file, `temp.file`, was created in the `/tmp` directory. `/tmp` is a public temporary directory that is periodically cleaned out by the system. It is best to create your temporary files in the `/tmp` directory.

The shell offers a processing alternative that allows the output of one command to be read directly as input by another command without the need for a temporary file. It is called a *pipeline*, or just a *pipe*, and is represented by the `¦` metacharacter. A pipeline connects processes by making the standard output of one command the standard input of the other. One command reads input directly from the output of another, so there is no need for a temporary file.

A pipeline lets you print `who`'s output by sending it directly to the `lp` command via a pipeline:

```
$ who ¦ lp
request is laser-344 (1 file)
```

This command line is executed by two separate processes, one for `who` and one for `lp`. The processes are created in a special way that connects the standard output of the `who` process to the standard input of the `lp` process.* The shell creates a separate process for each

---

*`lp`, like `cat`, reads from the standard input if no arguments are passed to it.

command in a pipeline (there can be several), as shown in figure 2.6. Thus, like background commands, pipelines are a kind of concurrent processing where each piece of the pipeline is run simultaneously.

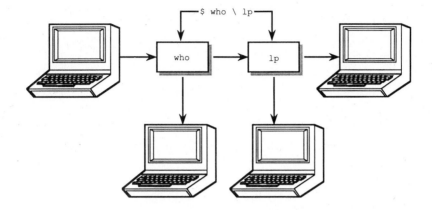

Fig. 2.6.   *The shell starts a process for each command in a pipeline.*

Pipelines show the flexibility of the UNIX design at its best. A process is independent of the data it uses, so it doesn't care where its input stream comes from, even if it's another process. In fact, a pipeline is really a specialized type of a redirection, where the output of one process is redirected to be the input of a second process rather than of a file.

Like semicolons, pipelines are executed left to right. Thus, parentheses can be used to send the output of several commands down a pipeline. The following command uses `lp` to print the date and the names of users currently on the system:

```
$ (date ; who) ¦ lp
request is laser-345 (1 file)
```

Table 2.2 shows the shell's process control metacharacters.

Table 2.2.   *Shell process control metacharacters.*

Metacharacters	Function
cmd &	Put the cmd in the background
cmd1 ; cmd2	Run cmd1, then cmd2
(cmds)	Execute cmds in a subshell
`cmd`	Substitute cmd's output for cmd
cmd1 ¦ cmd2	Pipe the output of cmd1 into the input of cmd2

Pipelines are an extremely useful tool that play a large role in creating the applications described in this book. In fact, one of the most powerful features of the UNIX System is its capability to execute several processes connected together in a pipeline.

File Name-Matching Metacharacters

So far, the metacharacters we've covered describe how to create a process or processes that execute the entered command line. The shell also recognizes other types of metacharacters. One set provides a shorthand way of specifying arguments on a command line. Specifically, the shell offers file name-matching metacharacters that you can use to identify one or more file names.

Brackets

Suppose you want to print the files `chapter.1` through `chapter.5`. One solution is to run `lp`, listing the five file names as arguments.

```
$ lp chapter.1 chapter.2 chapter.3 chapter.4 chapter.5
request is laser-346 (5 files)
```

This is too much repetitive typing.

Because file names are common command-line arguments, the shell provides a set of metacharacters that act as *wildcards* for file names. A wildcard can match one or more characters in a file name.

For example, in the previous `lp` command, the five file names are quite similar. In fact, only the last character is different. Another way to list all five file names is to take all the files beginning with `chapter.` and then add a single character that is a 1, 2, 3, 4, or 5 to the end of the file name. In essence, you want to specify a *range* of possible characters that can be put on the end of `chapter.` to make a valid file name.

The shell provides a file name-matching range metacharacter, represented by brackets, `[]`. The range of characters to match is listed inside the `[]`s. Thus, the five file names can be abbreviated as `chapter.[12345]`. The following command also schedules all five files to be printed by `lp`:

```
$ lp chapter.[12345]
request is laser-347 (5 files)
```

Characters inside `[]` match only a single character. That is, the file name `chapter.[12345]` will match only a file named `chapter.` followed by either a 1, 2, 3, 4, or 5. It will not match `chapter.12`. That would require `chapter.1[12345]`, `chapter.[12345]2`, or `chapter.[12345][12345]`. Note that none of these three would match `chapter.2`.

It is important to understand how the shell interprets file name-matching metacharacters. Earlier in this chapter, we saw that the shell scans each command line for metacharacters and that the shell implements any metacharacters it sees before the shell creates a process to execute the resulting command line. The entire purpose of file name-matching metacharacters is to ask the shell to alter the command line by expanding a file name pattern into all the file names that match that pattern before the command line is executed.

Thus, the shell expands `chapter.[12345]` into all the files that match that pattern *before* the command line is executed. If you enter the command*

```
$ lp chapter.[12345]
```

in a directory that contains all five of the matching file names, the shell converts that command line into

```
$ lp chapter.1 chapter.2 chapter.3 chapter.4 chapter.5
```

and then creates a process running `lp`, sending it the five file names as arguments. `lp` does not know whether the original command line you entered contained a file name metacharacter or not, because all it sees is the result of the expansion of the file name-matching metacharacter.

If the current directory contains only the first two chapters, the command line

```
$ lp chapter.[12345]
```

gets expanded into

```
$ lp chapter.1 chapter.2
```

because the shell can find only two file names that match the pattern. Note that the files identified by file name-matching metacharacters are listed in alphabetical order. This is how the shell reports the names that match file name-matching metacharacters.

---

*The output of the `lp` command has been omitted.

What happens if a file name pattern doesn't identify any files in the current directory? The shell assumes that the argument is to be passed *as is* to the command being executed.* For example, this can happen if you are in the wrong directory and use a file name pattern that doesn't match any file in that directory. In this case, the shell looks at all the files in the current directory. When it doesn't find any that match, the shell sends the file name pattern as it was entered to the command, which then treats it like any other argument.

As an illustration, the error message printed by lp with the command line

```
$ lp listing.[1234]
lp: can't access file "listing.[1234]"
lp: request not accepted
```

shows that the shell passed the file name listing.[1234] as entered to lp because no files in the current directory matched the pattern. lp can't find a file named listing.[1234] either, so it prints the error messages and fails. Note that the shell interpreted the file name metacharacters and that lp simply took the 14 characters passed to it as the name of a single file, listing.[1234]. Thus, lp doesn't check for shell file name-matching metacharacters; rather, it treats argument(s) as the exact name(s) of the files to be printed. Incidentally, in a different directory, the results could very easily be different.

If the range of characters you want to match is sequential, such as 1 through 5, you can identify the range by its endpoints and a dash. Thus, [12345] becomes [1-5]. Also, a range can be mixed with other characters. The pattern file[adhc1-5] matches this list of files, but no others:

```
filea
filec
filed
fileh
file1
file2
file3
file4
file5
```

---

*The C shell doesn't do this by default, but it can be set to pass nonmatching patterns on to commands.

For a range to be valid, the character before the dash must be lex-icographically less than the one after the dash. The range [x-c] is invalid.*

Suppose you wanted to print each of the first nine chapters except the fifth one. You could use any one of these commands:

```
lp chapter.[1-46-9]
lp chapter.[12346789]
lp chapter.[6-91-4]
```

The shell also has an *exclusion* range metacharacter, represented by an exclamation point inside brackets, [!]. Assuming that chapter files have only numeric extensions, the pattern chapter.[!5] matches all the files beginning with chapter. and not ending with a 5.

Although chapter.[!5] is an even shorter way to write chapter[1-46-9], there is a meaningful difference between the two notations. The pattern chapter[1-46-9] specifically lists all the characters that can appear at the end of the file name. chapter.[!5] simply says that any character but a 5 can be the last character. chapter.[!5] should also match such file names as

```
chapter.x
chapter.#
chapter.=
chapter.D
chapter.z
chapter.+
```

Because we assumed that only numbers are used as extensions for chapter file names, none of these file names, or any of the other possible matches, would appear in the current directory. However, if any such file names were found, their names would be matched by chapter.[!5] and their contents printed by lp.

Question Mark

In addition to specifying a range of characters, you can use another shell file name metacharacter, the ?, to match any single character. The pattern chapter.? matches all files that begin with the characters chapter. followed by one (and only one) character. The pattern

---

*The range doesn't generate an error message but instead matches the character c.

`chapter.??` matches all the file names that begin with `chapter.` followed by exactly two characters. The pattern `chapter.??` does not match `chapter.1`, because `chapter.1` has only one character after the period.

Asterisk

The most general file name metacharacter is `*`, which matches zero or more of any characters. To match every file name that starts with `chapter.`, use `chapter.*`. Because an asterisk represents zero or more of any characters, the pattern `chapter.*` also matches the file name `chapter.` (the name `chapter` followed by a period). Depending on what other file names are in the current directory, any of the following patterns could work just as well and require less typing.

```
c*
ch*
chap*
chapter*
```

Note that an `*` matched any characters. This includes periods, control characters, spaces, or any other legal file name character.

When used by itself, the `*` matches all file names in the current directory. This can be demonstrated with the `echo` command:

```
$ echo *
chapter.1 chapter.2 file1 file2 file3
```

Again, note that the shell expands `*` to the five files in the current directory (in alphabetic order) and then executes the `echo` command, sending the five file names as arguments.

Table 2.3 shows all the file name-matching metacharacters.

Table 2.3. *The shell's file name-matching metacharacters.*

Metacharacters	Function
[ ]	Range of single characters to match
[!]	Range of single characters to exclude
?	Any single character
*	Zero or more of any characters

Matching Other File Names

All the previous examples show the file name-matching metacharacters appearing at the end of a name. This placement is not required. File name-matching metacharacters can appear anywhere in a string of characters and anywhere on a command line. If the previous `echo` command listed all the fles in the current directory, the pattern `*2` would identify `chapter.2` and `file2`, `c*2` would uniquely match `chapter.2`, and `f*[12]` is `file1` and `file2`. Table 2.4 lists some other file name patterns.

Table 2.4.   *Some shell file name patterns.*

Pattern	Meaning
`*file`	Any name ending in `file`
`*file*`	Any name containing `file` anywhere
`[abc]*`	Any name starting with either an a, b, or c
`???`	All three-character file names
`???*`	All file names with three or more characters
`*[!123]`	All file names not ending in 1, 2, or 3

File name-matching metacharacters can also appear in a larger path name. For example, to find all the files named `junk` in first-level subdirectories in your home directory, you could use the following:

```
$ ls /usr/ray/*/junk
/usr/ray/Acct/junk
/usr/ray/C/junk
/usr/ray/Classes/junk
/usr/ray/Labels/junk
/usr/ray/Letters/junk
/usr/ray/UNIX.book/junk
```

The `*` represents only one file name. Thus, this command searches only the directories directly under my home directory. It didn't find the file `/usr/ray/Acct/1989/junk`.

File-Naming Considerations

The UNIX System lets a file name contain *any* character, except the forward slash (/). The forward slash is a UNIX file system metacharacter that separates directories in a path name. As a result, a file name can contain control characters, spaces, tabs, even newlines and backspaces—any character but a /.*

Because a file name can use virtually any character, it is perfectly legal for a file name to contain shell metacharacters. This leads to a perverse situation: Some file names don't match their own names!

Consider a file named due.may[3-8], which holds work due during the week of May third through eighth. To print the contents of the file, you enter the following command:

```
$ lp due.may[3-8]
```

The first thing the shell does is check for a file name that matches the pattern: due.may followed by a 3, 4, 5, 6, 7 or 8:

```
due.may3
due.may4
due.may5
due.may6
due.may7
due.may8
```

If none of these file names exists in the current directory, the shell sends the pattern entered, in this case the actual file name you want, to lp as an argument. Thus, the previous lp command may or may not work, depending on the names of the other files in the current directory. Note that if any of the six files that match due.may[3-8] exist, the pattern is replaced by the matching file name(s) and the actual file due.may[3-8] is not printed.

In addition to creating files that don't match themselves, it is possible to create file names that match themselves, plus additional names. Be careful with file names such as ideas? or *important*. Although they may describe their files' contents, such file names also could match several other file names when they are part of a command line.

It is a bad idea to put a shell metacharacter in a file name. As a general rule, it is best to use only alphabetic characters, digits, and periods in file names.

---

*Different versions of UNIX let file names have a different number of characters. Versions based on AT&T UNIX typically allow 14. Versions based on Berkeley UNIX typically allow 255.

Hands-on Exercise 2.4

How would each of these commands fail?
  a. `cat msgs&mail>tom`
  b. `cat ideas;ch.[1-3]`
  c. `cat memo.vp(sales)`

Quoting Metacharacters

Is there anything you can do to avoid the conflict between shell metacharacters and legal UNIX file names? Put more broadly, is there anything you can do if you need to use as part of a command line a character that happens to have a special meaning to the shell?

The shell contains a separate set of metacharacters that remove the special meaning of other shell metacharacters. When a character loses its meta-meaning, it is said to be *quoted*. You've already seen one shell-quoting metacharacter: the backquotes (command substitution). The shell does not see any metacharacter inside backquotes as part of the command line, but rather as part of the command whose output is to be substituted.

Backslash

Because backquotes cause command substitution, it is not practical to use backquotes to quote metacharacters. Rather, the shell offers the backslash (\) to quote any single character, and single quotes for quoting several characters. Thus, although the command `cat files1&2` results in several errors, quoting the `&` with a backslash turns `files1&2` into a file name:

```
$ cat files1\&2
```
contents of files1&2

The shell removes the quoting metacharacters from the command line before executing it. When the shell scans the command line `cat files1\&2` for metacharacters, it finds the backslash, removes the backslash, ignores the following character (in this case the `&`), and then executes the resulting command line.

Single Quotes

The single quotes are a shorthand way of putting a backslash in front of every character in a sequence of characters. The command line `cat mail.ray\<-\>bob` works, as do the commands `cat 'mail.ray<->bob'` and `cat mail.ray'<->'bob`. The shell removes the single quotes from the command line, ignoring the special meaning of any characters inside them.

An important distinction exists between backquotes and single quotes. The shell looks inside backquotes, executing the command line it finds. The shell doesn't look inside single quotes, but passes everything between the quotes on to the command as a single argument (even if spaces are inside the quotes).

A type of quoting occurs for certain characters inside `[]`. The `*`, `?`, and `[` characters lose their special meanings. Thus, the pattern `file[*]` matches only the name `file*`.

Hands-on Exercise 2.5

Suppose the current directory contains the following files:
```
$ ls
file*
file-
file.1
file1
file2
file3
xx&yy
xx'yy
xx(yy
xx;yy
xx?yy
xx]yy
xyz
```
Use `ls` to list:
  a. all the files whose names begin with `file`
  b. `file*` only
  c. `file-`, `file1`, and `file3`
  d. all five character file names beginning with `xx`
  e. the files `xx&yy`, `xx'yy`, and `xx]yy`

Hands-on Exercise 2.6

Given the files in exercise 2.5, explain this output:

```
$ ls xx[[]]yy
xx[[]]yy not found
```

Summary

This chapter discusses in great detail specific metacharacters understood by the shell. The entire chapter can be summarized by one important statement: The shell scans each command line entered for metacharacters, which are interpreted and implemented before the command line is executed.

Although it is important to know which metacharacters the shell provides and what each one does, you can identify them by checking a shell command summary.* The key concept is to understand the steps taken by the shell before it creates one or more processes to execute the entered, and possibly modified, command line. A great many mistakes can be traced back to "misunderstandings" between you and the shell.

---

*See Appendix A for a shell metacharacter summary.

Part Two

USING UNIX TOOLS

Among the major benefits of the UNIX System are the hundreds of commands it offers. Many of these commands are system commands to be used in configuring, managing, or programming on the system. However, an important subset of UNIX commands implement data processing tools such as searching and sorting.

The purpose of this part is twofold. First, it discusses the major UNIX data processing tools. Second, it shows how to combine these tools to create applications that solve everyday problems.

3

UNIX Filters

$\mathbf{T}$he UNIX System uses its multiprocessing capabilities in two ways. First, it lets you create background processes, providing a way for you to do more than one task at a time. Second, multiprocessing makes command pipelines possible. Recall that a command pipeline processes data through a number of concurrently executing programs by connecting the output of one to the input of another.

Pipelines are very handy in everyday work on a UNIX System and in creating applications. Pipelines let you apply several processing steps sequentially to get a job done in a single, efficient command line.

To work, a pipeline requires commands that handle input and output in a specific way. Because commands in a pipeline have both their input and output redirected, commands used in a pipeline must read input from the standard input, send output to the standard output, and report errors to the standard error. Without these characteristics, pipelines won't work.

As was demonstrated in Chapter 2 , the `date` command doesn't read from its standard input. Instead, it accesses the system clock. Redirection has no effect on `date`'s input. This also means that `date` can't be used inside a pipeline.

```
$ ls ¦ date
Tue May 25 08:18:19 PDT 1989
```

The output of `ls` is redirected into the pipe, but `date` ignores `ls`'s output and discards it on termination.

`ls` doesn't read its standard input either. If you reverse the two commands in the previous pipeline, `ls` ignores `date`'s output:

```
$ date | ls
book.notes
book.outline
chapter.1
chapter.2
chapter.3
```

Both `ls` and `date` send output to the standard output but ignore their standard input. These commands fit into a pipeline only if they are the head of the pipeline.

```
$ date | cat
Tue May 25 08:21:23 PDT 1989
```

This pipeline works because `cat` does read its standard input. Thus, the characters sent to the pipe by `date` are read from the pipe and sent to `cat`'s standard output.

The `cat` command is different from `date` and `ls` because it reads its standard input, sends output to its standard output, and reports errors on the standard error. For this reason, `cat` is called a *filter*.

Using Filters

UNIX provides many commands that are filters. Filters are important for two reasons. First, you can use them anywhere in pipelines to create applications and solve problems simply. Second, they often implement data processing tools that can be used to create applications.

Filters are an important part of the UNIX environment. The more you know about the UNIX filters and their use, the more productive you are on the UNIX System.

For example, consider this common computer application. You have a file containing names and addresses (such as a list of customers or prospects, or a Christmas card list) and you want a list of those in California, sorted by ZIP code, on one-up labels. This task may be easy to do if you own a database management system and the names are stored in it or if you have special list management software tied into a word processor.

However, if you don't have such software or the names aren't in the proper format, what do you do? You no doubt can buy software to solve the problem, although you may have to massage the data first. Another idea is writing your own program to read the file and print the labels. Unfortunately, these solutions take either time, money, or both.

UNIX offers a quicker and cheaper answer: a pipeline of UNIX filters. To see how this is done, let's break the job down into its constituent parts. The list contains people from all over, so the first step is to find those who are in California. This task is easily done with a *searching* filter.

After you have a list of people with California addresses, you need to put them in ZIP code order. You can use a *sorting* filter to do this. To print the names on one-up labels requires a *formatting* filter. Actually printing the labels can be done by redirecting the output of the pipeline to the printer device or using the print spooler (either `lp` or `lpr`). Figure 3.1 shows this pipeline.

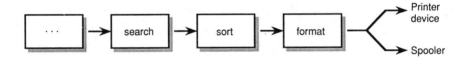

Fig. 3.1.   *A label-printing pipeline.*

The pipeline in figure 3.1 has a number of advantages. It can be created quickly, in less than five minutes from start to finish. Further, the entire pipeline uses existing software that comes with UNIX. The filters being used are available on all versions of UNIX, so the pipeline is completely portable.

However, the most important part of this pipeline is its flexibility. The output of the search segment is a list of names of people with California addresses. Changing one of the pipeline's components (or just one of its arguments) can result in an entirely different list.

For example, if the customer list also contains the purchase and payments dates, you can transform the label-printing pipeline into an accounts-receivable tracking system by changing how the data is searched. The key is mixing and matching programs in the pipeline until the desired output is achieved.

Creating pipelines is an important part of both interactive use and application development on the UNIX System. Your ability to solve problems using pipelines relies on your knowledge of UNIX utility programs and filters. Thus, the first step in learning how to create pipelines is becoming familiar with the important UNIX tools.

The UNIX documentation lists considerably more than 200 utility programs. One approach is to look at each one as a potential component in a pipeline. However, this is not the way to go about it. Although it is valuable to know what is available on UNIX, when you create applications the most useful commands are the UNIX filters. Table 3.1 provides a brief list of the important UNIX filters.

Table 3.1.   *Important UNIX filters.*

Filters	Functions
awk	A flexible text-formatting tool that has its own C-like programming language
cat	Prints a file on the standard output
comm	Reports common and noncommon lines in two files
cut	Prints pieces of each line in a file (System V only)
diff	Reports the differences between two files
grep	Searches for lines in a file that contain a pattern
join	Combines lines containing a common field from two files into a single line
nl	Numbers the lines in a file
nroff	Formats lines according to embedded formatting codes in the text
od	Prints the individual characters in a file
paste	Combines lines from two or more files into one line (System V only)
pr	Paginates a file
sed	Edits text in a stream
sort	Sorts the lines in a file
tail	Prints the last lines in a file
tee	Sends the standard input to two separate files
tr	Translates individual characters
uniq	Prints unique lines in a file

The important thing about filters is that they can be placed anywhere in a pipeline. This increases your processing options. Also, filters implement general processing tasks, such as searching or sorting. Nonfilter UNIX commands usually perform system-related tasks, like ls or date. As you will see later on, both types of commands are important when creating applications.

A Computerized Phone List

Although the UNIX System views all data as moving in a stream of characters, UNIX filters assume that their data is made up of *lines* of text. That is, the file consists of lines containing zero or more characters terminated by a newline*. The `sort` command sorts lines of text into their proper order, sending the sorted data to the standard output. The search command compares each line it reads to a specified pattern and sends only those lines containing the pattern to the standard output.

The best way to learn about filters is to use them with a meaningful example. We will use a simple solution to a common problem in most organizations, a company phone list. The task is to put the employee phone list "on-line."

For simplicity, we will use the list stored in the file `phone.list`.

```
$ cat phone.list
Smith, Terry    7-7989
Adams, Fran     2-3876
StClair, Pat    4-6122
Brown, Robin    1-3745
Stair, Chris    5-5972
Benson, Sam     4-5587
```

The phone list has a very specific format:

Last name, First name <tab> Phone number <newline>

Every line begins with a last name, which is always followed by a comma and a space, then the first name, a tab, and the phone number. The phone number is a single number, a dash, and then four digits. No characters appear after the phone number.

The phone list will be used throughout Parts 2 and 3 of this book to demonstrate the capabilities of various UNIX filters. To get the most out of the following chapters, you should enter the phone list on your computer and try the interactive examples. This not only gives you experience with using these commands, but it also lets you experiment with the concepts discussed.

---

*The UNIX System views a newline as a line terminator. Generally, a newline maps onto a single linefeed (ASCII 10).

Summary

Because commands in a pipeline have both their input and output redirected, commands used in a pipeline must read input from the standard input, send output to the standard output, and report errors to the standard error. You can use filters in a pipeline because they handle input, output, and errors in this way. All commands in a pipeline, except the first and last commands, must be filters so that the output of each command in the pipeline is connected to the input of the next command.

A filter can be placed anywhere in a pipeline. Most UNIX filters assume that their data is made up of lines of text containing zero or more characters and ending with a newline line terminator. This chapter introduced the concept of UNIX filters and showed examples of how they can be used.

4

The *grep* Command

One of the most useful UNIX tools is the searching filter. You will find yourself using it all the time. The name of this command is `grep`. (The derivation of this name is discussed later.)

How to Use *grep*

As was mentioned in Chapter 3, `grep` reads lines from its standard input, or from the file(s) listed on the command line, and sends only those lines containing a specified pattern to the standard output.

For example, to find all the lines containing a capital S anywhere on the line, use

```
$ grep S phone.list
Smith, Terry    7-7989
StClair, Pat    4-6122
Stair, Chris    5-5972
Benson, Sam     4-5587
```

Note that three of the lines printed begin with S and that one simply contains an S.

Because the file name `phone.list` is listed on the command line, `grep` read the lines out of the file. In addition, `grep` will read data from the standard input if no file name is listed. In the commands

```
$ grep S < phone.list
```

and

```
$ cat phone.list ¦ grep S
```

grep reads lines from its standard input. In the first case, the standard input is redirected from the file. The second command is a pipeline, and grep searches the output of cat.

Options

Most UNIX utilities recognize options that further specify what the command does. One of the more obvious options that the grep command recognizes is the -v option, which tells grep to print the lines that don't match the pattern. This command prints the lines that don't contain an S.

```
$ grep -v S phone.list
Adams, Fran      2-3876
Brown, Robin     1-3745
```

Note that the -v is the first argument on the command line, before the pattern. grep, like most UNIX utility programs, requires that its options be listed first.

grep recognizes several additional options. The most useful options are listed in table 4.1. The -c option tells grep to print the number of matched lines only. The -i option instructs grep to search for the pattern in both upper- and lowercase characters. If you just want to identify files that contain the pattern, use -l, which tells grep to output only file names. If you want to know where the matched line occurs, use -n, which tells grep to precede each matched line with its line number. The -s option tells grep to suppress error messages if a file doesn't exist or is not readable.

It is not unusual to use more than one option. For example, to find all lines that don't contain an either an S or s, you would use

```
$ grep -v -i s phone.list
Brown, Robin      1-3745
```

Table 4.1.   grep *options.*

Option	Meaning
-c	Prints number of matches only
-i	Ignores case when searching for pattern
-l	Prints only the names of files containing pattern
-n	Precedes each matched line with its line number
-s	Suppresses file error messages
-v	Prints all lines that don't contain a pattern

Taking another step, if you only wanted to find out how many lines in the file didn't contain either a lower- or uppercase S, you could add -c to the previous command:

```
$ grep -v -i -c s phone.list
1
```

The order of the options is unimportant.

In addition to listing the options individually, you can combine them. Thus, the command grep -v -i -c s phone.list can also be written grep -vic s phone.list.

Quoting Arguments

Sometimes, options interfere with the pattern. The phone list file contains a dash between the first digit in the phone number and the four-digit extension. If you want to find all the people whose phone extensions begin with 5, you might enter

```
$ grep -5 phone.list
grep: illegal option -- 5
...
```

However, this doesn't work because grep assumes that whenever the first argument begins with a dash, it is an option. grep doesn't have a -5 option, so it prints the error message.

To solve this potential problem, you must tell grep that the dash in front of the 5 does not identify an option but rather is part of the pattern. Unfortunately, grep doesn't provide an option to do this, although some commands do. Instead, you can use a trick.

Like the shell, `grep` understands that backslashes are quoting characters. If `grep` sees `\-5` as a pattern, it will throw away the backslash (as a quote for the following character) and search for `-5`. Further, because this argument now starts with a backslash and not a dash, `grep` no longer sees it as an option.

To make this work, you must remember that the shell looks at each command line before it is executed. Thus, you can't simply enter `\-5` as the pattern. If you do, the shell will gobble up the backslash before sending the argument to `grep`. The backslash must be quoted from the shell. This can be done with single quotes, `'\-5'` or the more unsightly `\\-5`.

```
$ grep '\-5' phone.list
Stair, Chris     5-5972
Benson, Sam      4-5587
```

Figure 4.1 shows how the command is passed to `grep`.

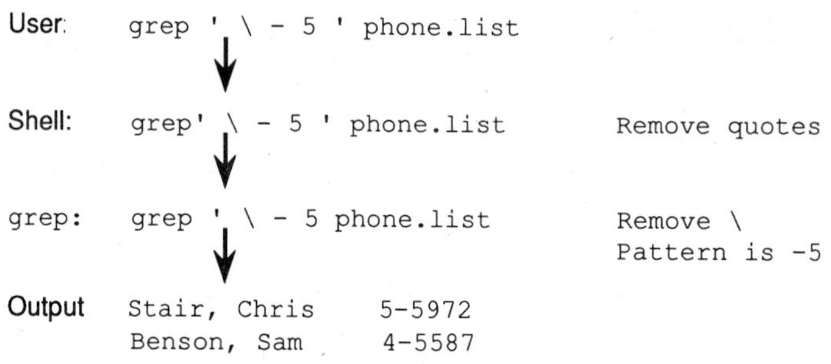

User: grep ' \ - 5 ' phone.list

Shell: grep' \ - 5 ' phone.list   Remove quotes

grep: grep ' \ - 5 phone.list   Remove \
                                                 Pattern is -5

Output   Stair, Chris   5-5972
           Benson, Sam   4-5587

Fig. 4.1.   *Passing -5 as a pattern to* grep.

The most important aspect of searching a line is to search for the proper text in the appropriate place. For example, if you wanted to find all the people whose first names started with C, you could use

```
$ grep C phone.list
StClair, Pat     4-6122
Stair, Chris     5-5972
```

But this doesn't quite do the job. In addition to finding Chris Stair, it also found Pat StClair. The problem stems from looking for a capital C in the wrong place.

The command line `grep C phone.list` looks for a C anywhere on the line. However, first names appear in a specific place on every line, after the last name, a comma, and a space. The reason the previous `grep` command got the wrong answer is because it was looking for the correct pattern in the wrong place.

The correct pattern must include information that identifies where on the line the text is located. In the case of a first name, the pattern must be preceded by a comma and a space:

```
$ grep , C phone.list
grep: Cant open C
phone.list: Smith, Terry      7-7989
phone.list: Adams, Fran       2-3876
phone.list: StClair, Pat      4-6122
phone.list: Brown, Robin      1-3745
phone.list: Stair, Chris      5-5972
phone.list: Benson, Sam       4-5587
```

Although the pattern appears correct, the result is clearly wrong. What happened? The problem is due to our old friend the shell.

Remember that before the shell creates a process to run `grep`, it scans the line for metacharacters (there aren't any) and then separates the command line into arguments at whitespace (space and tab characters). Thus the shell actually splits the pattern you sent to `grep` into two arguments. The shell views the space after the comma (in the pattern) as an argument separator.

The process created by the shell passes `grep` three arguments: a comma, the single character C, and `phone.list`. As instructed, `grep` searches the two files: C and `phone.list` for a comma. The first line is an error message telling you that `grep` couldn't find a file C. Then it prints every line in `phone.list` that contains a comma, which is all of them. The file name `phone.list` precedes every line because when you send `grep` more than a single file name, it displays which file contained the matched line being printed.

The solution to this problem is to hide the space from the shell using single quotes or a backslash. The correct command is

```
$ grep ', C' phone.list
Stair, Chris    5-5972
```

The command `grep ,\ C phone.list` will also work.

A similar problem occurs when you are trying to search for certain phone numbers that begin with a specified number. For example, to find all the phone numbers that begin with a 4, you might use, as a pattern, a tab* followed by a 4. However, as you can see, the command

```
$ grep <tab>4 phone.list
StClair, Pat     4-6122
Brown, Robin     1-3745
Benson, Sam      4-5587
```

doesn't quite work. It found Robin Brown's entry, which merely contains a 4, along with the two that start with a 4. The problem is again caused by whitespace.

In addition to using spaces as an argument separator, the shell also uses tabs and newlines. In fact, the shell uses *whitespace* characters (those characters that appear as spaces when printed) as argument separators. The correct command is

```
$ grep '<tab>4' phone.list
StClair, Pat     4-6122
Benson, Sam      4-5587
```

A backslash in front of the tab would also work.

Hands-on Exercise 4.1

There is another way to search for lines whose phone numbers begin with 4. What is it?

These two examples demonstrate an important point. When you enter command-line arguments, it is always a good idea to enclose them in single quotes, especially if they contain any unusual characters such as spaces, tabs, and asterisks. Also, quoting any argument that includes a nonalphanumeric character is an excellent habit to acquire. That way, you won't make a mistake by incorrectly using a metacharacter you are unaware of or just didn't notice. You will find a "quoting habit" comes in handy long after you learn all the shell metacharacters and, presumably, know whether quotes are required or not.

---

*When a tab must be shown as part of a pattern, it is listed as *<tab>*.

Searching for Two Patterns

and Search

Up to now, you've searched only for patterns that occur in a single place on a line. What if you need to search for a line that contains two separate patterns? For example, suppose you need to locate a phone number and you believe that it starts with a 4 and contains a 6. This requires an *and* search. That is, you need to find a line whose phone number starts with a 4 *and* contains a 6.

   and searches can be implemented as two separate searches connected by a pipeline. Each command in the pipeline performs another step of the *and* search. This example requires two searches, one for lines whose numbers starting with 4 and one for those containing a 6. The pipeline is

```
$ grep '<tab>4' phone.list ¦ grep 6
StClair, Pat    4-6122
```

Hands-on Exercise 4.2

Suppose you want entries that don't begin with a 4 but do contain a 6. How would you search for this line?

---

or Search

Another type of search is called an *or* search. An example is looking for phone numbers beginning with either a 4 or a 5. Unlike *and* searches, where each search must deal with the results of the previous one, *or* searches are independent of one another. Thus, to implement an *or* search requires two separate commands.

   Finding all the phone numbers that begin with a 4 or a 5 can be done in two ways. One method involves using a temporary file to hold the results of the two searches.

```
$ grep '<tab>4' phone.list > /tmp/phone.tmp
$ grep '<tab>5' phone.list >> /tmp/phone.tmp
$ cat phone.tmp
StClair, Pat    4-6122
Benson, Sam     4-5587
Stair, Chris    5-5972
```

Note the output redirection in the second `grep` command is append redirection.

The problem with this approach is twofold. First, you must use a temporary file. Second, you must type two separate command lines.

A better solution is to remove the need for a temporary file by using the shell's grouping metacharacter, parentheses, to combine the output of two commands into a single output stream.

```
$ (grep '<tab>4' phone.list ; grep '<tab>5' phone.list)
StClair, Pat    4-6122
Benson, Sam     4-5587
Stair, Chris    5-5972
```

Search Combinations

By combining *or* searches with *and* searches, you can create some fairly specific patterns. For example, suppose you recall that Robin's phone number (you can't remember the last name) begins with a 1 or a 4, but you can't remember which. You could just search for Robin and look at all of them. However, to look for an entry with a first name of Robin and a phone number beginning with a 1 or a 4, you could use the command line.

```
$ (grep '<tab>1' phone.list ; grep '<tab>4' phone.list) |
> grep ', Robin<tab>'
Brown, Robin    1-3745
```

Note the > at the beginning of the second line of this command. This is not a redirection metacharacter. In fact, it is not a metacharacter at all. It is the shell's *secondary* prompt.

The shell displays its secondary prompt when a command line ends without being completed. In essence, the shell is saying to you, "I see that the previous line ends with a pipe symbol and that means the command must be continued on the next line. So I'll print a secondary prompt to tell you it's all right with me." Pipe symbols, semicolons, quoted newlines*, and shell logical operators (covered in Part 3) produce secondary prompts when they are the last character on a command line.

---

*Newlines are quoted by a backslash, single quotes, double quotes (not yet covered), backquotes, or parentheses.

Hands-on Exercise 4.3

Create a command line that searches for all the lines in `phone.list` whose first names begin with either S or T and whose phone numbers begin with 5 or contain an 8.

Summary

The `grep` command is a powerful filter that searches a file for lines that contain a pattern and sends these lines to the standard output.

Like most UNIX utilities, `grep` recognizes options that further specify what the command does. Also like most UNIX utility programs, `grep` requires that its options be listed as the first arguments on the command line and start with a leading dash; the order of the options is unimportant. When multiple options are used they can be separated by spaces, tabs, or newlines.

This chapter demonstrated various ways to perform a search, such as looking for two separate patterns in the same line with an *and* search using a pipeline.

5

Regular Expressions

So far, we have used *fixed* patterns with `grep`. That is, the patterns have stated exactly what characters to look for. If we wanted to find a phone number that begins with a 4, we used the pattern `' <tab>4'`.

Fixed patterns are useful when you know *exactly* what you want to find. However, you often don't know. For example, exercise 4.3 asks you to find the lines whose first names begin with an S or T. In this case, the search is expressed as either of two acceptable patterns.

Although the use of pipelines and command groupings provides a good deal of flexibility in finding certain patterns, there are several things that a fixed pattern cannot handle at all. As a simple example, it is not possible to locate lines whose last names start with a specific character using fixed patterns. This is because a fixed pattern cannot specify the start of a line (which is how the last name is identified). A similar problem exists for finding phone numbers that end with a certain digit.

In addition to fixed patterns, `grep` also understands a pattern-matching language called *regular expressions*. Regular expressions provide two additional pattern pieces: location and character ranges.

Location of a Pattern

Caret

The location of a pattern can be set as the beginning or ending of a line. A caret (^) represents the start of a line and a dollar sign ($) the line's end. To find all the entries whose last names begin with an S, use

```
$ grep '^S' phone.list
Smith, Terry      7-7989
StClair, Pat      4-6122
Stair, Chris      5-5972
```

Quoting a Regular Expression

Note the single quotes around the pattern. The shell scans every pattern first, so you should always quote the pattern. You never know when you will encounter some weird shell option. As a real-life illustration, in the early days of UNIX, the caret was used as the pipeline metacharacter (now represented by ¦). For compatibility reasons, some shells still interpret a caret as a pipeline. Without the quotes, these shells print the ambiguous response

```
$ grep ^S phone.list
S: not found
Usage: grep -blcnsvi pattern file . . .
```

These messages make more sense if you replace the caret with a pipe symbol. The first line is a shell error reporting that the "command" S (the first argument after a pipe symbol must be a command) cannot be found. The second line is a grep error message reminding you of how to use grep. This error occurs because grep is called without any arguments. The point of this example is to show why you should make a habit of putting single quotes around patterns, whether the quotes are strictly needed or not.

Dollar Sign

To locate phone numbers that end with a 5, use the end-of-line marker—the dollar sign—as part of the pattern.

```
$ grep '5$' phone.list
Brown, Robin      1-3745
```

grep treats the caret and the dollar sign as special only if they begin and end a line, respectively. Thus, a pattern cannot span more than one line. grep is not able to search beyond the end of a line. The pattern 5$S looks for the fixed pattern of a 5 followed by a dollar sign and an S. The same is true of an embedded caret.

Matching a Range of Characters

Single Dot

In addition to beginning and ending line anchors for our patterns, regular expressions also provide ways to match a range of possible characters. The most general character range is represented by a single dot. The dot is regular-expression shorthand for *any single character*. Although a dot in a pattern matches any single character, it matches only one character. The pattern `.S` identifies lines containing the two character sequence, the second character of which is a capital S.

```
$ grep '.S' phone.list
Benson, Sam     4-5587
```

None of the lines beginning with S was printed because the S in those lines appears at the start and are not preceded by a character.

The dot is often useful when you know the two ends of a pattern but not what's in the middle. For example, suppose the business card you have in your wallet has been mutilated to the point that you can make out only the first and last digits of a person's phone number. To search for a phone number that begins with a 4 and ends with a 2, you can use dots to "pad out" the pattern. The search pattern is `'4-...2'`, which says a 4, followed by a dash, followed by exactly three characters, followed by a 2.

```
$ grep '4-...2' phone.list
StClair, Pat    4-6122
```

This works because every phone number in this example is represented the same way: a number, a dash, and four numbers. Note that the three unknown digits in the middle of the phone number are represented by three dots, one for each number.

Because the phone number is the last thing on a line, the end of the pattern is also the end of the line. To more fully specify the phone number (to stop it from getting confused by other numeric information in the file, such as an office number), you could add a dollar sign on the end: `4-...2$`. This says to look for the pattern at the end of each line. Another way to find the same lines is the pipeline `grep '4-' phone.list | grep '2$'`.

Hands-on Exercise 5.1

Find all the entries in the phone list with three-character first names.

Hands-on Exercise 5.2

Find all the entries that have an 8 as the second to the last digit in the phone number.

Often, a pattern contains any one of a set of specific characters. For example, Exercise 4.3 asks you to find the entries whose last names begin with an S or T. In this pattern, a dot is not appropriate. Instead, you want to say "match either an S or a T."

Brackets

In regular expressions, you specify a range of characters by enclosing them in brackets. The characters S and T are represented by the pattern [ST]. To find all the people whose last names begin with S or T, combine the previous range with the caret (the beginning of the line).

```
$ grep '^[ST]' phone.list
Smith, Terry    7-7989
StClair, Pat    4-6122
Stair, Chris    5-5972
```

The brackets are treated the same in regular expressions as with shell metacharacters. Thus, you can specify a range of characters using a dash. For example, the pattern [A-F] is a shorthand for [ABCDEF].

```
$ grep '[A-F]' phone.list
Adams, Fran     2-3876
StClair, Pat    4-6122
Brown, Robin    1-3745
Stair, Chris    5-5972
Benson, Sam     4-5587
```

The characters listed inside brackets are matched against individual characters. This means that the pattern `[23]` will identify lines that contain either a 2 or a 3.

```
$ grep '[23]' phone.list
Adams, Fran     2-3876
StClair, Pat    4-6122
Brown, Robin    1-3745
Stair, Chris    5-5972
```

Character ranges match only a single character. The pattern `[23]` will not look for the two-character sequence 23.

A character range can contain any set of characters, including those specified with dashes. For example, the range, `[A-DF3h#S-V]`, matches A, B, C, D, F, 3, h, #, S, T, U, or V.

Character ranges are commonly used with other regular expression symbols. For example, to find all the people whose last names begin with an A, B, or C, the brackets are combined with the caret.

```
$ grep '^[A-C]' phone.list
Adams, Fran     2-3876
Brown, Robin    1-3745
Benson, Sam     4-5587
```

A similar example is finding phone numbers that end with a 2 through 5.

```
$ grep '[2-5]$' phone.list
StClair, Pat    4-6122
Brown, Robin    1-3745
Stair, Chris    5-5972
```

Hands-on Exercise 5.3

Find all the entries in the phone list whose phone numbers begin with a 2 through 5.

Hands-on Exercise 5.4

Find all the entries in the phone list whose first names begin with a C through R.

Hands-on Exercise 5.5

Find all the entries in the phone list whose phone numbers begin with a 2 through 5 and end with a 5, 6, or 7.

The Exclusion Range

In addition to listing a range of characters to find, you also can list a set of characters not to search for. An exclusion range is specified by putting a caret inside the brackets. Thus, the pattern [^567] matches all characters that are not a 5, 6, or 7.

The exclusion range comes in handy when it is easier to list what isn't to be matched than what is. For example, suppose you want to find all the phone numbers that don't begin with a 4 or a 5. Using the pattern [^45]- requires less typing than [12367890]- but finds the same lines.

```
$ grep '[^45]-' phone.list
Smith, Terry    7-7989
Adams, Fran     2-3876
Brown, Robin    1-3745
```

Table 5.1 lists some common range patterns.

Table 5.1. *Common regular expression ranges.*

Pattern	Meaning
[A-Z]	All uppercase characters
[0-9]	All digits
[A-Za-z]	All upper- and lowercase characters
[A-Za-z0-9]	All alphanumeric characters

Hands-on Exercise 5.6

Find all the entries in the phone list whose phone numbers don't end with a 5, 6, or 7.

In addition to providing a character range, brackets also quote what's listed inside them. If a dot, dollar sign, beginning bracket, or backslash is listed inside brackets, `grep` doesn't treat it as a regular expression character, but rather as the character itself. The pattern [4$] looks for either a 4 or a $ in the file.

Dashes and carets have a special meaning inside brackets. However, if a dash is the first character inside brackets, it is seen as the dash character only. Just the opposite is true for carets. If a caret appears anywhere but the first character after a beginning bracket, it is seen as the caret character only. The treatment of these characters is shown in table 5.2.

Table 5.2. *Using dash and caret in regular expressions.*

Pattern	Meaning
[A-D]	The characters A, B, C, D
[-AD]	The characters -, A, D
[^56]	All characters but 5 and 6
[5^6]	The characters 5, ^, 6

Wildcard Characters

Earlier you used the pattern 4-...2$ to find phone numbers beginning with a 4 and ending with a 2. Consider the similar task of finding someone whose last name begins with an S and whose first name begins with a C.

At first glance, it might seem that you can identify names in the same way that you can identify phone numbers, that is, using dots to represent "unknown" parts of the pattern. In a previous example, the dots were substituted for the middle three digits of the phone number.

The problem with this approach is that phone numbers are different from names. Phone numbers have a fixed format: a number, a dash, and four numbers. Names are not a set number of characters in length. As a result, you don't know how many characters are between the S and the C.

What you need is a *wildcard* character: a character that means "skip everything between the S and the C." Regular expressions use the asterisk as a wildcard.

Asterisk

In a regular expression, an asterisk says to match zero or more of the preceding character. That is, an asterisk is the second part of a two-part pattern. The first part of the wildcard pattern is the character (or range) to match; the second part is the asterisk.

The asterisk must be used properly or else a meaningless pattern results. The pattern A* reads zero or more As. The odd result is that every character matches this pattern. A lowercase x matches zero every character matches this pattern. A lowercase x matches zero As. In fact, every line in phone.list contains zero or more As.

```
$ grep 'A*' phone.list
Smith, Terry      7-7989
Adams, Fran       2-3876
StClair, Pat      4-6122
Brown, Robin      1-3745
Stair, Chris      5-5972
Benson, Sam       4-5587
```

Typically, the asterisk is used in combination with the dot to represent zero or more of any character. Thus, the regular expression version of the shell's asterisk is .*. The dot is any single character; the asterisk is zero or more of what the dot matches. Together, they match the pattern zero or more of any characters.

You can use the .* pattern to help search for last names that begin with an S and first names that begin with a C. The entire pattern is made from three different parts:

    ^S   Last name starts with an S

    .*   Skip rest of last name

    , C   First name starts with a C

When the pattern is assembled, it is '^S.*, C'.

```
$ grep '^S.*, C' phone.list
Stair, Chris      5.5972
```

In addition to being combined with the dot, the asterisk is often used with brackets. Table 5.3 shows some typical patterns.

Table 5.3. *Useful patterns containing an asterisk.*

Pattern	Meaning
[A-Z]*	Zero or more uppercase characters
[a-z]*	Zero or more lowercase characters
[A-Za-z]*	Zero or more alphabetic characters
[0-9]*	Zero or more digits

Hands-on Exercise 5.7

Find all the entries in the phone list whose last names begin with a J through Z and whose phone numbers end with a 2, 3, 6, or 8.

In the pattern '^S.*, C', the .* matches whatever characters appear between an S at the beginning of the line and a comma. The .* can also match the comma and the space, so can you shorten the pattern to '^S.*C'?

The answer is no, because the comma and space in the pattern represent position in the line, not just characters. The comma and the space identify the C as the first character of the first name. Without the comma and space, the pattern simply says to look for an S at the beginning of the line followed by a C somewhere in the line.

```
$ grep '^S.*C' phone.list
StClair, Pat    4-6122
Stair, Chris    5-5972
```

The pattern '^S.*C' is too general, because it matches StClair. The point is that you need to be precise in the patterns you specify. This is especially true when using wildcards.

Earlier, you matched a phone number with the pattern 4-...2. Another way to identify a phone number pattern is to combine the digit range with the asterisk. You know the two ends of the phone number, so you can use the pattern [0-9]* to skip all the numbers between the 4 and the 2. The complete pattern would be 4-[0-9]*2$. Now the dollar sign is required to ensure that the 2 is treated as the end of the phone number.

Which pattern, 4-...2 or 4-[0-9]*2$, is better? The pattern 4-[0-9]*2$ specifically states that only digits appear after a dash and before the 2 at the end of the line. The pattern 4-...2 doesn't identify what characters are between the dash and the 2, but it does define how many there are. The best pattern is the one that gets exactly the correct result with the minimum of effort. I would rate these two about equal. Note that the more detailed pattern `4-[0-9][0-9][0-9]2$` exactly matches what you're looking for, though it does require a lot of typing.

Regular expression characters are treated differently by `grep` than other characters, so what do you do if you want to match a character that has a special regular expression meaning? Like the shell, programs that use regular expressions also use backslashes to quote things. Thus, the command `grep '\$' filename` searches the file for a dollar sign. Note that the backslash is inside the single quotes so the shell can't see it.

The asterisk matches zero or more instances of a specified character. What gets matched if there is more than one possible match as a result of using an asterisk in a pattern? For example, the pattern `'S.*7'` looks for an S followed by a 7. Consider the line

```
Smith, Terry    7-7989
```

from the phone list file. Which 7 is the one being matched by `'S.*7'`? The rule is that regular expressions always match the longest possible string of characters. Thus, the pattern `'S.*7'` matches the string

```
Smith, Terry    7-7
```

When using `grep`, it makes little difference since you are only looking for a line matching the pattern. However, with other tools that use regular expressions, the character matched by a regular expression will be important.

Quoted Braces

In addition to the asterisk, regular expressions offer a more limited wildcard mechanism. Instead of using the range zero or more, you can specify your own minimum and maximum number of pattern repeats. The syntax for enumerating your own minimum and maximum is to use quoted braces: `\{min,max\}`. Thus, the pattern `'5\{2,4\}'` says to look for two, three, or four 5s in a line.

```
$ grep '5\{2,4\}' phone.list
Benson, Sam    4-5587
```

The pattern would also match 4-5557 and 4-5555.

In addition to fixed patterns, you can use other regular expressions with quoted braces. In exercise 5.1, you were asked to find all entries with three-character first names. Suppose you wanted to find all the entries with three- or four-character first names. You could use the quoted braces with the dot.

```
$ grep ', .\{3,4\}<tab>' phone.list
Adams, Fran     2-3876
StClair, Pat    4-6122
Benson, Sam     4-5587
```

Incidentally, the pattern is a comma, a space, a dot, \{3,4\}, and a tab.

There are two other ways to use quoted braces. You can search for an exact number of matches by putting only one number inside the braces. The pattern '[345]\{2\}' looks for two 3s, 4s, or 5s in a row.

```
$ grep '[345]\{2\}' phone.list
Brown, Robin    1-3745          45 matches pattern
Benson, Sam     4-5587          55 matches pattern
```

You can also search for a minimum number of matches (but no maximum) by removing the second number inside the quoted braces but leaving the comma. The pattern '^.\{6,\},' looks for last names, at least six characters in length.

```
$ grep '^.\{6,\},' phone.list
StClair, Pat    4-6122
Benson, Sam     4-5587
```

Hands-on Exercise 5.8

Find all the entries in the phone list that contain between two and four 7s, 8s, or 9s.

Hand-on Exercise 5.9

Find all the entries with five-character last names and three- or four-character first names.

If all this seems more like the characters displayed by modem noise than it does pattern matching, maybe a practical example will help. The format of the phone list file is very specific: First names are supposed to appear after a comma and a space. A problem arises for people with titles after their last names. Consider these names:

Jackson, Ph.D., Jerry

Thomas, Jr., Lynn

Lynn's and Jerry's first names will be found with the usual searches as well as with some others. In addition to matching the `, J` pattern, Jerry Jackson's entry matches the `, P` because it has more than one comma. To find all the entries in the phone list with more than one comma, use `grep ',\{2,\}' phone.list`. The current list has no names matching this pattern.

Quoted Parentheses

Until now, you have had to specify the pattern being matched. What if your pattern involves a character that matched a previous pattern? For example, suppose you wanted to locate all the entries that contain a double character, like 55. The pattern `[0-9][0-9]` won't work because that simply matches any two digits. Instead, you want to find lines where the second character is the same as the first one. The problem is that you don't know which character matched the first range, so how can you look for that character again?

The solution to this problem is using another regular expression construct called *bracketed regular expressions*. Nine registers are maintained that can hold what is matched by a regular expression. The contents of these registers can be used elsewhere in the pattern to represent what was matched previously.

Characters are put into the registers by bracketed regular expressions, which are identified by quoted parentheses `\(...\)`. The registers are assigned in order. That is, the first register gets what matches the first bracketed regular expression, the second register gets what matches the second regular expression, and so on. To refer to what is held in a register, use a backslash in front of the register's number: `\1` for the first register, `\2` for the second one, and so on.

A bracketed regular expression is nothing more than any regular expression enclosed in quoted parentheses. The regular expression inside the quoted parentheses is interpreted as if the quoted parentheses weren't there. Thus, the pattern `\(.\)` matches any single character and stores that character into register 1. The pattern \(.\)\1 identifies a two-character sequence where both characters match.

```
$ grep '\(.\)\1' phone.list
Smith, Terry      7-7989
StClair, Pat      4-6122
Benson, Sam       4-5587
```

The pattern matched the `rr` in `Terry` and the `22` and `55` in the phone numbers.

Let's take one more look at how the pattern \(.\)\1 works. Consider the first line in the phone list file:

```
Smith, Terry      7-7989
```

Because a dot matches any character, the bracketed regular expression \(.\) matches S, the first character on the line, and puts S in register 1. On seeing the \1 in the pattern, grep takes the S out of the register and compares it to the second character on the line, the m. This doesn't match, so the pattern begins anew, putting m in register 1. This continues until the rr is actually matched, at which point the line is sent to the standard output and the search terminates.

As another example, suppose you wanted to find phone numbers that have the same digit on both sides of the dash. You must first store what is to the left of the dash in register 1, \(.\)-, and then see if what's after the dash is the same character. The final pattern is \(.\)-\1.

```
$ grep '\(.\)-\1' phone.list
Smith, Terry      7-7989
Stair, Chris      5-5972
```

As an example of using two registers, this command finds lines that contain a double character and have the same digit on both sides of the dash.

```
$ grep '\(.\)\1.*\(.\)-\2' phone.list
Smith, Terry      7-7989
```

Register 1 holds an r when the match occurs; register 2 holds a 7 when the second match is found.

Creating Regular Expressions

The key to using regular expressions is learning how to combine different pieces of a pattern to look for exactly the characters you want to find. As an example of constructing a pattern, consider the task of finding all last names containing two uppercase characters. Incidentally, these need not be the same character and they don't need to be next to one another.

Before you begin writing a pattern, let's try to rephrase the task into a more pattern-like description, given that we know what a last name looks like. Finding a last name with two uppercase characters could also be stated as looking for an uppercase character followed by zero or more lowercase characters, followed by another uppercase character. The pattern should now be evident as `'[A-Z][a-z]*[A-Z].*,'`.

```
$ grep '[A-Z][a-z]*[A-Z].*,' phone.list
StClair, Pat    4-6122
```

Creating regular expressions is an acquired skill. It takes some time before you can create complicated regular expressions that match exactly what you are searching for. However, regular expressions are a key part of many UNIX tools and filters. All of the editors on the UNIX System—vi, ex, ed, and sed (covered in Chapter 6)—use them. The time you spend learning to use regular expressions will be paid back many fold. Here are three exercises to get you started.

Hands-on Exercise 5.10

Find all entries whose first names start with T and whose phone numbers don't begin with a 4 or a 6.

Hands-on Exercise 5.11

Find all the entries whose first names contain more than one uppercase character.

Hands-on Exercise 5.12

Find all the entries whose phone numbers contain a duplicate digit, not necessarily next to each other.

Shell Metacharacters Versus Regular Expression Characters

It is common for users to confuse the shell's file-matching meta-characters with regular expression characters. This makes sense since some characters represent both shell metacharacters and regular expression characters, namely the asterisk and the brackets. There is no easy way to distinguish them, so you must learn which is which.

However, a few points may make it easier to tell the difference. First, the shell's file-matching metacharacters do not include a way to mark either the beginning or the end of a pattern, Instead, an asterisk is used to match everything before or after a set of characters. For example, `*c` identifies all file names that end in a c. A dollar sign is required for all regular expressions to match the same thing: `c$`.

In the shell, an asterisk by itself matches every file name in the directory. In regular expressions, an asterisk by itself is meaningless. In fact, it is a fixed pattern that only matches an asterisk. In most regular expressions that use an asterisk, an asterisk will follow either a dot or a set of brackets.

The most important distinction between shell metacharacters and regular expressions is that the shell interprets metacharacters. Thus, you should adopt the style of putting regular expressions inside single quotes, so the shell can't see them. This way, any characters inside single quotes are not meant for the shell. The converse is also true: anything outside single quotes should be treated as something that the user wants the shell to see.

The *fgrep* and *egrep* Commands

Chapter 4 discussed the `grep` command without showing how to use it with regular expressions. This chapter shows how to extend the power of `grep` by creating powerful patterns using regular expressions. Although only one `grep` command was covered in Chapter 4, the `grep` command is actually part of a three-filter family of searching tools. The two other commands that claim the `grep` name are `fgrep` and `egrep`. The subtle distinction between these three commands is how they handle their searching expressions.

The `grep` command can handle only a single search pattern. Both `fgrep` and `egrep` can handle several patterns and perform their searches in parallel; that is, they look for several patterns at the same time. The difference between `fgrep` and `egrep` is that `fgrep` doesn't recognize any regular expression characters and `egrep` does.

To handle multiple patterns, `fgrep` and `egrep` use the `-f` option, which tells these commands to find the search patterns in the file listed after the `-f` on the command line. In the file, the patterns are stored one per line. For example, to find the phone numbers of all the people in your department, you could use `fgrep` with a pattern file that held the last names of everyone in your group.

```
$ cat dept.list
Smith,
Brown,
StClair,
$ fgrep -f dept.list phone.list
Smith, Terry    7-7989
StClair, Pat    4-6122
Brown, Robin    1-3745
```

`egrep` differs from `grep` in two ways. `egrep` can match several patterns in a single pass through the file. Also, `egrep` recognizes an extended set of regular expression characters.

With the exception of bracketed regular expressions (the `\( \)` and `\{ \}` constructs), `egrep` can interpret the same regular expression characters that `grep` does. In addition, `egrep` recognizes the +, ?, ¦, and (). Table 5.4 describes what these characters mean.

Table 5.4.   egrep's *extended regular expression characters.*

Character	Function
r+	One or more matches of r
r?	Zero or one matches of r
a¦b	Either a or b
(r)	Treat r as a single regular expression

Although `egrep` accepts the `*`, it also provides two additional ranges: zero or one, represented by the `?`, and one or more, represented by the `+`. With an `*`, you have no control over how long the matching string might be. With `?`, you can specify that you want to match a line containing *no more than* one match of the pattern. Note that a `?` pattern matches zero occurrences as well. Thus,

```
$ egrep '5?' phone.list
Smith, Terry    7-7989
Adams, Fran     2-3876
StClair, Pat    4-6122
Brown, Robin    1-3745
Stair, Chris    5-5972
Benson, Sam     4-5587
```

matches every line in the phone list because every line contains zero or one 5.

The `+`, on the other hand, requires that there be at least one match in the line, although there can be more than one. Note the difference in output between the 5? and the \5+.

```
$ egrep '5+' phone.list
Brown, Robin    1-3745
Stair, Chris    5-5972
Benson, Sam     4-5587
```

Only the lines that actually have a 5 are matched. The pattern 5+ does the same thing as 55*.

`egrep` can search for several patterns at the same time. The ¦ symbol is used to contruct patterns that consist of several others. For example, to find all the Smiths or Browns in the phone list file, use the pattern `Smith,¦Brown`.

```
$ egrep 'Smith,¦Brown,' phone.list
Smith, Terry    7-7989
Brown, Robin    1-3745
```

The real power of `egrep` comes with the fourth added regular expression character, the parentheses. The parentheses tell `egrep` to treat whatever is inside them as a single regular expression. This lets you to apply regular expression characters to larger patterns. For example, to find someone named either Robin Brown or Robin Smith, you could use

```
$ egrep '^(Smith,|Brown,) Robin' phone.list
Brown, Robin    1-3745
```

Table 5.5 shows other `egrep` patterns.

Table 5.5.   *Some egrep patterns.*

Patterns	Functions
(ab)+	One or more occurrences of ab
(ab)?	None or one ab string
(a|b)+	One or more occurrences of a or b

Some *egrep* Patterns

As a (somewhat contrived) example, to find lines containing at least two rs or two 5s, you can use

```
$ egrep '(rr|55)+' phone.list
Smith, Terry    7-7989
Benson, Sam     4-5587
```

`fgrep`'s capabilities are a subset of those for `egrep`, so I'm not sure why you would use `fgrep`. One reason you might choose `fgrep` is that a tool designed for fixed pattern searching (`fgrep`) should run faster than a program able to handle regular expressions (`egrep`) looking for a fixed pattern. Although it seems that this theory should hold true, tests show that `fgrep` is, in fact, slower than either `grep` or `egrep`, even with fixed patterns.

```
$ time fgrep 'a' chapter.* > /dev/null
        real        12.2
        user        10.1
        sys          0.8
$ time egrep 'a' chapter.* > /dev/null
        real         9.9
        user         8.7
        sys          0.2
```

```
$ time grep 'a' chapter.* > /dev/null
        real        9.6
        user        8.1
        sys         0.3
```

Therefore, I can't see any reason why you would use `fgrep`. It is included here merely for the sake of completeness.

As for the choice between `grep` and `egrep`, if you need to use a bracketed regular expression, you must use `grep`. To use the ?, +, |, or (), you must use `egrep`. Except for these requirements, the choice between `grep` and `egrep` is one of personal preference only. I prefer to use `grep`, if for no other reason than that its name is one character shorter than `egrep`.

Summary

In addition to understanding fixed patterns, `grep` also understands regular expressions. These are a key part of many UNIX tools and filters, including all of the editors on the UNIX System. The key to using regular expressions is learning how to combine different pieces of a pattern to look for exactly the characters you want to find.

Regular expressions provide the capability to search for the location of a pattern and for characters within a range. Regular expressions are so important that I included several tables in this chapter listing regular expression characters and their meanings.

6

The *sed* Command

Text editing is a common computer task, typically involving an interactive, full-screen editor that lets you move through the text, making changes where they are needed.

UNIX supplies vi, an interactive screen editor. It can edit text on a terminal but is virtually of no use in editing text in a stream (i.e., a pipeline) being read from the standard input. Further, vi doesn't easily write its edit file to the standard output. In other words, vi is not a filter and is of no use in a pipeline.

In addition to vi, UNIX supplies sed, a stream editor. sed is a filter that reads its standard input,* performs the requested edits, and sends the output to the standard output. Because sed is a filter, it prints the results of any edits to the standard output, not back into the file being read. Thus, any changes made by sed are not reflected in the file. Updating the file with the changes is discussed later in this chapter.

Editors need two pieces of information: what text is to be edited and then what changes are to be made. Interactive editors let you select text by moving the cursor to it using keystrokes or a pointing device. After you are at the proper spot in the file, you issue the edit command.

The sed filter works the same as other editors except it is not interactive and must provide another way to identify where an edit is to occur. Because sed is editing a stream of characters, it uses either line numbers or regular expressions to locate the line(s) to edit.

---

*Like most other filters, sed only reads the standard input if no file names are listed on the command line.

sed requires that it receive at least one argument: the editing command. Additional arguments are names of files to edit:

```
sed 'edit-command' [filenames]
```

sed edit commands often contain spaces or other special characters and should always be enclosed in single quotes to protect them from shell interpretation.

The edit command consists of two parts, an *address* to identify the line to edit and an *instruction*, which tells sed what to do with the line.

```
sed 'address instruction' [filenames]
```

If the address part of the command is omitted, every line is chosen for editing. It is an error if there is no instruction in a sed command. Incidentally, one way that sed tells you it didn't understand your command is with the message command garbled.

There are three kinds of addresses you can use with sed. First, you can edit every line by leaving the address blank. This is fairly common. Second, you can specify a single line number or a range of lines. Third, you can use a single regular expression or a range of them.

sed is a full-featured editor containing many editing instructions. However, I have found only three of them to be truly useful in my UNIX work. This is not to say that the other instructions are useless. Rather, the work I've done either hasn't needed them, or other tools perform the same tasks more easily. The three instructions are *substitute*, *delete*, and *print*.

The Substitute Instruction

The substitute instruction is represented by s and requires two pieces of information: what is to be changed and what is to take its place. sed uses delimiters to separate the parts of the command. Traditionally, a forward slash is used with the substitute command, although any delimiter (not contained in the substitution strings) will work.

Substituting for Fixed Patterns

The format of the sed substitute command is

```
sed 's/string to change/string to insert/' filename
```

For example, suppose you are told that Terry Smith's last name is really Smythe. To make such a change, substitute Smythe for Smith.

```
$ sed 's/Smith/Smythe/' phone.list
Smythe, Terry  7-7989
Adams, Fran    2-3876
StClair, Pat   4-6122
Brown, Robin   1-3745
Stair, Chris   5-5972
Benson, Sam    4-5587
```

Keep in mind that the contents of the phone list file haven't been changed. Instead, the file has been displayed on the standard output after going through the sed filter.

```
$ cat phone.list
Smith, Terry   7-7989
Adams, Fran    2-3876
StClair, Pat   4-6122
Brown, Robin   1-3745
Stair, Chris   5-5972
Benson, Sam    4-5587
```

Recall that a sed command consists of an address to locate the lines to edit and the edit instruction. In this sed command, the address was omitted, leaving just the substitute instruction. In such a case, every line is chosen for editing. However, only those lines containing the string Smith are affected by the command. In the phone list file, there is only one line where the substitution is made.

The address for a sed command goes in front of the instruction. Because sed is editing the first line, you could add the numeric address 1.

```
$ sed '1s/Smith/Smythe/' phone.list
Smythe, Terry 7-7989
Adams, Fran   2-3876
StClair, Pat  4-6122
Brown, Robin  1-3745
Stair, Chris  5-5972
Benson, Sam   4-5587
```

You may be wondering why all the lines are printed even though you specified that only the first one was to be edited. Unlike `grep`, whose job it is to print only certain lines, `sed` is an editor, and it prints every line it reads, regardless of whether it was edited. As you'll see shortly, it's possible to suppress the display of unchanged lines.

The address chooses only the lines to edit. Thus, if you chose lines 1 through 5, the result would be the same because lines 2, 3, 4, and 5 don't contain the string `Smith`. To identify a range of line numbers, put a comma between them.

```
$ sed '1,5s/Smith/Smythe/' phone.list
Smythe, Terry   7-7989
Adams, Fran     2-3876
StClair, Pat    4-6122
Brown, Robin    1-3745
Stair, Chris    5-5972
Benson, Sam     4-5587
```

The only way to change the output of this `sed` command is to omit line 1 from the address range. In the following example, the address tells `sed` to check lines 2 through the end of the file. Because none of these lines contains Smith, no edit is performed. In an address, the end of the file is represented by a dollar sign.

```
$ sed '2,$s/Smith/Smythe/' phone.list
Smith, Terry    7-7989
Adams, Fran     2-3876
StClair, Pat    4-6122
Brown, Robin    1-3745
Stair, Chris    5-5972
Benson, Sam     4-5587
```

In addition to numeric addresses, you can also identify lines to edit using regular expressions. To ensure that a regular expression address is not confused with an editing instruction, `sed` requires you to enclose regular expression addresses in forward slashes. Another way to identify the first line for editing is to use `/Smith/` as the address.

```
$ sed '/Smith/s/Smith/Smythe/' phone.list
Smythe, Terry   7-7989
Adams, Fran     2-3876
StClair, Pat    4-6122
```

```
Brown, Robin    1-3745
Stair, Chris    5-5972
Benson, Sam     4-5587
```

The command `'/Smith/s/Smith/Smythe/'` says to select lines containing Smith and then to substitute Smythe for Smith.

Often the regular expression that identifies the lines to edit also specifies what is to be changed by the substitute instruction. `sed` lets you use a shorthand in cases where the search expression also matches the characters being changed. The shorthand is simply to omit the first part of the substitute command. Thus,

```
$ sed '/Smith/s/Smith/Smythe/' phone.list
```

becomes

```
$ sed '/Smith/s//Smythe/' phone.list
```

You can select a range of lines by using regular expression addresses in the same way you choose a range of lines with a numeric address: by separating them with a comma. The address `/Smith/,/Stair/` identifies lines starting with the first one containing `/Smith/` through the first line containing `/Stair/`. You can select from a pattern to the end of the file by using a dollar sign. The range `/Smith/,$` chooses from the first line matching `/Smith/` to the end of the file.

Hands-on Exercise 6.1

Write three `sed` commands: one with no address, one with a numeric address, and one with a regular expression address that changes Brown to Browne in your phone list.

`sed` is a filter. That means it prints to the standard output. Thus, the "Smith" edits have no effect on the phone list file itself. The filter simply sent the edited character stream to the standard output. If you want to update the file, you must replace it with `sed`'s output. Your first thought might be to use redirection this way *(but don't enter this command)*:

```
$ sed 's/Smith/Smythe/' phone.list > phone.list
```

Worse than not working (and it doesn't work), this command erases the phone list file.

The problem involves the order of command interpretation. Recall that the shell always scans a command line for shell metacharacters before creating a process to execute the command. As a result, the shell sets up the redirection, which erases the contents of `phone.list`, before `sed` can get a chance to look at it.

Updating the `phone.list` file takes two steps. First, you need to create a temporary file to hold `sed`'s output. Second, you must replace the phone list with the temporary file.

```
$ sed 's/Smith/Smythe/' phone.list > /tmp/phone.tmp
$ mv /tmp/phone.tmp phone.list
```

If you want to keep a backup of the current phone list, add the command `mv phone.list phone.bak` between the `sed` and the `mv`. Note that the rest of the book assumes that the phone list has not been updated.

Using Regular Expressions in Commands

In addition to substituting for fixed patterns, such as Smith, `sed` allows regular expressions as the first part of a substitute command. For example, this command replaces a 2 at the end of a line with a 3.

```
$ sed 's/2$/3/' phone.list
Smith, Terry    7-7989
Adams, Fran     2-3876
StClair, Pat    4-6123
Brown, Robin    1-3745
Stair, Chris    5-5973
Benson, Sam     4-5587
```

Hands-on Exercise 6.2

What does the command `sed '2,4s/2$/3/' phone.list` do?

Hands-on Exercise 6.3

Write a command that removes the first two characters of the phone number and replaces them with an X.

Not only can the substitute command add text to a line, but it also can remove text by substituting nothing for it. For example, to convert the phone list into a name list, you have to get rid of the phone number. Because the phone number starts after a tab and goes to the end of the line, the regular expression <tab>.*$, matches it.

```
$ sed 's/<tab>.*$//' phone.list
Smith, Terry
Adams, Fran
StClair, Pat
Brown, Robin
Stair, Chris
Benson, Sam
```

The empty substitution string represents just what it says. It replaces the matched text with nothing.

Another example is deleting the last name from each entry. The last name goes from the beginning of the line to a comma and a space. One pattern that matches the last name is ^.*, (a space follows the comma in the pattern).

```
$ sed 's/^.*, //' phone.list
Terry    7-7989
Fran     2-3876
Pat      4-6122
Robin    1-3745
Chris    5-5972
Sam      4-5587
```

So far, the sed commands have replaced text. Often you want to add text to the line without removing anything from it. For example, suppose the company has expanded to the point where employees have to use seven-digit phone numbers instead of five. The prefix to add is 72. Because the phone number is preceded by a tab, it might seem that this command would work.

```
$ sed 's/<tab>/72/' phone.list
Smith, Terry727-7989
Adams, Fran722-3876
StClair, Pat724-6122
Brown, Robin721-3745
Stair, Chris725-5972
Benson, Sam724-5587
```

However, it doesn't quite do the job. True, it did add the 72, but it also removed the tab between the first name and the number.

Remember that sed's substitute command replaces text. The first substitution pattern is removed from the line, and the second one is put in its place. Often, the first pattern is simply used as a line marker to tell sed where to add text. That is the purpose of the tab in the previous command. The correct way to do this is, in effect, to remove the pattern from the line and then to reinsert it. Thus, the command you should use to add a 72 prefix to the phone number is

```
$ sed 's/<tab>/<tab>72/' phone.list
Smith, Terry    727-7989
Adams, Fran     722-3876
StClair, Pat    724-6122
Brown, Robin    721-3745
Stair, Chris    725-5972
Benson, Sam     724-5587
```

Hands-on Exercise 6.4

Remove the first name from the phone list.

Hands-on Exercise 6.5

Put the word "Phone:" in front of the phone number.

Handling Multiple Instructions

Suppose your company expands into another building and those employees with phone numbers beginning with 1 through 4 are now in building 1 and everyone else is in building 2. You want the phone list to reflect this. This edit requires two different substitute instructions: one for those people in building 1 and one for people in building 2.

You can perform both substitutions in a single sed command by using multiple instructions. All instructions are sent to sed as the first argument. Each instruction must be on its own line.

```
$ sed '/[1-4]-/s/$/ (Bldg 1)/
> /[05-9]-/s/$/ (Bldg 2)/' phone.list
```

```
Smith, Terry    7-7989  (Bldg 2)
Adams, Fran     2-3876  (Bldg 1)
StClair, Pat    4-6122  (Bldg 1)
Brown, Robin    1-3745  (Bldg 1)
Stair, Chris    5-5972  (Bldg 2)
Benson, Sam     4-5587  (Bldg 1)
```

Note that text was added to the end of a line by substituting for the $. You can't remove the new line through substitution, but you can use it as a place marker. Text can be added at the beginning of the line by substitution for ^.

To insert a new line with sed, you must quote the new line with a backslash. For example, you can add a heading to the output by substituting the heading for the beginning of the first line and then putting a new line at the end of it.

```
$ sed '1s/^/Name<tab> <tab>Phone Number\
> /' phone.list
Name            Phone Number
Smith, Terry    7-7989
Adams, Fran     2-3876
StClair, Pat    4-6122
Brown, Robin    1-3745
Stair, Chris    5-5972
Benson, Sam     4-5587
```

Recall that bracketed regular expressions let you store in registers the text on a line that matches a regular expression. Bracketed regular expressions can be quite useful in sed substitute commands. For example, suppose you want to abbreviate everyone's first name to just their first initial and a period.

This is easily done by storing the first character after a comma and a space in register 1 and then substituting that for the entire first name.

```
$ sed 's/, \(.\).*<tab>/, \1<tab>/' phone.list
Smith, T. 7-7989
Adams, F. 2-3876
StClair, P.    4-6122
Brown, R. 1-3745
Stair, C. 5-5972
Benson, S.    4-5587
```

Let's take a closer look at this command. The pattern part of the substitute instruction, , \(.\).*<tab>, matches each employee's first name. Remember that a pattern containing \(...\) matches the same thing as it would without the bracketing—in this case, , ..*<tab>. The bracketing stores the first character after the space in register 1. This is the first character in the first name. Because everything in the first part of a substitute instruction is removed from the line, you must put the comma, space, and tab back in the line along with the contents of register 1 and a period. The result is the second part of the substitute instruction: , *.<tab>.

Hands-on Exercise 6.6

Substitute the first initial of the last name for the entire last name.

Hands-on Exercise 6.7

Substitute the first initial of the last name for the last name and the first initial of the first name for the first name.

Hands-on Exercise 6.8

Assume that everyone's building number is the same as the first number in the phone number. Add the building number to the end of each phone entry.

---

sed uses forward slashes as the delimiter in substitute commands. What happens if the substitution to be made involves forward slashes? Suppose you need to convert a UNIX path name to a DOS path name. DOS path names use back slashes as directory separators. Thus, the UNIX path /usr/ray becomes the DOS path \usr\ray.

Before you can perform this edit, you need to know that the sed substitute command performs only the first substitution it finds on a line. If you want to make the change to every occurrence of the pattern on the line, you must add a g (for global) to the end of the substitute instruction.

```
$ echo xxx ¦ sed 's/x/Y/'
Yxx
$ echo xxx ¦ sed 's/x/Y/g'
YYY
```

Using `echo` as the first command in a pipeline is a simple way to introduce text into the pipeline data stream. This technique will be important when you create applications.

You have two choices in making the path name substitution. First, you can quote the nondelimiting forward slashes with backslashes.

```
$ pwd
/usr/ray/book
$ pwd ¦ sed 's/\//\\/g'
\usr\ray\book
```

`sed` recognizes the backslash as a quoting character. A literal backslash is represented by two backslashes. Two are required because the first is needed to quote the second one.

`sed` lets you use any character as the substitute instruction delimiter. Because forward slashes are the substitution pattern, let's use semicolons as the substitution delimiter.

```
$ pwd ¦ sed 's;/;\\;g'
\usr\ray\book
```

The Delete Instruction

`sed`'s delete instruction is represented by d. It simply removes the identified line from the output stream. The following command deletes all the lines:

```
$ sed d phone.list
```

Use the delete instruction to delete lines that match regular expressions or specifically numbered lines.

```
$ sed '/^S/d' phone.list
Adams, Fran    2-3876
Brown, Robin   1-3745
Benson, Sam    4-5587
```

```
$ sed '1,3d' phone.list
Brown, Robin    1-3745
Stair, Chris    5-5972
Benson, Sam     4-5587
```

When used to delete lines matching a regular expression, a `sed` command is equivalent to a `grep -v` command with the same pattern.

```
$ sed '/^[A-J]/d' phone.list
Smith, Terry    7-7989
StClair, Pat    4-6122
Stair, Chris    5-5972
$ grep -v '^[A-J]' phone.list
Smith, Terry    7-7989
StClair, Pat    4-6122
Stair, Chris    5-5972
```

Hands-on Exercise 6.9

Delete all the entries whose phone numbers begin with a 2, 3, or 7.

The Print Instruction

`sed`'s print instruction is represented by p. Normally, the `sed` command puts every line it reads onto its standard output. Thus, it may seem redundant to use a print instruction. In fact, when used with a regular `sed` command, the print instruction does produce redundant output.

```
$ sed p phone.list
Smith, Terry    7-7989
Smith, Terry    7-7989
Adams, Fran     2-3876
Adams, Fran     2-3876
StClair, Pat    4-6122
StClair, Pat    4-6122
Brown, Robin    1-3745
Brown, Robin    1-3745
Stair, Chris    5-5972
```

```
Stair, Chris    5-5972
Benson, Sam     4-5587
Benson, Sam     4-5587
```

One copy of each line is passed through by sed and one copy is printed because of the print instruction.

By itself, the print instruction is not of much value. It is mainly used with sed's −n option. The −n option tells sed not to put lines read to the standard output. When −n is used, the only output from a sed command is that explicitly printed with the print instruction.

```
$ sed -n p phone.list
Smith, Terry    7-7989
Adams, Fran     2-3876
StClair, Pat    4-6122
Brown, Robin    1-3745
Stair, Chris    5-5972
Benson, Sam     4-5587
```

In this case, sed doesn't copy its input to standard output. All the output is due to the print instruction.

When used with a regular expression, the print instruction is equivalent to a grep command.

```
$ sed -n '/[1-4]-/p' phone.list
Adams, Fran     2-3876
StClair, Pat    4-6122
Brown, Robin    1-3745
Benson, Sam     4-5587
$ grep '[1-4]-' phone.list
Adams, Fran     2-3876
StClair, Pat    4-6122
Brown, Robin    1-3745
Benson, Sam     4-5587
```

One advantage that sed's print command has over grep is that grep can't search for lines by number. Because sed can handle numeric addresses, the print instruction does this easily.

```
$ sed -n '1,3p' phone.list
Smith, Terry    7-7989
Adams, Fran     2-3876
StClair, Pat    4-6122
```

This comes in handy when you want to select a few lines from a file by number.

Options

sed takes two other options in addition to -n. The -f option tells sed to take its editing commands from the file whose name follows the -f.

```
$ cat cmd.file
s/<tab>/<tab>phone: /
$ sed -f cmd.file phone.list
Smith, Terry    phone: 7-7989
Adams, Fran     phone: 2-3876
StClair, Pat    phone: 4-6122
Brown, Robin    phone: 1-3745
Stair, Chris    phone: 5-5972
Benson, Sam     phone: 4-5587
```

The -e option sends several editing commands to sed from the command line. Instead of putting all the commands in a single argument, you can precede each one with a -e. The following command converts the comma and space after the last name into a tab and changes all phone numbers that start with 2 to start with a 4:

```
$ sed -e 's/, /<tab>/' -e 's/2-/4-/' phone.list
Smith          Terry     7-7989
Adams          Fran      4-3876
StClair        Pat       4-6122
Brown          Robin     1-3745
Stair          Chris     5-5972
Benson         Sam       4-5587
```

Summary

The sed command comes in handy when you need to make changes that are within a line of text. You will find that sed is useful in both interactive use and within larger applications. This chapter only covered three of sed's many instructions. It is worthwhile to read your system's documentation on the sed command to discover other instructions that you might find useful.

7

The *awk* Command

UNIX provides several tools that perform similar tasks. An example of two such commands are `sed` and `awk`. The `sed` command edits text. The `awk` command formats text. There is a large overlap in the capabilities of the two commands. Both can perform edits and format text.

What is the difference between editing and formatting? In my opinion and in the context of UNIX tools, editing means changing the characters that make up a line of text. Formatting is changing the words in the line. It is editing to substitute a 4 at the end of a line with a 2, to change Smith into Smythe, or to replace someone's first name with only an initial. It is formatting to switch the first name and last names or to put the word "Number" in front of the phone number.

The `awk`* command works similarly to `sed`. An `awk` command takes an instruction as its first argument. The instruction consists of a pattern and an action. The action is always enclosed in braces.

awk `'pattern { action }'` `[files]`

awk is a filter, so the input files are optional.

awk performs the specified action on lines that match the pattern. The pattern can be a regular expression or a logical test. As with `sed`, a regular expression pattern must be enclosed in forward slashes. If no pattern is listed, the action is performed on every input line.

---

*If you are wondering what awk stands for, the name of the command is derived from the first characters of the last names of the people who wrote the command—Aho, Weinberger, and Kernighan.

Using the Default Print Action

awk provides a default action: to print the line. Thus, when a pattern is listed without an action, it performs grep's job, that is, it displays all lines that match the pattern.

```
$ awk '/^S/' phone.list
Smith, Terry    7-7989
StClair, Pat    4-6122
Stair, Chris    5-5972
```

In addition to an implied print command, awk also offers a print action. The preceding grep-like command could also be written

```
$ awk '/^S/ {print}' phone.list
Smith, Terry    7-7989
StClair, Pat    4-6122
Stair, Chris    5-5972
```

awk is very sensitive to its syntax. If you forget a forward slash or a brace, your awk command will fail, usually issuing the somewhat renowned error message awk: bailing out near line 1.

```
$ awk '/^S/ print' phone.list
awk: syntax error near line 1
awk: bailing out near line 1
```

Defining and Counting Fields

What makes awk so good at formatting is that it separates every line it reads into *fields*. awk considers a field to be any sequence of characters separated by whitespace (spaces and tabs). It numbers each field, starting at 1, and identifies each field by its number preceded by a dollar sign. The line

```
Smith, Terry    7-7989
```

consists of three fields:

```
$1    Smith,
$2    Terry
$3    7-7989
```

When you refer to a field identifier (i.e., $1), awk substitutes the current line's field for it. To print a field, list the field identifier with a print statement. The action `print $1` prints the first field in the selected line.

```
$ awk '{print $1}' phone.list
Smith,
Adams,
StClair,
Brown,
Stair,
Benson,
```

In addition to breaking each line into fields, awk also counts the number of fields on each line and the number of lines read. awk refers to the number of fields as NF and the number of lines read as NR. This command prints the line number and the first and third fields of each line.

```
$ awk '{print NR, $1, $3}' phone.list
1 Smith, 7-7989
2 Adams, 2-3876
3 StClair, 4-6122
4 Brown, 1-3745
5 Stair, 5-5972
6 Benson, 4-5587
```

Note the commas in the print command. They tell print to separate its output with spaces. A print statement without commas runs its output together. Spaces between print's arguments have no effect.

```
$ awk '{print NR $1 $3}' phone.list
1Smith,7-7989
2Adams,2-3876
3StClair,4-6122
4Brown,1-3745
5Stair,5-5972
6Benson,4-5587
```

Printing Fixed Strings

You also can print fixed strings by enclosing them in double quotes. The tab between the first name and the phone number is removed by awk because the tab is a delimiter. To add it back in, simply put a quoted tab in the print statement.

```
$ awk '{print $1, $2 "<tab>" $3}' phone.list
Smith, Terry    7-7989
Adams, Fran     2-3876
StClair, Pat    4-6122
Brown, Robin    1-3745
Stair, Chris    5-5972
Benson, Sam     4-5587
```

Note that there are no commas on either side of the tab. If commas were used, spaces would be printed on both sides of the tab, and the format of the output wouldn't match the format of the phone list file.

Hands-on Exercise 7.1

Print the phone list with the word ''phone'' inserted in front of each phone number.

Rearranging words on a line is easily accomplished with awk. You simply tell awk how to print them. For example, the following command prints the phone list with the first name followed by the last name and then the phone number.

```
$ awk '{print $2, $1 "<tab>" $3}' phone.list
Terry Smith,    7-7989
Fran Adams,     2-3876
Pat StClair,    4-6122
Robin Brown,    1-3745
Chris Stair,    5-5972
Sam Benson,     4-5587
```

Hands-on Exercise 7.2

For phone numbers beginning with a 4, 5, or 6, print the phone list in the following format:

Last name, (First name) *tab* Phone number

Hint: You need to use both a pattern and an action.

Printing Nothing

In addition to printing something, you can also print nothing with the print command. However, you must use the proper print command. Recall that the print command, if called by itself, prints the entire input line. If you use the print command with a null string as the argument, it simply prints an extra blank line. A null string is represented by an empty set of double quotes (**" "**). Also, to print a blank line, you can put the string **"\n"** (the double quotes are required) in a print command.

For example, suppose you want to print the phone list with each name and phone number entry occupying two lines. On one line the name is to be preceded by "Name:"; on the second line, each phone number is to be preceded by "Number:"; and the entries are to be separated by a blank line.

Printing several lines for a single input line requires that multiple commands be contained in a single action, as long as each command is on its own line or separated by semicolons.

```
$ awk'{print "Name:", $1, $2
> print "Number:",$3
> print "" }' phone.list
Name: Smith, Terry
Number: 7-7989

Name: Adams, Fran
Number: 2-3876

Name: StClair, Pat
Number: 4-6122
```

```
Name: Brown, Robin
Number: 1-3745

Name: Stair, Chris
Number: 5-5972

Name: Benson, Sam
Number: 4-5587
```

If written using semicolons instead of new lines and "\n" instead of the empty string, the command looks like this:

```
$ awk '{print "Name:", $1, $2; print "Number:", $3,"\n"
> print "\n" }' phone.list
```

Until now, the awk commands used either regular expression patterns or had no pattern at all. As was mentioned earlier, awk also can select lines based on logical tests. awk provides the logical tests listed in table 7.1.

Table 7.1.   *Logical tests.*

Symbol	Meaning
==	Equal
!=	Not equal
<	Less than
<=	Less than or equal to
>	Greater than
>=	Greater than or equal to
~	Matches a regular expression
!~	Doesn't match a regular expression
||	Logical or
&&	Logical and

When using a regular expression with either the ~ or the !~ tests, you must enclose the regular expression in forward slashes. When comparing anything to a string, enclose the string in double quotes.

For example, to change Smith into Smythe, you can use the equality test to find the entries with a last name of Smith.

```
$ awk '$1 == "Smith," { print "Smythe,", $2 "<tab>" $3}'
phone.list
Smythe, Terry   7-7989
```

Note that the spaces around the == are not required. The pattern
$1=="Smith," also works.

When you did the same thing with sed, both the changed and
unchanged lines were printed. This is the way sed works. awk, however, prints only the lines it is told to print. To print all the lines in the
file, you have to add another pattern to the awk command that·explic-
itly prints the unchanged lines.

The logical *and* and the logical *or* allow you to look for several
things on a line. For example, suppose you need to find the entries
whose phone numbers start with a 1 or 2 or whose last names start
with A or B. In this search, you want to match one or the other pattern.
This calls for the logical *or*.

```
$ awk '$1 == "Smith," { print "Smythe,", $2 "<tab>" $3}
> $1 != "Smith,"' phone.list
Smythe, Terry   7-7989
Adams,  Fran    2-3876
StClair, Pat    4-6122
Brown,  Robin   1-3745
Stair, Chris    5-5972
Benson, Sam     4-5587
```

The second pattern takes advantage of awk's default print action.
From the length of this awk command, you can see why sed is often
used to do simple formatting.

There is a subtle distinction between using the pattern
/Smith,/ and using the logical test $1 == "Smith,". The pattern
/Smith,/ searches the entire line for the characters "Smith,". The
logical test $1 == "Smith," searches only the first field (the last
name) for "Smith,".

```
$ awk '$1 ~ /^[AB]/ ¦¦ $3 ~ /^[12]/' phone.list
Adams,  Fran    2-3876
Brown,  Robin   1-3745
Benson, Sam     4-5587
```

The regular expression position characters work within single fields in
awk. Thus, you can use a caret to identify the beginning of a field. You
also can use a dollar sign to denote the end of a field. Remember, a
regular expression in awk must be enclosed by forward slashes.

Hands-on Exercise 7.3

Find all the entries whose phone numbers either begin or end with a 5.

Hands-on Exercise 7.4

Find all the entries with last names of at least five characters and first names with four or more characters.

Each entry in our phone list has three fields: a last name, a first name, and a phone number. You can verify this with awk.

```
$ awk 'NF != 3' phone.list
```

This command prints all lines that don't have three fields. Because there is no output, all lines in the phone list have only three fields. Incidentally, the variables NF and NR are used without dollar signs. In awk, only field identifiers need dollar signs.

Options*

awk recognizes two options. The -f option tells awk to read its instructions from the file whose name follows the -f.

```
$ cat chklist'
$ $1 ~ /^[AB]/ ¦¦ $3 ~ /^[12]/
$ awk -f chklist phone.list
Adams, Fran      2-3876
Brown, Robin     1-3745
Benson, Sam      4-5587
```

Single quotes aren't necessary for the instructions in chklist because the shell doesn't see what's in chklist, which is read directly by awk.

The other awk option, represented by -F, lets you choose a delimiting character other than whitespace. The single character listed after the -F is what awk uses to separate fields on a line. For example,

---

*awkptions?

if the dash (–) is used as the delimiter, the phone extension is the second field.

```
$ awk -F- '{print $2}' phone.list
7989
3876
6122
3745
5972
5587
```

awk allows only one character delimiter with –F. Thus, trying to set two delimiters with –F, such as –F'–,' or –F'–' –F',', has no effect beyond setting the dash as the delimiter (the first character after a –F). awk's –F option is quite useful and will come in handy later.

    As a final demonstration of the difference between formatting and editing, consider the comma after the last name. When the names are rearranged into first followed by last name, the comma seems out of place. Because the comma occurs within a field, awk would have trouble removing it. However, it is easy to get rid of the comma with sed, although the actual formatting is best done with awk. Both can be done in a single pipeline, with awk formatting each line and sed removing the comma.

```
$ awk '{print $2, $1 "<tab>" $3}' phone.list ¦
> sed 's/,//'
Terry Smith      7-7989
Fran Adams       2-3876
Pat StClair      4-6122
Robin Brown      1-3745
Chris Stair      5-5972
Sam Benson       4-5587
```

It doesn't matter which command is first, since the results are the same in either case.

Hands-on Exercise 7.5

Create a memo distribution list from the phone file by printing each entry in the following format:

_____ T. Smith

Hint: One way to do this is to use bracketed regular expressions.

Hands-on Exercise 7.6

Your company is upgrading its phone system and any phone numbers that begin with a 4 or 5 will now have a prefix of 73. Thus, the number 5-5972 becomes 735-5972. Create a list of just the new phone numbers printed in first name-last name format and get rid of the comma. *Hint:* Use a pipeline.

Summary

This chapter has demonstrated only the basic features of awk. In addition, awk contains a complete C-like programming language for use with complicated formats. The awk programming language is covered in Chapter 19. Chapter 19 provides a detailed example of writing awk programs to create reports.

The *sort* Command

We've covered three of the four main UNIX filters: `grep` searches, `sed` edits, and `awk` formats. The fourth filter sorts. As odd as it may seem given the names of the other three filters, the sorting command is named `sort`. To sort the phone list, run `sort` on the file.

```
$ sort phone.list
Adams, Fran    2-3876
Benson, Sam    4-5587
Brown, Robin   1-3745
Smith, Terry   7-7989
StClair, Pat   4-6122
Stair, Chris   5-5972
```

If this were all `sort` did, it wouldn't require an entire chapter to describe. In fact, `sort` has a large number of options and capabilities that make it a truly useful tool.

Take a closer look at the output of the previous `sort phone.list` command. `StClair` appears before `Stair`; that is, a capital C sorts before lowercase a. `sort` compares characters by using their numeric (ASCII) codes. All uppercase characters have lower numeric codes than lowercase a. However, this subtlety is lost on people not familiar with how computers represent stored data.

`sort` solves this possible ambiguity with the `-f` option. The `-f` option tells `sort` to ignore case.

```
$ sort -f phone.list
Adams, Fran     2-3876
Benson, Sam     4-5587
Brown, Robin    1-3745
Smith, Terry    7-7989
Stair, Chris    5-5972
StClair, Pat    4-6122
```

Options

sort offers several options to identify how the file is to be sorted. Some of these are shown in table 8.1.

Table 8.1.   sort *Options.*

Option	Function
-b	Ignore leading spaces and tabs
-d	Ignore nonalphanumeric characters
-f	Ignore case
-i	Ignore control characters
-m	Merge two sorted files
-M	Sort first three characters as month names
-n	Sort the data numerically, not as characters
-r	Sort the file from highest to lowest
-u	Output only one copy of identical lines

The *-r* Option

Some of these options are obvious in their use. To order the lines from highest to lowest, use -r.

```
$ sort -r phone.list
Stair, Chris    5-5972
StClair, Pat    4-6122
Smith, Terry    7-7989
Brown, Robin    1-3745
Benson, Sam     4-5587
Adams, Fran     2-3876
```

Note that sorting with −r has the same lowercase a and upper-case C problem. With −r, the uppercase C should come before the lowercase a. To reverse the output and ignore case requires both the −f and the −r options.

```
$ sort -r -f phone.list
StClair, Pat    4-6122
Stair, Chris    5-5972
Smith, Terry    7-7989
Brown, Robin    1-3745
Benson, Sam     4-5587
Adams, Fran     2-3876
```

The order of these options is not important, although the order is important in other options. Further, the options can be put together into a single argument.

```
$ sort -rf phone.list
StClair, Pat    4-6122
Stair, Chris    5-5972
Smith, Terry    7-7989
Brown, Robin    1-3745
Benson, Sam     4-5587
Adams, Fran     2-3876
```

The -*b* Option

You need the −b option because both spaces and tabs have very low numeric codes, lower than any character. As a result, the number of spaces and tabs in front of a line determines how that line is sorted. The −b tells sort to ignore the whitespace at the beginning of a line.

Another sorting problem caused by the ASCII numeric codes involves ordering numbers correctly. The numeric codes for the digits 0 through 9 increase from 0 to 9. The digit 1 sorts before the digit 2, which sorts before 3, and so on. The problem arises when you compare numbers with several digits. It turns out that the number 154 sorts before the number 23. To demonstrate this, you can use echo to put these two numbers into a pipeline to sort.

```
$ echo "154\n23" ¦ sort
154
23
```

The \n in the echo command represents a new line. The new line is needed because sort orders entire lines.

The -*n* Option

If you use the -n option, sort compares numbers as numbers, not a string of character digits. With -n, 154 and 23 are put in their ascending order.

```
$ echo "154\n23" | sort -n
23
154
```

Sort Fields

A sorting program needs a way to determine whether one line is to appear before another. This ordering is done based on comparing some or all of the characters from one line against some or all of the characters in the other. The characters that represent each line for this comparison are called a *sorting key*.

sort compares lines by using all the characters in each line. In addition to sorting on entire lines, sort can use only some of the characters on a line as the sorting key.

When sort reads a line, it splits the line into *fields* using spaces and tabs as delimiters. With the proper arguments, you can tell sort to use one or more of these fields as the sort key. To identify the sort key, use the + and − options. The argument +*n* tells sort to skip (i.e., not sort) the first n fields of each line.

Every line in the phone list contains three fields.

```
        Smith, Terry     7-7989
          ↑        ↑        ↑
Field   1        2        3
```

Thus, sort +1 will skip the last name on each line and sort the file starting at first name.

```
$ sort +1 phone.list
Stair, Chris    5-5972
Adams, Fran     2-3876
StClair, Pat    4-6122
Brown, Robin    1-3745
Benson, Sam     4-5587
Smith, Terry    7-7989
```

sort +2 sorts the phone list by phone number.

```
$ sort +2 phone.list
Brown, Robin    1-3745
Adams, Fran     2-3876
Benson, Sam     4-5587
StClair, Pat    4-6122
Stair, Chris    5-5972
Smith, Terry    7-7989
```

Establishing Delimiting Characters

Besides separating fields at spaces and tabs, you can tell sort to use a different delimiting character with the −t option. The character following the −t is treated as the delimiter. For example, to sort the phone list by the four digits after the dash in the phone number, you could set the delimiter as the dash and then simply sort on the second field.

```
$ sort -t- +1 phone.list
Brown, Robin    1-3745
Adams, Fran     2-3876
Benson, Sam     4-5587
Stair, Chris    5-5972
StClair, Pat    4-6122
Smith, Terry    7-7989
```

The −t option only lets you set a single character as the delimiter.

Noting the Beginning of a *sort*

The + option tells `sort` only where to begin the sort. The command `sort +2` sorts from the third field to the end of the line. You also can tell `sort` where to stop the sort key using the −n option, where n is a field number. Thus, the command `sort +1 −2` says to use only the second field on the line as the sort key.

Suppose that several Smiths previously worked at your company. When they were there, the phone list file looked like this:

```
$ cat phone.list.old
Smith, Terry    7-7989
Smith, Pat      9-3545
Smith, Gert     8-1906
Adams, Fran     2-3876
StClair, Pat    4-6122
Brown, Robin    1-3745
Stair, Chris    5-5972
Benson, Sam     4-5587
```

If you simply sort this list, the Smiths will be sorted by first name.

```
$ sort phone.list.old
Adams, Fran     2-3876
Benson, Sam     4-5587
Brown, Robin    1-3745
Smith, Gert     8-1906
Smith, Pat      9-3545
Smith, Terry    7-7989
StClair, Pat    4-6122
Stair, Chris    5-5972
```

However, suppose you want to sort the entries by last name and phone number. That is, when the last names match, sort the matching lines by phone number. This calls for sorting on the first field and, when last names match, on the third field. `sort` lets you identify secondary sort fields, those that only come into play if the primary sort doesn't distinguish one line from the next.

Identifying the Sort Key

Every +n argument identifies a sort field. The first one is the primary sort, the next one the secondary sort, and so on. If three sort fields were noted on the command line, the third field would only be used if the first two couldn't distinguish one line from another. In practice, when additional sort fields are used, a sort field usually is bounded by a −n argument as well.

Sorting the names in the old phone list by last name and then phone number requires a sort on the first field (+0 −1) and then on the third field (+2).

```
$ sort +0 -1 +2 phone.list.old
Adams,  Fran      2-3876
Benson, Sam       4-5587
Brown,  Robin     1-3745
Smith,  Terry     7-7989
Smith,  Gert      8-1906
Smith,  Pat       9-3545
StClair, Pat      4-6122
Stair,  Chris     5-5972
```

Note that the Smith lines are now sorted by phone number, not first name. Also, the secondary sort field has no effect on the other lines in the file, because none of their last names match. Incidentally, the argument +0 tells sort to skip no fields or, put another way, to use a sort key that starts at the beginning of the line.

What would happen if two people had the same last name and phone number? sort's two sort keys would not be enough to identify the order of the two lines. In a final attempt to sort them, sort would compare both entire lines, ordering them appropriately.

Regardless of the command line arguments, the final sorting key is always the entire line. There is no way to change this.

In addition to identifying entire fields as the sort key, you can select characters within a field. You do this by adding a *.n* to a + or − argument, where *n* is the number of characters to skip from the beginning of the field. For instance, the command sort +2.4 phone.list says to ignore the first two fields and the next four characters in each line and then to sort from there to the end of the line.

```
$ sort +2.4 phone.list
StClair, Pat    4-6122
Benson, Sam     4-5587
Brown, Robin    1-3745
Adams, Fran     2-3876
Stair, Chris    5-5972
Smith, Terry    7-7989
```

Note that this line is sorted by a key starting with the fifth character in the phone number field (with the dash counted as a character). The sorted column contains the numbers: 1, 5, 7, 8, 9, 9. `sort` counts the field delimiter (the tab between the first name and the phone number) as the first character in a field. The first four characters skipped in the third field of the first line are a tab, 4, -, and 6. The sort key is `122`.

For some reason, there is a difference between how `sort` handles the delimiter that precedes a field. If you use the default delimiters, each field starts with its delimiter. However, if you use the `-t` option to specify a delimiter, it is not considered the first character in each field. Because a tab separates the second and third fields, `sort +2.4 phone.list` should give the same results as `sort -t'<tab>' +1.4 phone.list`.

```
$ sort -t'<tab>' +1.4 phone.list
StClair, Pat    4-6122
Brown, Robin    1-3745
Stair, Chris    5-5972
Adams, Fran     2-3876
Benson, Sam     4-5587
Smith, Terry    7-7989
```

However, `sort -t'<tab>' +1.4 phone.list` sorts on the second to last character (the sort key is `22` in the first line), where the command `sort +2.4 phone.list` uses the third to the last character (the sort key is `122` in the first line). It is not clear why this distinction exists, although you should know about it.*

Hands-on Exercise 8.1

Sort the phone list by the four digits after the dash in the phone number without using the `-t` option.

---

*My guess is that it's a bug, not a feature.

As an extended example, consider the `membership` file, which holds the member names, numbers, and dues paid for an organization. The file contains four tab-separated fields: first name, last name, member number, and dues paid this year.

```
$ cat membership
Ray        Sanchez   55290-7865    34.42
Thomas     Hart      55389-7855    23.42
Pat        Bain      55490-7856    43.67
Mary       Jones     55488-7777    33.47
Randy      Wilson    55489-7765    9.00
Terry      Miller    55390-7965    24.24
```

Tabs are not allowed in the data fields. Thus, whenever a filter sees a tab, it can be sure that the tab is at the end of one field and the beginning of another. By using tabs as delimiters, you make it much easier to distinguish between fields.

The member number contains three pieces of information. The first three digits identify the chapter joined, the next two are the year joined, and the last four are the member's unique membership code. To sort by year joined, use the sort key of +2.4 -2.6.

```
$ sort +2.4 -2.6 membership
Mary       Jones     55488-7777    33.47
Randy      Wilson    55489-7865    9.00
Thomas     Hart      55389-7855    23.42
Pat        Bain      55490-7856    43.67
Ray        Sanchez   55290-7865    34.42
Terry      Miller    55390-7965    24.24
```

Incidentally, the sort key specifier, -2.6, is an inclusive range; that is, the sort key includes the character identified by -2.6. A two-character sort key is specified by +2.4 -2.6 (the fifth and sixth characters in the third field, including the delimiter).

Hands-on Exercise 8.2

Sort the membership list by membership code (the last four digits in the third field).

Hands-on Exercise 8.3

Sort the membership list by chapter (the first three characters in third field).

Hands-on Exercise 8.4

Sort the membership list by chapter number. Where the chapter number is the same for two lines, sort by last name.

Sorting Alphabetically

By default, `sort` compares sorting keys by character (ASCII) codes, that is essentially alphabetical. This is also true for secondary sorts. As an example of a situation where this might be a problem, consider sorting the membership list by chapter number (the first three numbers) and by amount paid.

```
$ sort +2 -2.4 +3 membership
Ray        Sanchez   55290-7865    34.42
Thomas     Hart      55389-7855    23.42
Terry      Miller    55390-7965    24.24
Mary       Jones     55488-7777    33.47
Pat        Bain      55490-7856    43.67
Randy      Wilson    55489-7865    9.00
```

This sort is incorrect. Nine dollars (in the last line) should sort before 33 and 43. The problem is that the codes for 3 and 4 are lower than the code for 9.

`sort` provides a way around this error with the `-n` option, which tells `sort` to compare characters as if they were numbers. The following command does the trick.

```
$ sort -n +2 -2.4 +3 membership
Ray        Sanchez   55290-7865    34.42
Thomas     Hart      55389-7855    23.42
Terry      Miller    55390-7965    24.24
Randy      Wilson    55489-7865    9.00
Mary       Jones     55488-7777    33.47
Pat        Bain      55490-7856    43.67
```

If you want one of the fields sorted as characters and one sorted as numbers, you must place the −n after the key specifier of the field you want to sort numerically. For example, if you want to sort the last name (as characters) and the amount paid (numerically), you could use the command sort +1 −2 +3n membership.

Using the Overwrite Option

Until now, we've been satisfied to print sorted files on the standard output. Often you will want to sort a file in place—that is, to put the sorted output back in the original file. Because this is a common need, sort provides a special *overwrite* option, represented by −o.* You must use the −o option with a file name that follows the −o on the command line. When −o is used with sort, nothing is sent to the standard output.

To sort the phone list by last name and to put the sorted list back into the phone list file, use −o phone.list.

```
$ sort phone.list -o phone.list
$ cat phone.list
Adams, Fran      2-3876
Benson, Sam      4-5587
Brown, Robin     1-3745
Smith, Terry     7-7989
StClair, Pat     4-6122
Stair, Chris     5-5972
```

The input file does not have to be the same as the output file.

Sorting Multiple Files

One final point: When sort is given more than one file to sort, it sorts the files together.

---

*sort is the only filter that provides such an option, although a −o option would be useful for other filters as well.

```
$ sort phone.list phone.list.old
Adams, Fran     2-3876
Adams, Fran     2-3876
Benson, Sam     4-5587
Benson, Sam     4-5587
Brown, Robin    1-3745
Brown, Robin    1-3745
Smith, Gert     8-1906
Smith, Pat      9-3545
Smith, Terry    7-7989
Smith, Terry    7-7989
StClair, Pat    4-6122
StClair, Pat    4-6122
Stair, Chris    5-5972
Stair, Chris    5-5972
```

To get rid of duplicate lines, use the −u option when sorting files together.

```
$ sort -u phone.list phone.list.old
Adams, Fran     2-3876
Benson, Sam     4-5587
Brown, Robin    1-3745
Smith, Gert     8-1906
Smith, Pat      9-3545
Smith, Terry    7-7989
StClair, Pat    4-6122
Stair, Chris    5-5972
```

Hands-on Exercise 8.5

Create (or modify) an appropriate data file and run the `sort` command using the −M, −d, and any other options you want to demonstrate. Be sure to try different entries so that you are sure how each option works.

Summary

The sort command provides a great deal of flexibility by allowing you to exactly identify how the lines in a stream are to be ordered. With the proper combination of arguments and options, you should be able to sort a file any way you need. As you will see, sort's capabilities often come in handy.

Pipelines

One of the most valuable benefits of the UNIX System comes in handy when you combine filters to create pipelines. Pipelines let you solve seemingly difficult problems quickly. Further, pipelines are quite flexible. Often a pipeline can be adapted to perform an entirely different task with the addition of one more filter or the substitution of one for another.

Extending the Capability of Commands

As an example of extending a command's capability, suppose you wanted to list the files in the current directory by size, the largest one first. Your first thought should be to check the options of ls. ls provides the -l and -s options, both of which report file sizes (-l in characters and -s in blocks). Unfortunately, both sort the files in alphabetic order by name.

ls supplies the information, but doesn't display it the way you want. The solution is to do it yourself by sending the output of ls to sort. There is one hitch to all this: The ls -s command prints the total number of blocks in the current directory as the first line of output.

```
$ ls -s
total 347
    5 book.outline
   30 chapter.1
   99 chapter.2
```

```
23 chapter.3
28 chapter.4
50 chapter.5
45 chapter.6
31 chapter.7
33 chapter.8
 1 membership
 1 phone.list
 1 phone.list.old
```

If you simply sort the output of ls -s, you get the line total 347 in the output.

```
$ ls -s | sort
   1 membership
   1 phone.list
   1 phone.list.old
   5 book.outline
  23 chapter.3
  28 chapter.4
  30 chapter.1
  31 chapter.7
  33 chapter.8
  45 chapter.6
  50 chapter.5
  99 chapter.2
 total 347
```

If you want to get rid of the total 347 line, you could insert a sed command between the ls and the sort to remove the first line of output. The command is sed 1d.

```
$ ls -s | sed 1d | sort
 1 membership
 1 phone.list
 1 phone.list.old
 5 book.outline
23 chapter.3
28 chapter.4
30 chapter.1
31 chapter.7
33 chapter.8
```

```
45 chapter.6
50 chapter.5
99 chapter.2
```

Hands-on Exercise 9.1

Modify the `ls -s ¦ sed 1d ¦ sort` pipeline to sort the list by decreasing file size. Note that BSD UNIX Systems don't list a file's group owner in an `ls -l` listing. Thus, on BSD, file size is the fourth field.

Hands-on Exercise 9.2

Sort the output of `ls -l` by file size. See the note in exercise 9.1.

Hands-on Exercise 9.3

The pipeline in exercise 9.2 sorts files of the same size by modification date. Modify the pipeline to sort files by name when they are the same size.

Extending Pipelines

After you have a pipeline that works, extending it to do even more is quite easy. For example, suppose you wanted to sort the files in the current directory and also total the blocks used by all of these files. You've already created a pipeline that sorts files by size. Is there a way to extend it to include the total?

In the pipeline, `ls -s ¦ sed 1d ¦ sort`, the entire purpose of the `sed` command is to remove the total line from `ls`'s output. If you remove `sed` from the pipeline, the shell puts the total line back into the output, and `sort` puts it at the end of the file listing. The problem with this solution, as shown in the previous section, is that the total line is in the wrong format. You want it to match the rest of the listing—that is, to list total blocks and then the word "total."

Because you want to change the format of a line, you should immediately think of `awk`. Thus, rearranging the total line is easy. You just replace the `sed` in the pipeline with `awk 'NR == 1 { print $2, $1 }'`. In addition to rearranging the total line, you have to print the rest of the lines unchanged. This requires a second line in the awk command of NR != 1 { print }.

```
$ ls -s ¦ awk 'NR == 1 { print " " $2, $1 }
> NR != 1 { print }' ¦ sort
    1 membership
    1 phone.list
    1 phone.list.old
    5 book.outline
   23 chapter.3
   28 chapter.4
   30 chapter.1
   31 chapter.7
   33 chapter.8
   45 chapter.6
   50 chapter.5
   99 chapter.2
  347 total
```

In awk, the test NR == 1 is true for the first line read. The test NR! == 1 is true for every line except the first one. Those two tests are required because the first line of ls -s is the total line, which is the only one whose format must be changed.

The space added to the front of the total line is needed to align the enties properly. Note how you didn't have to do anything to put the total at the bottom of the listing. This is a natural result, because total blocks should be larger than any single file. Thus, by reformatting the total line, you also sorted it properly.

Creating Applications with Pipelines

Creating pipelines is an acquired skill. It takes time to learn how the various UNIX filters work and to get the feel of putting them together into pipelines. Here is a two-step procedure to follow when writing a pipeline:

1. Break the task down into steps.
2. Find (or write) a filter that can perform each step.

For example, there is no way, using `ls`, to list those files that are executable by their owners. Creating a pipeline to do this requires four steps:

1. List all files with their permissions.
2. Remove the total line.
3. Find all files that are executable by their owner.
4. Format the output to owner and file names only.

Now that you have the steps, you can match commands to them. Step 1 is done by `ls -l`; step 2, by `sed 1d`; step 3, by `grep '^...x'`; and step 4, by `awk '{print $3 "<tab>" $9}'`. Because the current directory doesn't (yet) contain any executable files, I ran the pipeline in my home directory. As a result, the pipeline printed a number of directories with search permission.

```
$ cd
$ ls -l ¦ sed 1d ¦ grep '^...x' ¦
> awk '{print $3 "<tab>" $9}'
ray   Acct
ray   C
ray   Classes
ray   Invoices
ray   Letters
ray   Talks
ray   Unix.book
ray   cgrep
ray   laser
ray   preview
ray   reminder
```

The main purpose behind this two-step planning procedure is to separate the design of the pipeline from the commands that implement it. Often, programmers try to create pipelines using only those commands and filters that they know. This usually leads to poorly implemented pipelines. An example is programmers who aren't familiar with `awk` and who instead try to do all their formatting with `sed`.

What happens if you don't know of a command that can perform a certain step? Search through the UNIX manual or a UNIX command summary for one that can. It is much easier to locate a command after you know what that command has to do. Further, if, in fact, no command exists that can implement a certain step, you now can create a command that does just what is required.

Hands-on Exercise 9.4

Create a pipeline that prints the files in the current directory that are larger than 10,000 characters.

Formatting Data

An application consists of two parts: data and the tools that process the data. Before you can think about programs processing the data, you need to design the data's format. If the data aren't formatted properly, the programs required by the application get much more complicated. So far, you've had an easy time dealing with the data in the phone list. However, you've been lucky because, as it turns out, the data layout in the phone list is poorly designed.

The main problem with the phone list is that the first and second fields are separated by a comma and a space, characters that might appear as part of the data. Some people have names that contain spaces and/or commas. Consider these everyday names that might appear in someone's phone list:

```
Holden, Mary Ann        3-3451
Johnson, J. T. 2-2345
Smith, Ph.D., Marty     5-2213
```

Suppose you want to find all the entries whose first names start with a P. The command `grep ', P'` `phone.list` would find the following lines:

```
StClair, Pat    4-6122
Smith, Ph.D., Marty     5-2213
```

Identifying first names in a phone list containing such entries is much more complicated than simply looking for the characters following a comma and a space. Now you must look for characters that are preceded by a comma and a space, are followed by a tab, start with a specified character, and contain one or more upper- or lowercase characters, spaces (to handle Mary Ann), or periods (to handle J. T.).

```
$ cat phone.list.2
Smith, Terry    7-7989
Adams, Fran     2-3876
StClair, Pat    4-6122
Brown, Robin    1-3745
Stair, Chris    5-5972
Benson, Sam     4-5587
Holden, Mary Ann        3-3451
Johnson, J. T. 2-2345
Smith, Ph.D., Marty     5-2213
$ grep ', P[a-zA-Z. ][a-zA-Z. ]*<tab>' phone.list.2
StClair, Pat    4-6122
```

Hands-on Exercise 9.5

Find all the entries in phone.list.2 that include more than one-word first names.

The main problem with the phone list is that one of the delimiters might appear as part of the data. To avoid complications caused by badly formed data, it is best to pick a field delimiter that will not appear in the data. Many programmers use tabs to separate fields in a line.

```
$ cat phone.list.tab
Smith,      Terry   7-7989
Adams,      Fran    2-3876
StClair,    Pat     4-6122
Brown,      Robin   1-3745
Stair,      Chris   5-5972
Benson,     Sam     4-5587
Holden,     Mary Ann        3-3451
Johnson,    J. T.   2-2345
Smith, Ph.D.,   Marty       5-2213
$ grep '<tab>P.*<tab>' phone.list.tab
StClair, Pat    4-6122
```

The file `phone.list.tab` contains the same data as `phone.list.2`. The difference between the files is that `phone.list.tab` separates the last name and the first name with a tab. The file `phone.list.2` has a comma and a space separating last and first names. Note how much easier it is to find first names that start with P when you use tabs* as the delimiters.

Creating a List of Names

In Chapter 3, we talked about printing a list of names as labels, after finding the people in California and sorting them by ZIP code. This section explores how to design and implement such a list.

The first step is designing the data file. For simplicity, let's assume that the file stores each person's name, street address, city, state, and ZIP code. Obviously, more information could be put into the file, such as company name, phone number, and contact date. For simplicity, we will use only these five fields.

Because UNIX filters work on lines, each name is stored on a single line. Further, the tab is used as the delimiter. The format of the file is

```
name <tab> address <tab> city <tab> state <tab>zipcode
$ cat name.list
Robin Swan      1289 Broadway   New York        NY      10001
Terry Wilson    121 First St.   San Jose        CA      95131
Chris Nelson    412 Castro St.  Mountain View   CA      94041
Fran Thomas     2204 Main St.   Palatine        IL      60074
Pat Moleen      803 Pine St.    Santa Cruz      CA      95062
```

Hands-on Exercise 9.6

Sort the name list by state.

---

*When tabs are displayed on a terminal (and in this book when a terminal display is being simulated), the results are often ragged because tabs force the terminal to skip to the next tab stop. Tab stops usually are inserted after every eight characters. Thus, how a tab is displayed depends on the number of characters preceding the tab.

The labels from the name list are only for those people in California, in ZIP code order. As was noted in Chapter 3, this is a three-step process: search for those in California, sort them by ZIP code, and format them into labels. In UNIX parlance, `grep` to `sed` to `awk`.

One way to search for addresses in California is the pattern `'<tab>CA<tab>'`. However, this will only look for any field containing "CA". Because this is a list that could contain all kinds of information, it is best to be as specific as possible.

The state field is the second to last field on the line. To remove all chance of search error, your pattern should pinpoint this field exactly. Because the delimiter is a unique character (one that doesn't appear in the data), you can completely identify a field as zero or more non-delimiters, `[^<tab>]*`. This pattern matches a string of characters that do not contain a tab. By definition, anything that isn't a tab must be part of a field. The last field, then, would be matched by the pattern `<tab>[^<tab>]*$`, that is, a tab followed by zero or more nontabs at the end of the line.

```
$ grep '<tab>CA<tab>[^<tab>]*$' name.list
Terry Wilson    121 First St.  San Jose       CA      95131
Chris Nelson    412 Castro St. Mountain View CA       94041
Pat Moleen      803 Pine St.   Santa Cruz     CA      95062
```

Hands-on Exercise 9.7

Use `grep` to search the name list for anyone living in San Jose.

Because the pattern consists of an entire field, it is easier, in this case, to use `awk`. You have only to set the field separator (`-F` argument) to tab and then print all the lines with `$4 == "CA"`.

```
$ awk -F'<tab>' '$4 == "CA"' name.list
Terry Wilson    121 First St.  San Jose       CA      95131
Chris Nelson    412 Castro St. Mountain View  CA      94041
Pat Moleen      803 Pine St.   Santa Cruz     CA      95062
```

Hands-on Exercise 9.8

Use `awk` to look for addresses in California where the state abbreviation might be CA, ca, or Ca.

The second step is easily done by `sort`. The ZIP code is the fifth field if only tabs are used as field separators. The command is `sort -t'<tab>' +4`.

Formatting a line into a label is done with a multiline `awk` command. Before you start writing code, you need to know what a peel-off label looks like. These labels have six lines of printable space and one line between each label. The names in this example require three lines:

```
Name
Street Address
City, State ZIP code
```

You must then skip four lines to get to the next label.

Only lines being printed will be passed to `awk`, so it will format every line. No `awk` pattern is required. To identify the fields properly, you must tell `awk` to use a tab as a field separator. Do this with the `-F'<tab>'` option. Recall that `awk` prints blank lines with `"\n"`.

```
$ awk -F'<tab>' '{ print $1
> print $2
> print $3 ",", $4, $5
> print "\n\n\n" }'
```

Incidentally, the reason only three new lines (`\n`) are listed in the last `awk` print command is that `print` adds a new line at the end of each line it prints. That's where the seventh line comes from.

When put together, the entire pipeline prints the entries in the name list exactly to your specifications.

```
$ grep '<tab>CA<tab>[^<tab>]*$' name.list ¦
> sort -t'<tab> +4 ¦ awk -F'<tab>' '{ print $1
> print $2
> print $3 ",", $4, $5
>
> print "\n\n\n" }'
Chris Nelson
221 Castro St.
Mountain View, CA 94041

Pat Moleen
803 Pine St.
Santa Cruz, CA 95062
```

```
Terry Wilson
121 First St.
San Jose, CA 95131
```

If you want to print the labels, you could pipe the output of awk to `lp`. Another option is to redirect them into a file for printing later.

Hands-on Exercise 9.9

Add a new field in the name list for company name. Make company name field 2. How would this change the label-printing pipeline?

Hands-on Exercise 9.10

Currently, the name list puts both the first name and last name in the same field. After some thought, you decide this is a bad idea. Write a command that puts a tab between the first and last names. Don't assume that everyone has only one first name (although you can assume that everyone has only one last name).

Hands-on Exercise 9.11

Because the name list usually will be sorted by ZIP code, write a script to rearrange the name list file to put the ZIP code as the first field. Store the modified data back in the name list file.

Is it realistic to use pipelines to manage real-life data? It is a judgment call on your part. Clearly, as data files get larger, pipelines get slower. However, pipelines are useful in a number of areas.

In my experience, every business has a small number of large database applications. Generally, these applications manage data vital to the economic health of the company. This data must be available quickly, easy to modify, and correct. For the most part, it is not appropriate for pipelines to manage huge amounts of vital data. Pipelines are not interactive, can be quite slow, and are hard to use by those not familiar with UNIX. Typically, such applications are the responsibility of database management systems.

In contrast to these essential programs are a large number of everyday problems that can also be automated but only if done quickly without a great deal of trouble or expense. Examples are phone lists, travel reimbursement records, seminar attendance, and appointment calendars; the list is endless. It isn't worth the time and effort to put these into a full-scale database manager, and yet these tasks are tedious if you must use only pencil and paper. Such applications are excellent examples of where pipelines can be used to solve problems quickly and cheaply.

Although many of the tasks performed in a business are repetitive, they are not always automated. Often, the reason for not automating them is that no one has the time, the experience, or the training to do so. However, devising pipelines is much simpler than "real" programming. The creators of UNIX have already written the programs for you. All you have to do is piece them together into a problem-solving pipeline.

Many everyday problems can be solved with a small amount of data and a modest investment of time. A list of names is a good illustration. I use a name list file to write customized letters, to produce invoices for public seminars, and to remind me to make followup calls to people interested in my services. These lists hold anywhere from less than ten to several hundred names. Further, after you've taken the time to produce a pipeline that solves a common problem, you will be surprised how many times you can reuse or modify it to do a related task.

What is a "small amount" of data? At what point does the data requirement outstrip the usefulness of a pipeline? Clearly, this depends on your machine. However, some simple tests help determine what is acceptable response time.

The `test.list` file contains 1000 names and addresses.

```
$ wc test.list
   1000    8600   45240 test.list
```

To determine appropriate response time, let's search this file to see how long it takes. The UNIX `time` command will help you by reporting the amount of real, user, and system time consumed by a process. Adding the user and system times together is the amount of computer time* used (real time is actual elapsed time).

---

*The timing tests were done on a system based on an Intel 80286 CPU chip. It is one of the least powerful UNIX machines made.

```
$ time grep '<tab>9' test.list > /tmp/junk

real        2.0
user        1.4
sys         0.3
```

These times are reported in seconds. Thus, to search a 1000-line file took less than 2 seconds. Incidentally, the output of the timed `grep` command was redirected to get a better idea of execution time. If the output came to the terminal, the execution time would be much longer to account for the overhead of printing on the terminal.

Sorting takes longer than searching.

```
$ time sort test.list > /tmp/junk

real        3.5
user        2.5
sys         0.7
```

In fact, it takes almost twice as long. Further, more complicated commands eat up more execution time.

```
$ time sort -t'<tab>' +4 test.list > /tmp/junk

real       12.5
user       10.4
sys         0.8
```

How long does it take to create California mailing labels in ZIP code order? `time` can also handle pipelines.

```
$ time grep '<tab>CA<tab>[^<tab>]*$' /tmp/junk ¦
> sort -t'<tab>' +4 ¦ awk -F'<tab>' '{ print $1
> print $2
> print $3 ",", $4, $5
> print "\n\n\n" }' > /tmp/list
real       14.1
user       12.1
sys         1.5
$ wc /tmp/junk
    4200   5400  31006 /tmp/junk
```

It took just under 14 seconds to create 600 labels (4200 lines divided by 7 lines per label). Keep in mind these timings were done on a slow UNIX machine. The results on your machine will be different.

What happens when files get very big? The file `mailing.list` contains 12,638 names.

```
$ time grep '<tab>CA<tab>' mailing.list > /tmp/junk

real      2:10.6
user       50.3
sys        25.3
$ wc -l /tmp/junk
5596 junk
```

As you can see, even a simple search bogs down when the data files get large. Incidentally, the 25 seconds of system time were spent reading `mailing.list` and writing the 5596 lines to `junk`.

Clearly, there are applications that are too large for pipelines. But it is equally clear that many problems can be easily and completely solved by pipelines. What determines the difference? First, can what you need be done by a pipeline? Second, will the data get so large that the pipeline will become inefficient? Over time, as you gain experience with the UNIX filters and creating pipelines, you will learn how to spot applications that are easy to pipeline.

Summary

Pipelines are valuable computer processing tools that greatly enhance your ability to get work done quickly. Also, pipelines let users extend the commands in their environment to better match what they like. Pipelines are one of the main reasons why so many users like UNIX so much.

10

Other Tools in
the Pipeline

UNIX supplies many tools that can be used in pipelines. However, not every command deserves its own chapter. The purpose of this chapter is to cover those tools that are useful but have a narrow focus, don't accept many options, and/or can be demonstrated quickly.

The *wc* Command

An example is wc. wc prints the number of lines, words, and characters in a file, as well as the file's name.

```
$ wc chapter.9
    637     4047  23843 chapter.9
```

wc accepts three arguments: -c to count only characters, -w to count only words, and -l to count only lines. If one of these options is used, wc prints only the requested number and the file name. You can combine these three options to get the values you need.

Note that wc is not a filter, at least not in the same sense as grep, sed, sort, and awk. Although it does read its standard input and write to its standard output, it doesn't "filter" the data. Instead, wc summarizes its input into three numbers. For this reason, wc is generally used at the end of a pipeline. Two common uses are counting the number of files in a directory and counting the number of users currently logged on.

```
$ ls ¦ wc -l
17
$ who ¦ wc -l
2
```

No file name was printed because `wc`'s input is a pipeline.

The *cut* Command

One of the strengths of the `awk` command is its capability to refer to individual fields in a line. In fact, Chapter 7 discussed this as being the basis for the difference between formatting and editing. However, if all you want to do is print a few of the characters in a line, you don't have to use `awk`. Instead, you can use the `cut` command.

The `cut` command writes various characters to the standard output based on criteria listed on the command line. `cut` views a line as a set of characters or a set of fields. The default field delimiter is a tab. To extract entire fields from a line, use the `-f` option. To extract characters only, use the `-c` option.*

The fields can be specified in the `-f` option as a range, such as `-f1-3`, or a comma separated list, such as `-f1,2,3`, or both, as in `-f1,2-5,8`. The range `-f-3` prints the first three fields, and the range `-f4-` prints from the fourth field to the end of the line.

For example, in the `phone.list.tab` file, a tab separates the three fields on each line. To print each person's name, use the command `cut -f1,2 phone.list.tab`.

```
$ cut -f1,2 phone.list.tab
Smith,          Terry
Adams,          Fran
StClair,        Pat
Brown,          Robin
Stair,          Chris
Benson,         Sam
Holden,         Mary Ann
Johnson,        J. T.
Smith, Ph.D.,   Marty
```

---

*Note that the `cut` command is only available in System V UNIX. It will not be found on XENIX or BSD systems.

Fields 1 and 2 could also be specified as −f1−2 or −f−2. Incidentally, cut uses the field delimiter as the field separator when it outputs more than one field. This is why cut put a tab between these fields.

cut's −d option lets you select whatever character you want as the delimiter. For example, to print the last four digits in a phone number, you can use a dash as the delimiter and print field 2.

```
$ cut -d- -f2 phone.list.tab
7989
3876
6122
3745
5972
5587
3451
2345
2213
```

Note that cut allows you to specify a single delimiter character. If more than one character is listed with −d, only the first one is used.

Hands-on Exercise 10.1

Print all the last names, without the comma, in the phone list using the cut command.

To extract a set of characters out of a line, the same conventions that work with fields will work with the −c option. Thus, the command cut −c2−34,55− would print the second to the 34th characters and then the 55th character to the end of the line.

For example, the data in an ls −l listing is separated by an exact number of spaces. If you want to print just the owner's permissions and the file name in the current directory, you could use cut's −c option and identify exactly the characters you want.

```
$ ls -l ¦ sed 1d ¦ cut -c2-4,55-
rw-book.outline
rw-chapter.1
rw-chapter.10
rw-chapter.2
rw-chapter.3
```

```
rw-chapter.4
rw-chapter.5
rw-chapter.6
rw-chapter.7
rw-chapter.8
rw-chapter.9
rw-membership
rw-name.list
rw-phone.list
rw-phone.list.2
rw-phone.list.old
rw-phone.list.tab
```

Note that `cut` doesn't put a space between character 4 and 55. To add a space here, use

$ ls -l ¦ sed 1d ¦ cut -c2-4,55- ¦ sed' s/\(...\)/\1 /'
```
rw- book.outline
rw- chapter.1
rw- chapter.10
rw- chapter.2
rw- chapter.3
rw- chapter.4
rw- chapter.5
rw- chapter.6
rw- chapter.7
rw- chapter.8
rw- chapter.9
rw- membership
rw- name.list
rw- phone.list
rw- phone.list.2
rw- phone.list.old
rw- phone.list.tab
```

Recall that the purpose of the `sed 1d` command is to remove the total line that `ls -l` prints.

Hands-on Exercise 10.2

Create a pipeline to print the owner's permissions and name, as well as the file name in the current directory.

Hands-on Exercise 10.3

Create a pipeline to print the terminal ports currently being used.

One problem with using `cut` is that it treats two delimiters next to one another as an *empty* field. This is different from `awk` or `sort`, which treat a set of contiguous delimiters as separating a *single* field. For a demonstration of this, consider printing only a file's permissions and the file's name. This is easy using `awk`.

```
$ ls -l ¦ sed 1d ¦ awk '{print $1, $9}'
-rw-rw-rw- book.outline
-rw-rw-rw- chapter.1
-rw-rw-rw- chapter.10
-rw-rw-rw- chapter.2
-rw-rw-rw- chapter.3
-rw-rw-rw- chapter.4
-rw-rw-rw- chapter.5
-rw-rw-rw- chapter.6
-rw-rw-rw- chapter.7
-rw-rw-rw- chapter.8
-rw-rw-rw- chapter.9
-rw-rw-rw- membership
-rw-rw-rw- name.list
-rw-rw-rw- phone.list
-rw-rw-rw- phone.list.2
-rw-rw-rw- phone.list.old
-rw-rw-rw- phone.list.tab
```

Because `ls -l` separates its fields with spaces, it would seem that using `cut` with space as the delimiter would work the same way. But, it doesn't. The problem is caused by `cut` treating two consecutive spaces as an empty field. The following output includes a ninth field, but because it's empty, nothing was output for that field:

```
$ ls -l ¦ sed 1d ¦ cut -d' ' -f1,9
-rw-rw-rw-
-rw-rw-rw-
-rw-rw-rw-
-rw-rw-rw-
-rw-rw-rw-
```

```
-rw-rw-rw-
-rw-rw-rw-
-rw-rw-rw-
-rw-rw-rw-
-rw-rw-rw-
-rw-rw-rw-
-rw-rw-rw-
-rw-rw-rw-
-rw-rw-rw-
-rw-rw-rw-
-rw-rw-rw-
-rw-rw-rw-
```

If a line doesn't contain a delimiter, `cut` can't extract fields out of it. Instead, `cut` prints the entire line. `cut` offers a `-s` option that tells `cut` not to print lines that do not contain delimiters.

The *uniq* Command

When creating applications with pipelines, you occasionally must either get or remove lines that are unique to a file. This is the purpose of the `uniq` filter. Actually, `uniq` has three capabilities. It will print only one copy of duplicate lines (the default option), print only unmatched (unique) lines, or print only duplicated lines.

So far, three different phone list files have been referred to in this book: `phone.list`, `phone.list.2`, and `phone.list.old`. It is not uncommon to find several, similarly named files in a directory. After looking at each file, you might be interested in seeing exactly what data is represented by all three. This is where `uniq` comes in.

It's too much to ask of `uniq` to try to locate duplicate lines in unsorted data. Instead, `uniq` assumes that its input is sorted. Thus, to find all the names in the three phone lists, without duplication, requires that you sort the files and pipeline them to `uniq`.

```
$ sort phone.list phone.list.2 phone.list.old ¦ uniq
Adams, Fran    2-3876
Benson, Sam    4-5587
Brown, Robin   1-3745
Holden, Mary Ann        3-3451
Johnson, J. T.          2-2345
Smith, Gert    8-1906
```

```
Smith, Pat      9-3545
Smith, Ph.D., Marty     5-2213
Smith, Terry  7-7989
StClair, Pat  4-6122
Stair, Chris  5-5972
```

Incidentally, you can get the same result by replacing `uniq` with `sort -u` in the previous pipeline.

How many lines were removed? This can be determined by `wc`.

```
$ cat phone.list phone.list.2 phone.list.old ¦ wc -l
23
$ sort phone.list phone.list.2 phone.list.old ¦ uniq ¦ wc -l
11
```

As you can see, there are 12 duplicate names in the three files.

`uniq` offers three options. `-c` not only tells `uniq` to print both unique and duplicate lines but also asks it to count the number of duplicates. `-d` tells `uniq` to print only one copy of matched lines and to ignore unique lines. `-u` tells `uniq` to print only the unique lines. All three options are demonstrated as follows:

- `-c` tells `uniq` to print both unique and duplicate lines as well as to count the number of duplicates:

  ```
  $ sort phone.list phone.list.2 phone.list.old ¦ uniq -c
  3 Adams, Fran    2-3876
  3 Benson, Sam    4-5587
  3 Brown, Robin 1-3745
  1 Holden, Mary Ann      3-3451
  1 Johnson, J. T.        2-2345
  1 Smith, Gert    8-1906
  1 Smith, Pat     9-3545
  1 Smith, Ph.D., Marty    5-2213
  3 Smith, Terry 7-7989
  3 StClair, Pat 4-6122
  3 Stair, Chris 5-5972
  ```

- `-d` tells `uniq` to print only one copy of matched lines and to ignore unique lines:

  ```
  $ sort phone.list phone.list.2 phone.list.old ¦ uniq -d
  Adams, Fran     2-3876
  Benson, Sam     4-5587
  Brown, Robin    1-3745
  ```

```
Smith, Terry    7-7989
StClair, Pat    4-6122
Stair, Chris    5-5972
```

- -u tells uniq to print only the unique lines:

```
$ sort phone.list phone.list.2 phone.list.old ¦ uniq -u
Holden, Mary Ann      3-3451
Johnson, J. T.        2-2345
Smith, Gert 8-1906
Smith, Pat 9-3545
Smith, Ph.D., Marty   5-2213
```

Like most filters, uniq can also take its input from a file named on the command line. However, uniq takes input only from a single named file. Similarly, you can send output to a file via redirection or by listing an output file on the command line. The output file name must be the second file listed on the command line. This means an output file cannot be identified on the command line unless an input file is also listed.

So far, uniq has compared entire lines looking for duplicates. uniq can also match parts of lines. The part of each line to compare for uniqueness is specified in much the same way as sort identifies its sort key.

uniq provides the *-n* and **+***n* options. The *-n* option says to ignore the first *n* fields. The **+***n* option says to skip the first *n* characters. The **+***n* and *-n* options only tell uniq where to begin comparing lines to each other. The comparison always goes from the specified starting point to the end of a line.

Although uniq works closely with the sort command, uniq doesn't have sort's flexibility. uniq provides the capability to choose where to start the comparison, but not where to stop it, always using the rest of the line. This is unfortunate because it occasionally would come in handy to stop the comparison before the end of the line.

In Chapter 9, you used the name.list file to create a set of one-up labels. When doing large mailings, you often can save money by counting the number of pieces being sent to each ZIP code. At first glance, this might seem easy. Because the name.list file has five tab-separated fields, the command uniq -4 name.list should work. Unfortunately, it won't. The reason is that uniq uses both spaces and tabs to identify fields. Using these delimiters gives the lines in name.list different numbers of fields. To show this, use awk's NF (number of fields on a line) variable.

```
$ awk '{print NF}' name.list
9
8
9
8
9
```

Because you don't need anything but the ZIP code to count them, why not just delete everything else on the line and process only the ZIP code? You can use sed or awk to do this.

```
$ awk '{print $NF}' name.list ¦ sort ¦ uniq -c
   1 10001
   1 60603
   1 94041
   1 95062
   1 95131
```

Recall that the NF variable in awk equates to the number of fields on a line. Also, dollar signs are used only with field numbers. Thus, $NF is an easy way to print the last field on every line.

Hands-on Exercise 10.4

Count the ZIP codes in name.list, using sed instead of awk to extract them from each line.

Hands-on Exercise 10.5

Use uniq to print a unique list of the users currently logged on. If a user is logged on more than once, that user only appears once in this listing.

The *join* Command

A command similar to uniq is join. Like uniq, join searches for lines with duplicate fields. However, instead of printing such lines, join merges them.

join implements a relational database *join* operation. In a relational database, a join combines the lines from several files (tables) by matching them on a single field (key). The UNIX version of join can handle lines from only two *sorted* files.

Unless told otherwise, join compares the first fields of lines read from two files. If the fields match, the line from the first file combined with everything from the second file, except the matching field, is sent to the standard output.

For example, the file room.list contains a list of names and office numbers separated by a tab character.

```
$ cat room.list
Smith, Terry      492
Adams, Fran       423A
StClair, Pat      339
Brown, Robin      387
Stair, Chris      221
Benson, Sam       444C
```

join can be used to combine the lines in the phone list and room list files so that you end up with names, phone numbers, and office numbers in a single file.

You must first sort both files before sending them to join.

```
$ sort phone.list > phone.list.s
$ sort room.list > room.list.s
$ join phone.list.s room.list.s
Adams, Fran 2-3876 Fran 423A
Benson, Sam 4-5587 Sam 444C
Brown, Robin 1-3745 Robin 387
Smith, Terry 7-7989 Terry 492
StClair, Pat 4-6122 Pat 339
Stair, Chris 5-5972 Chris 221
```

As with the other field-oriented commands, join identifies fields as characters separated by whitespace. It sees consecutive delimiters as a single delimiter and ignores leading delimiters. Thus, join compares lines on last name only. When the lines match, join prints the entire line from the first file and the line minus the matching field from the second. In this example, the first name is printed twice because it appears in both files.

One way to get around printing the first name twice is to tell `join` to use only a tab as the field delimiter. `join`'s field delimiter is set by the `-t` option.

```
$ join -t'<tab>' phone.list.s room.list.s
Adams, Fran    2-3876  423A
Benson, Sam    4-5587  444C
Brown, Robin   1-3745  387
StClair, Pat   4-6122  339
Stair, Chris   5-5972  221
```

Note that `join` separated the output fields with a tab, which was the field delimiter. The character specified by a `-t` option is always used as the output delimiter. If `-t` is not used, `join` separates output fields with a space.

Hands-on Exercise 10.6

Add the words "Phone" and "Room Number" to the output of the combined `phone.list` and `room.list` files.

Another solution to the repeated-field problem is the `-o` option that tells `join` which fields from which files to print. The syntax for `-o` is *n*.*m*, where *n* is a file number (either 1 or 2) and *m* is a field number. To print only last name, first name, phone number, and office number, use `-o 1.1 1.2 1.3 2.3`.

```
$ join -o 1.1 1.2 1.3 2.3 phone.list.s room.list.s
Adams, Fran 2-3876 423A
Benson, Sam 4-5587 444C
Brown, Robin 1-3745 387
Smith, Terry 7-7989 492
StClair, Pat 4-6122 339
Stair, Chris 5-5972 221
```

To change the order of the fields being output, rearrange the file-field pairs. This command prints the first name before the last name by putting `1.2` in front of `1.1`.

```
$ join -o 1.2 1.1 1.3 2.3 phone.list.s room.list.s
Fran Adams, 2-3876 423A
Sam Benson, 4-5587 444C
Robin Brown, 1-3745 387
Terry Smith, 7-7989 492
Pat StClair, 4-6122 339
Chris Stair, 5-5972 221
```

Note that the fields are separated by spaces because $-t$ wasn't used.

So far, join has been used as a stand-alone command. join can be used as a filter by reading the first input file from the standard input, which join does if a dash is listed as the first file name.

```
$ cat phone.list.s ¦ join -t'<tab>' - room.list.s
Adams, Fran      2-3876   423A
Benson, Sam      4-5587   444C
Brown, Robin     1-3745   387
StClair, Pat     4-6122   339
Stair, Chris     5-5972   221
```

Incidentally, this works for the first file name only.

join offers three additional options. The $-a$n option tells join to print unmatched lines as well. The *n* (a 1 or 2) identifies which file to print the unmatched line from. The $-e$ str option tells join to print str in place of an empty field. The $-j$n m option tells join to use field *m* in file *n* as the field to match. By default, join doesn't print unmatched lines, leaves blank fields blank, and matches the lines using the first field on each line.

Hands-on Exercise 10.7

Display the start-up program (field 7 in the /etc/passwd file) for the people currently logged on the system. *Hint:* The output of who and the contents of /etc/passwd are not compatible. You must change one of them before join can do its job.

The *pr* Command

UNIX filters output a stream of characters. Often you will want to format this output in a specific way. You can use awk or sed to do this.

However, UNIX provides a tool, the `pr` command, whose sole job is to paginate text.

`pr` can paginate, double space, make columns, regulate page width and length, indent or number lines, set tabs, and print substitute headers, in addition to other tasks. The default option is to paginate, putting five lines at both the top and bottom of each page and adding a header showing the file's modification date and time, file name, and page number.

```
$ pr phone.list
```

```
Sep 15 12:43 1989   phone.list Page 1




Smith, Terry     7-7989
Adams, Fran      2-3876
StClair, Pat     4-6122
Brown, Robin     1-3745
Stair, Chris     5-5972
Benson, Sam      4-5587

rest of page
```

Table 10.1 lists useful `pr` options.

One of the main uses of `pr` is to format a multipage file, so that, when the file is printed, the pages break at the proper spots. Generally, when `pr` is used in a pipeline, the `-t` option is specified so you can format without paginating. Here are some examples of using `pr`.

Number each line (`-n` default is equivalent to `-n5<tab>`):

```
$ pr -tn phone.list
      1      Smith, Terry     7-7989
      2      Adams, Fran      2-3876
      3      StClair, Pat     4-6122
      4      Brown, Robin     1-3745
      5      Stair, Chris     5-5972
      6      Benson, Sam      4-5587
```

Table 10.1. *Useful* pr *options.*

Option	Meaning
-d	Prints double-spaced output
-e*cp*	Replaces tabs or character *c*, if specified, in input with *p* spaces
-h *str*	Replaces the header text with *str*
-i*cp*	Sets tab stops to every *p* characters (8 if *p* is omitted) and replaces whitespace with *c* every *p* character
-l*n*	Sets page length to *n* lines
+*n*	Begins printing at page *n*
-*n*	Prints *n* columns
-n*cn*	Numbers lines by putting a *c* character between line numbers and text and using *n* significant digits
-o*n*	Offsets *n* characters from left
-p	Waits for user to enter Return before printing each page
-s*c*	Separates columns with *c* character (tab is default)
-t	Omits the top and bottom spacing in the headers and doesn't paginate (acts like cat)
-w*n*	Sets the line width to *n* characters if displaying multicolumn output

Create two columns (-2) separated by % (-s%):

```
$ pr -2s%t phone.list
Smith, Terry        7-7989%Brown, Robin     1-3745
Adams, Fran         2-3876%Stair, Chris     5-5972
StClair, Pat        4-6122%Benson, Sam      4-5587
```

Set tab stops every 15 characters and replace the dash with spaces (default is a tab stop every 8 characters and output spaces for tabs):

```
$ pr -te-15 phone.list
Smith, Terry    7   7989
Adams, Fran     2   3876
StClair, Pat    4   6122
Brown, Robin    1   3745
Stair, Chris    5   5972
Benson, Sam     4   5587
```

Replace whitespace at every 9 characters with a %:

```
$ pr -ti%9 phone.list
Smith, Terry%7-7989
Adams, Fran%2-3876
StClair,%Pat%4-6122
Brown, Robin%1-3745
Stair, Chris%5-5972
Benson, Sam%4-5587
```

It is worth noting that the `nl` filter numbers the lines in a file just like the `pr -tn` command.

```
$ nl phone.list
     1  Smith, Terry    7-7989
     2  Adams, Fran     2-3876
     3  StClair, Pat    4-6122
     4  Brown, Robin    1-3745
     5  Stair, Chris    5-5972
     6  Benson, Sam     4-5587
```

Further, `nl` has other options that dictate how a line is numbered and when and how the line numbers are incremented. This chapter will not cover `nl` in greater detail. Refer to your UNIX documentation for more information.

The *tee* Command

A pipeline works by sending characters from one command to another. Sometimes, you need to capture the characters in the middle of a pipeline. For example, to use `uniq` or `join` you have to send it sorted input. Suppose that, in addition to the output of the pipeline, you also want to save a sorted version of your input file. To save `sort`'s output while still continuing the pipeline is one example for using the `tee` command.

`tee` reads its standard input and sends it to its standard output and to the file listed on the command line. The command `... | tee sorted.file | ...` stores what is going through the pipe in the file `sorted.file`.

Earlier, you used the following command line to find the unique lines in several phone list files:

```
$ sort phone.list phone.list.2 phone.list.old ¦ uniq
Adams, Fran      2-3876
Benson, Sam      4-5587
Brown, Robin     1-3745
Holden, Mary Ann          3-3451
Johnson, J. T.            2-2345
Smith, Gert      8-1906
Smith, Pat       9-3545
Smith, Ph.D., Marty       5-2213
Smith, Terry     7-7989
StClair, Pat     4-6122
Stair, Chris     5-5972
```

If you want to store a copy of all the phone lists sorted together in
sorted.phfile, simply put tee between sort and uniq.

```
$ sort phone.list phone.list.2 phone.list.old ¦
> tee sorted.phfile ¦ uniq
Adams, Fran      2-3876
Benson, Sam      4-5587
Brown, Robin     1-3745
Holden, Mary Ann          3-3451
Johnson, J. T. 2-2345
Smith, Gert      8-1906
Smith, Pat       9-3545
Smith, Ph.D., Marty       5-2213
Smith, Terry     7-7989
StClair, Pat     4-6122
Stair, Chris     5-5972
$ cat sorted.phfile
Adams, Fran      2-3876
Adams, Fran      2-3876
Adams, Fran      2-3876
Benson, Sam      4-5587
Benson, Sam      4-5587
Benson, Sam      4-5587
Brown, Robin     1-3745
Brown, Robin     1-3745
Brown, Robin     1-3745
Holden, Mary Ann          3-3451
Holden, Mary Ann          3-3451
Johnson, J. T.            2-2345
```

```
Johnson, J. T.           2-2345
Smith, Ph.D., Marty      5-2213
Smith, Ph.D., Marty      5-2213
Smith, Terry    7-7989
Smith, Terry    7-7989
Smith, Terry    7-7989
StClair, Pat    4-6122
StClair, Pat    4-6122
StClair, Pat    4-6122
Stair, Chris    5-5972
Stair, Chris    5-5972
Stair, Chris    5-5972
```

The *tail* Command

There are times when you don't want to see an entire file. Instead, you may just need the last few lines. An example is when you want to see if any new information has been added to a file.

UNIX offers a tool designed especially for reading the ends of files, the `tail` command. By default, `tail` prints the last ten lines in a file. `tail` takes three arguments, which tell it where to start printing and when to stop.

If you need to see more or less than the last ten lines, use the **+***n* argument, which instructs `tail` to start printing *n* lines from the beginning of the file. The **-***n* argument says to begin printing n lines from the end of the file. These arguments can also have an l, b or c after *n*. l says to deal in lines; b says to deal in data blocks (usually 1K); c says to deal in characters. Thus, `tail -100c file` would print the last 100 characters in `file`. l and b set the value of *n* accordingly.

Here are two `tail` examples:

- Print the last four lines of the phone list:

  ```
  $ tail -4 phone.list
  StClair, Pat    4-6122
  Brown, Robin    1-3745
  Stair, Chris    5-5972
  Benson, Sam     4-5587
  ```

- Print the last 46 characters of the phone list:

  ```
  $ tail -46c phone.list
  1-3745
  Stair, Chris    5-5972
  Benson, Sam     4-5587
  ```

Most commands terminate when they read the end of a file. The -f argument tells `tail` not to stop at a file's end but to keep reading. This allows you to see what is added to the end of a file whenever the file is updated.

For example, suppose you wanted to know if any new people were added to the phone list. You can run `tail -f phone.list` in the background and whenever data is added, you will see it on your terminal.

```
$ cp phone.list /tmp/plist
$ tail -4f \tmp\plist &
3452
StClair, Pat    4-6122
Brown, Robin    1-3745
Stair, Chris    5-5972
Benson, Sam     4-5587
$ echo 'Wilson, Jerry    5-0911' >> /tmp/plist
Wilson, Jerry  5-0911                   Output from tail
```

The `tail -f` command will terminate when you log out or when you kill it. In this case, you can kill `tail` with `kill 3452`.

The *tr* Command

In addition to the `sed` command, which is a line editor, UNIX offers `tr`, a character editor. `tr` can change, delete, or "squeeze" characters in a file.

By default, `tr` takes two arguments and converts the characters in the first argument into those of the second. The command `tr x y` would convert xs into ys. For example, to convert tabs into tildes (~), enter the following:

```
$ tr '<tab>' '~' < phone.list
Smith, Terry~7-7989
Adams, Fran~2-3876
StClair, Pat~4-6122
Brown, Robin~1-3745
Stair, Chris~5-5972
Benson, Sam~4-5587
```

Note that the input file was redirected into `tr` and not sent as an argument. This was done because `tr` doesn't take a file name off the command line.

To delete characters, use the `-d` option. To get rid of the dash in the phone number, use the following:

```
$ tr -d - < phone.list
Smith, Terry     77989
Adams, Fran      23876
StClair, Pat     46122
Brown, Robin     13745
Stair, Chris     55972
Benson, Sam      45587
```

To delete several characters, simply put all of the characters that you want deleted in the first argument. To remove both the commas and the dashes in each line, use the following:

```
$ tr -d ,- < phone.list
Smith Terry      77989
Adams Fran       23876
StClair Pat      46122
Brown Robin      13745
Stair Chris      55972
Benson Sam       45587
```

The squeeze operation, represented by the `-s` option, replaces repeated characters with a single character. Many UNIX commands pad fields with several spaces. The `who` command is an example.

```
$ who
ray         console      Oct  9 07:14
rich        /dev/tty1    Oct  9 08:24
```

To collapse all the spaces into a single space, use `tr`.

```
$ who ¦ tr -s ' ' ' '
ray console Oct 9 07:14
rich /dev/tty1 Oct 9 08:24
```

`-s` requires two arguments. The first is the repeated character to look for and the second one is what to put in place of the repeated characters. Note that `who ¦ tr -s ' '` works as well.

Suppose you want to replace two different characters with with the same character. For example, you decide to separate the fields in the phone list with tildes. To convert the existing phone list to this format requires both the space and the tab to become tildes. `tr` is a literal command. Although it seems that `tr '<space> <tab>' '~'` should work, it doesn't.

```
$ tr '<space><tab>' '~' < phone.list
Smith,~Terry    7-7989
Adams, ~Fran     2-3876
StClair,~Pat    4-6122
Brown, ~Robin    1-3745
Stair,~Chris    5-5972
Benson, ~Sam     4-5587
```

As you see, it substitutes tildes for spaces only, leaving the tabs alone.

`tr` does a one-for-one substitution. If there are two characters in the first argument, there should be two in the second argument as well. Thus, one way to turn spaces and tabs into tildes is put two tildes in the second argument.

```
$ tr '<space><tab>' '~~' < phone.list
Smith,~Terry~7-7989
Adams, ~Fran~2-3876
StClair,~Pat~4-6122
Brown, ~Robin~1-3745
Stair,~Chris~5-5972
Benson, ~Sam~4-5587
```

`tr` recognizes character ranges using a shorthand involving brackets. As with the shell and regular expressions, a range of characters can be identified with brackets and a dash. To specify all lower-case characters, use the range `[a-z]`. Ranges can be used to capitalize all characters in the phone list.

```
$ tr '[a-z]' '[A-Z]' < phone.list
SMITH, TERRY    7-7989
ADAMS, FRAN     2-3876
STCLAIR, PAT    4-6122
BROWN, ROBIN    1-3745
STAIR, CHRIS    5-5972
BENSON, SAM     4-5587
```

Note that in both arguments, the ranges have the same number of characters, 26 in this example.

An extension of the range argument is a numbered argument. To identify a set number of characters, use [$c*n$], where c is a character and n is a number. This range is up to n of character c. If n is 0 or left out completely, the range is seen as infinite.

Previously, you had to put two tildes into the second argument to make both spaces and tabs into tildes. The range [~*] would also work.

```
$ tr '<space> <tab> '[~*]' < phone.list
Smith,~Terry~7-7989
Adams,~Fran~2-3876
StClair,~Pat~4-6122
Brown,~Robin~1-3745
Stair,~Chris~5-5972
Benson,~Sam~4-5587
```

Hands-on Exercise 10.8

Create a pipeline that deletes the commas and dashes from the phone list and separates the fields with tildes.

Several UNIX utilities operate on fields within a single input line. Unfortunately, there are inconsistencies with how these utilities work. Table 10.2 shows the default delimiter, how each utilty treats adjacent delimiters, and how an alternative delimiter is identified for the five tools covered that work with fields, namely, awk, cut, join, sort, and uniq.

Table 10.2. *Tools that work with fields.*

Utility	Default delimiter	Treats adjacent delimiter as	Alternative delimiters
awk	Whitespace	Whitespace	-F
cut	Tabs	Separate fields	-d
join	Space, tab	Whitespace	-t
sort	Space, tab	Whitespace	-t
uniq	Space, tab	Whitespace	None

Summary

The purpose of Part 1 has been to acquaint you with the data processing tools available on the UNIX System. Entire chapters were devoted to the main tools (`grep`, `sed`, `awk`, and `sort`) and to regular expressions. This chapter covered eight tools that are more focused than the aforementioned major tools. I feature these 12 tools because I have found that they are the ones I use in my own applications. However, there are many other UNIX filters. Check table 3.2 for a list of important UNIX filters and commands. It should be emphasized that the more you are familiar with UNIX commands, the more you can do on the UNIX System.

## Part Three

BOURNE SHELL PROGRAMMING

The shell offers a full set of metacharacters that can be used interactively to change the source or destination of data, control how a process is executed, and expand the command line, along with other useful features. In addition, the shell contains a fully functional command language that lets you create command files, called shell scripts, that often have the power of applications written in traditional programming languages.

When shell metacharacters and programming commands are combined, the result is an application development environment that allows you to quickly and easily get computerized solutions up and running. What's more, these shell script applications often completely solve the problem at hand.

The purpose of this part is to take you, step by step, though the programming features of the Bourne shell. For consistency, the phone list application serves as the example. In the course of phone list automation, the shell's programming capabilities are described and demonstrated.

Not everything in this part concerns shell programming. The last chapter takes a more detailed look at some programming features of `awk`. `awk`, too, offers a powerful programming language that makes it possible to process and format complex information.

11

Creating Shell Scripts

In addition to executing commands entered on the command line, the shell has the capability to execute commands stored in a text file. After the shell scans the command line for metacharacters, it checks the file whose name is the first argument remaining on the command line to see if it is directly executable.

Command Execution

First, the shell checks the execute permissions on the file. If the user has the proper permission, the shell then checks inside the file to determine whether it is directly executable; that is, whether the file contains a compiled program. This is determined by the so-called file magic number.* If the file does not contain the proper magic number, the shell assumes it is a text file containing shell command lines. It then checks whether the user has read permissions on the file. If so, then the shell begins reading and executing the lines in the file as if they were typed at the command line. If you want to determine what a file contains, use the `file` command.

---

*The language compiler inserts the magic number at the beginning of an executable file.

```
$ file phone.list
phone.list:  ascii text
$ file /bin/cat
/bin/cat:    pure executable...
```

The shell is not very discriminating in deciding whether to treat a file as set of commands. Consider what happens when you make the phone list file executable and try to execute it. You can change the executable permissions, if you own the file, by using the `chmod +x` command.

```
$ ls -1 phone.list
-rw-rw-rw-    ray     users      ...... phone.list
$ chmod +x phone.list
-rwxrwxrwx    ray     users      ...... phone.list
```

Now you can execute the `phone.list` file simply by entering its name on the command line.

```
$ phone.list
<msg>
```

The shell treats the lines in the file as individual commands to be executed. Because the phone list contains names that aren't legal UNIX commands, the shell prints an error message after reading each name.

As an example of a somewhat useful command file, consider the `phsmith` file.

```
$ cat phsmith
grep '^Smith,' phone.list
```

If this `grep` command is entered directly after the shell prompt, it will search the phone list for all the lines that begin with `Smith,`.

```
$ grep '^Smith,' phone.list
Smith, Terry   7-7989
```

The same result can be achieved by executing `phsmith`.

```
$ phsmith
Smith, Terry   7-7989
```

Incidentally, shell command files are typically called shell *scripts*.

Application Programming Language

In addition to executing UNIX command lines, the shell provides an entire application programming language. At first glance, the shell's application language appears similar to other computer languages. However, it is quite different. The distinction is that the shell is a command processor, thus, the main purpose of its programming language is to identify which command to execute.

In contrast, computer programming languages involve the implementation of algorithms, the manipulation of memory, and the creation of executable programs. Although a computer programmer thinks in terms of variables, control flow, and function calls, a shell "programmer" combines existing UNIX commands, shell metacharacters, and shell programming constructs to create application scripts that can be executed directly by the shell.

The `phsmith` script searches the phone list for a fixed pattern, which limits its usefulness. `phsmith` is valuable because it lets anyone search the phone list for `Smith`, without knowing anything about the underlying data file, such as its name, location, or format. An obvious extension is to let users search the phone list for whatever pattern they want without having to use `grep` directly or know about `phone.list`.

A user can communicate the search pattern to a phone number lookup script in two ways. One way is to have the user pass the pattern to the script via an argument on the command line. The other is to have the script prompt for the search pattern. The shell can do either. This chapter will demonstrate the former. The latter method is an exercise in Chapter 14.

Command-Line Arguments

After the shell scans the line for metacharacters and interprets them, it prepares to execute the resulting command by breaking the command line into arguments at whitespace characters. Not only does the shell determine the arguments, but it also stores them in metacharacters available to shell scripts.

You can identify the arguments on a command line by a dollar sign followed by a number. The first argument is referred to as $1, the second argument as $2, and so on. If there are no arguments, $1 equates to an empty string. The same would be true of $*n*, if there are only *n* [-] 1 arguments.

In addition to giving you the individual command-line arguments, the shell also hands over other valuable information. In $0, it puts the name of the command it executed. The number of command line arguments is stored in $#. Last, the shell takes all the command-line arguments, minus the command name, and puts them in $*.

For example, when the command line `grep '^Smith' phone.list` is entered, the shell scans it, sees the single quotes, removes them, and sets `^Smith` as the first argument ($1) and `phone.list` as the second argument ($2). The shell also sets other command-line information:

```
$0       grep
$1       ^Smith
$2       phone.list
$*       ^Smith phone.list
$#       2
```

The numbered metacharacters are called *positional parameters*, although they often are referred to simply as command line arguments.

To fully understand how positional parameters work, consider the following simple shell script.

```
$ cat show.args
echo There are $# command line arguments
echo The file executed is $0
echo The first argument is $1
echo The second argument is $2
echo The third argument is $3
echo All of the arguments are $*
$ show.args arg1 arg2 arg3 arg4

There are 4 command line arguments
The file executed is show.args
The first argument is arg1
The second argument is arg2
The third argument is arg3
All of the arguments are arg1 arg2 arg3 arg4
$ show.args arg1
There are 1 command line arguments
The file executed is show.args
The first argument is arg1
```

```
The second argument is
The third argument is
All of the arguments are arg1
```

Note that when you access a nonassigned argument, the result is an empty string. It is not an error. In fact, that's why nothing is printed for $2 and $3 in the second run of show.args.

Hands-on Exercise 11.1

What would the command show.args 'arg1 arg2' output?

Phone System Interface

So far, you have a file containing a list of names and phone numbers. Unfortunately, to get information out of the file you need to know about shell metacharacters, regular expressions, and various UNIX tools. It is unreasonable to expect users, casual or otherwise, to learn all about the UNIX System just to find someone's phone number. Instead of trying to educate your user community on the subtleties of the UNIX System, you can write a shell script that acts as an interface to the phone list.

Writing an Interface

The phfind script searches for the pattern the user puts on the command line. Thus,

```
$ orig.phfind Smith
Smith, Terry     7-7989
$ orig.phfind 4-55
Benson, Sam      4-5587
```

The shell passes the pattern listed on the command line to orig.phfind as $1. All orig.phfind does is to take the first argument and pass it to grep along with the name of the file to search.

```
$ cat orig.phfind
grep $1 phone.list
```

Because `orig.phfind` is a shell script, it must be readable and executable by the people who will use it. In this case, that means everyone.

```
$ ls -l orig.phfind
-rwxr-xr-x  1  ray    user   19  Oct 24 8:46  orig.phfind
```

How Command-Line Arguments Are Passed

`orig.phfind` looks at only the first argument passed to it. Thus, someone looking for Tom Adams finds all the `Adams,` entries.

```
$ orig.phfind Adams, Tom
Adams, Fran     2-3876
```

Suppose the user knows something about UNIX and suspects that the space in the person's name is the reason Tom Adams isn't found. Instead, the user tries `orig.phfind`, quoting the space in the name.

```
$ orig.phfind Adams,\ Tom
grep: Can't open Tom
phone.list: Adams, Fran 2-3876
```

Not only doesn't that work, but it also isn't clear just what happened.

You know that every time the shell executes a command line, it scans the line for metacharacters. Also, after a metacharacter is interpreted, the shell removes it from the line. Keeping this in mind, let's analyze how the shell executes the previous command. First, the shell scans the command line and sees the backslash. Because the backslash is quoting the space between `Adams,` and `Tom`, the shell sends `orig.phfind` only one argument: `Adams, Tom`.

When the shell invokes `orig.phfind`, it knows it is a shell script and begins executing each line in the file. The line `grep $1 phone.list` is scanned and the first positional parameter—`Adams, Tom`—replaces the `$1`. Then the resulting command, `grep Adams, Tom phone.list`, is executed. The space between `Adams,` and `Tom` is no longer quoted because the shell ate the backquote the first time it looked at the command line. These steps are shown in figure 11.1.

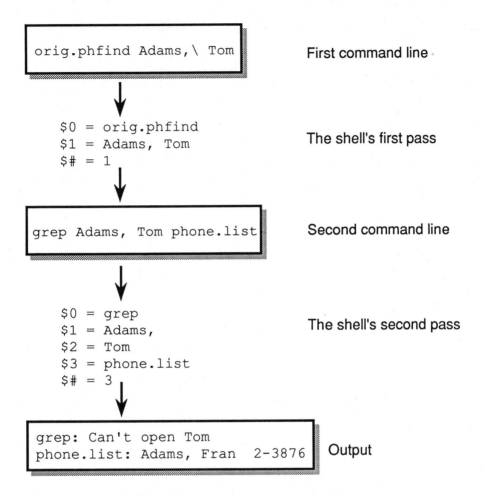

Fig. 11.1. *The shell's step-by-step execution of* orig.phfind.

Recall that grep takes only the first argument as the search pattern. Any additional arguments are seen as files to search. Now, the output of orig.phfind Adams,\ Tom can be understood. After the shell interprets the command line, which becomes grep Adams, Tom phone.list, grep looks for Adams, in the files Tom and phone.list. grep can't find Tom and tells you so. grep then searches phone.list, where it finds Fran Adams. grep prefixes the name of the file to a line when more than one file name is listed on the command line.

The erroneous output results because the shell scans the command line twice, once when it reads the orig.phfind command line and once just before executing the grep command that is executed by `orig.phfind`. However, the initial backslash is discarded by the shell's first pass.

The problem in this case is caused when the shell inserts the first argument into the `grep` command in `orig.phfind` and then re-scans the inserted argument. It's this second look that breaks the original single command line argument into a pattern and a file name (i.e., two arguments) because the space that separates the two names is no longer quoted.

Using Double Quotes

The shell provides an answer to this "second scan" problem—the double quotes. The double quotes are like the single quotes with an important exception: Double quotes don't quote dollar signs ($) or backquotes (`). However, double quotes do hide the result of the shell's substitution of these metacharacters.

For example, if `orig.phfind` is changed so that $1 is enclosed in double quotes (`grep "$1" phone.list`) the shell sees the $1 and replaces it with the first command line argument, as if there were no quotes there at all. However, when the shell scans the line a second time, to break it into arguments for `grep`, the shell treats what it substituted for $1 as a *single argument*.

To demonstrate the subtle effect of the double quotes, place them around the $1 in `orig.phfind`.

```
$ cat phfind
grep "$1" phone.list
```

Now, when you send `phfind` a name with a quoted space, it works properly.

```
$ phfind 'Adams, Tom'
$ phfind 'Adams, Fran'
Adams, Fran    2-3876
$ phfind Benson\ Sam
Benson, Sam    4-5587
```

The steps followed by the shell when the double quotes are added to `phfind` are shown in figure 11.2.

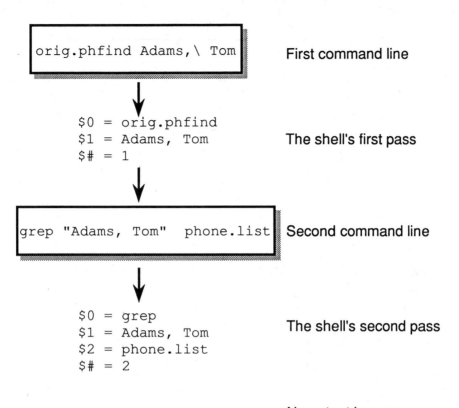

Fig. 11.2. *The shell's step-by-step execution of* phfind *when double quotes are added.*

There is no output to the command phfind 'Adams, Tom' because the phone list doesn't contain an entry for Tom Adams, which is what phfind now searches for.

The double quotes can also be used to protect the result of command substitution (i.e., backquotes).

```
$ phfind "`echo Adams,` Fran"
Adams, Fran      2-3876
```

In this example, the backquotes force the execution of the echo command. The double quotes combine the output of echo and the listed word Fran into a single argument, which is sent to phfind. Without the double quotes, the shell would treat Adams, and Fran as separate arguments.

Note that the command substitution output of backquotes is not quoted by the shell; that is, after the shell executes the command, the shell sees its output as if that output had been entered directly on the command line. To demonstrate this, search for Adams, Tom and then search for the result of the command echo Adams, Tom.

```
$ phfind Adams, Tom
Adams, Fran     2-3876
$ phfind `echo Adams, Tom`
Adams, Fran     2-3876
```

The results are the same because the shell doesn't treat these two commands differently. In both cases, $1 is set to Adams, and $2 to Tom.

Because $ and ` are not quoted by double quotes, there should be a way to quote such characters inside double quotes. Otherwise, neither of these characters could be quoted when included in a shell argument that contains a $ or ` to be interpreted. For example, suppose you want to search for the first argument at the end of a line. You would have to send grep the pattern 1. To preserve whatever the user sends as the first argument requires double quotes: "1". However, this pattern doesn't quote either of the dollar signs. To quote the ending dollar sign, simply put a backslash in front of it: "$1\$".

Hands-on Exercise 11.2

The price.list file contains the prices of various items that your company sells. Write a shell script that takes a number as an argument, which the shell script uses to search the price.list file. The prices in price.list have a dollar sign in front of them. You will have to create your own price.list file.

The phfind script works if the user is savvy enough to quote the spaces in someone's name. Another approach is to simply assume that the user is always searching for a single name. In this case, you can use $* to search the phone list. Recall that $* evaluates to all the positional parameters separated by spaces.

```
$ cat phname
grep "$*" phone.list
```

```
$ phname Adams, Fran
Adams, Fran     2-3876
$ phname Adams, Tom
$
```

The problem with using $* is that you assume the user wants to look for a single name only. What if the user enters phname Smith Jones? Here the user wants to look for two people in the list. Neither phfind nor phname addresses this problem. It will be solved in Chapter 12.

Hands-on Exercise 11.3

In phname, the $* is enclosed in double quotes. What happens if the $* is not quoted?

When should you use double quotes and when not? The answer is simple: Always enclose dollar signs in double quotes unless you have a good reason not to do so. No harm is done by quoting characters that don't need it. Using double quotes on dollar signs is a good habit to acquire.

Summary

You write a shell script by simply putting UNIX commands in a file. However, a subtle interaction occurs when you send arguments to a shell script. To control these side effects, be sure to put double quotes around dollar signs or back quotes.

The *case* Statement

Although `phfind` is only a one-line shell script, it performs a useful function. Furthermore, `phfind` hides its implementation from the user. That is, the user no longer needs to know the name of the data file or how `grep` works. What's more, `phfind` provides a consistent interface to the phone list. If the data file has to change to accommodate future needs or if another command is used to search the phone list, the user continues running `phfind`, unaware that anything has changed.

Limitations of *phfind*

The `phfind` script is useful, but only if the user does exactly what is expected. You already saw what happens when `phfind` passes an argument containing a quoted space. `phfind` has other shortcomings that need to be fixed:

- The user may not send `phfind` an argument.
- The user may send `phfind` several arguments.
- The script doesn't tell the user that the pattern isn't found.

These problems can be solved by introducing shell programming features to handle them.

What happens if `phfind` isn't passed an argument?

```
$ phfind
grep: RE error ...
```

The error message is coming from `grep` complaining that something is wrong with its pattern. To understand what has happened, we need to delve into how `phfind` is executed.

As always, the shell scans the (`phfind`) command line for meta-characters before actually executing the resulting command. In this case, the shell finds no metacharacters or arguments and creates a process running `phfind`. `phfind`'s process scans the single command line in that file, `grep "$1" phone.list`, and sees the meta-characters "`$1`". The problem is that no arguments were passed to this process so there is no `$1` to substitute.

When the shell encounters a reference to an argument that doesn't exist, the shell simply replaces the reference with an empty string. Actually, that isn't the problem. The real problem involves the interaction of the empty string and the double quotes. The double quotes tell the shell to perform argument substitution within the quoted string but to treat the resulting string as a single argument.

The current `grep` command, `grep "$1" phone.list`, becomes `grep ""` `phone.list` after the shell interprets the `$1`. Now `grep`'s first argument is an empty string. Because `grep` can't handle an empty pattern, it reports the error that you have already seen.

Note the distinction between putting double quotes around the `$1` and leaving it unquoted, and the effect of not sending any arguments to `phfind`. If `$1` is not quoted, the shell replaces it with an unquoted empty string, and the command line becomes `grep phone.list`. Although this command doesn't fail, it probably will confuse the user because it searches the standard input, most likely the terminal keyboard, for `phone.list`. The system sits idle waiting for the user's typed input. What's worse, what is entered is echoed on the screen. You should be very careful not to do this to inexperienced users.

If more than one argument is sent to `phfind`, unbeknownst to the user, only the first pattern is searched for. `phfind` silently ignores the other pattern. `phfind` should print an error message instead. If `phfind` finds a match to the first pattern sent, it prints out the matched line or lines. If no matches are found, nothing gets printed. This lack of output might confuse an inexperienced user. It would be better if `phfind` displayed a message if the pattern isn't matched.

Hands-on Exercise 12.1

The pattern `phone.list` actually searches for more than just the string `phone.list`. What else will it match?

A Conditional Statement

To handle different numbers of positional parameters, phfind must become, in essence, three separate commands. One version of phfind takes no arguments, a second version takes a single argument, and a third handles more than one argument. The problem is that all three of these versions must coexist inside a single command file, because you can't anticipate how the user will run the command.

The solution is to use a *conditional* statement. A conditional statement chooses which command to execute based on a preset condition. In phfind, the condition is the number of arguments listed on the command line, which the shell conveniently supplies to you in $#.

The shell uses the case statement to implement one type of conditional execution. The case statement chooses what to do based on *pattern matching*. Each set of commands is associated with a pattern. The commands with the pattern that matches the case's target string are executed. If no pattern is matched, none of the commands in the case statement is run.

Syntax of the *case* Statement

Like all of the shell's programming constructs, the case statement has a very specific syntax.

```
case string in
    pattern1) commands ;;
    pattern2) commands ;;
    pattern3) commands ;;
esac
```

The first line of the case statement must contain three things: the keyword case, the *string* to match, and the keyword in. In this context, the string is simply a set of characters.

How *case* Operates

The case statement works by matching the string to the patterns that begin each command set. Note that each pattern is terminated with a closing parenthesis. The commands to be executed, if a pattern is matched, are listed next. Any number of command lines can be associated with a single pattern. Note that each conditional command section (both the pattern to be matched and the commands to run) ends with a double semicolon. This pattern line

```
0) echo "Usage: phfind pattern"
   echo "pattern is what to look for in the phone list" ;;
```

executes the two `echo` commands, if the case *string* matches the character `0`. Note that the double semicolon appears at the end of the last command.

The shell matches the patterns from top to bottom. Further, because `case` is a shell construct, the patterns can include shell file-matching metacharacters. Table 12.1 lists some sample `case` patterns. The case statement matches patterns using the shell's file name-matching metacharacters.

Table 12.1. *A sample of* case *patterns.*

Pattern	Matches
`*`	Anything
`y*`	A string that begins with a *y*
`-?`	A two-character string beginning with a dash
`[Yy]*`	A string that begins with *Y* or *y*
`[!abc]*`	A string that doesn't begin with an *a*, *b*, or *c*

In addition to file name-matching metacharacters, the shell can identify a command line in a `case` statement by one or more separate patterns. In a `case` pattern, the vertical bar means *or*. For example, the pattern *a* ¦ *b* matches either an a or a b. You can put spaces between the pattern pieces and the pipe symbol.

Hands-on Exercise 12.2

What do these patterns match?
a. `[Hh][Ee][Ll][Pp]`
b. `[A-Z]*`
c. `stop ¦ exit ¦ quit`
d. `abc$`

In phfind, the test condition involves the number of arguments on the command line. The shell passes this information to the script in-$#. There are three conditions: none, one, or more than one command-line arguments. Here is how such a `case` statement would look:

```
case $# in
    0) what to do if there are no arguments ;;
    1) what to do if there is one argument ;;
    *) what to do if there are two or more arguments ;;
esac
```

Note how an *, in the last `case` option, is used as a "catchall" pattern. Because patterns are compared top to bottom, and * matches zero or more of any characters, be sure to put the * as the last pattern in a `case` statement.'

phfind1 Script

If no arguments are passed to `phfind`, you should tell the user how to use the script. A sample of such a pattern line was shown earlier.

```
0) echo "Usage: $0 pattern"
   echo "pattern is what to look for in the phone list" ;;
```

Note the $0 in the first `echo` statement. Although you stored the initial script in a specific file, that doesn't mean the script will be accessed with that same name. Instead, it is much better to refer to the current script with the same name used on the command line, which is supplied by the shell as $0.

If there is one argument on the command line, you want to search the phone list for the listed pattern.

```
1) grep "$1" phone.list ;;
```

What should you do if there is more than one argument? For the moment, the best solution is simply to tell the user that `phfind` can handle only a single argument. A better solution is implemented in Chapter 14.

```
*) echo "Too many patterns - only one allowed" ;;
```

When these three patterns are assembled into a `case` statement, the
result is the `phfind1` script.

```
$ cat phfind1
case $# in
    0) echo "Usage: $0 pattern "
       echo "pattern is what to look for in the phone list" ;;
    1) grep "$1" phone.list ;;
    *) echo "Too many patterns - only one allowed" ;;
esac
```

Incidentally, I have a habit of enclosing `echo`'s arguments in
double quotes. No doubt this is a habit from by BASIC programming
days. The double quotes in the `echo` command are not necessary, so
you can omit them if you like.

The following example demonstrates each of `phfind1`'s `case`
sections.

```
$ phfind1
Usage: phfind1 pattern
pattern is what to look for in the phone list
$ phfind1 Smith,
Smith, Terry     7-7989
$ phfind1 Smith, Jones, Brown,
Too many patterns - only one allowed
```

Hands-on Exercise 12.3

Modify `phfind1` to handle two pattern arguments by searching for
both of them on the same line. More than two arguments should be
handled as they are now (by printing the error message).

Hands-on Exercise 12.4

Modify `phfind1` to print the entire phone list if the user sends `-a` as `phfind1`'s single argument. *Hint:* You will have to put a `case` statement inside a `case` statement. This is allowed, as long as you remember to put `;;` at the end of each option. Remember that the end of a `case` statement can also be the end of another `case`'s section.

Hands-on Exercise 12.5

Modify `phfind1` to assume that the command line argument is a last name. To search for the first name, the script takes a `-f` option followed by the first name to search for. To search for a phone number, the script takes two arguments: a `-p` option followed by the phone number pattern.

Summary

Because `phfind` was written as an interface script to be used by novice users, it must be capable of handling an incorrect number of arguments. Using the shell's conditional `case` statement, you can write `phfind1` to handle the three possible argument sets—none, one, and more than one—and act accordingly. The `case` statement allows `phfind1` to execute one of three commands based on the user's input.

Logical Operators

The `phfind1` script successfully handles any number of command line arguments. It tells users when they have entered too much or too little information. `phfind1` is a useful command because it protects users from making confusing errors. However, the `phfind1` script still needs work. What happens if the user looks for someone who isn't in the phone list?

```
$ phfind1 Swartz
$
```

The answer is nothing. Because `grep` doesn't find any lines matching the pattern, it doesn't send any lines to the standard output.

Although this is perfectly acceptable behavior from `grep`, users of `phfind1` might become confused after they get no response. Many users will try the command a second time. When the results are the same (no output), the user's next response is unpredictable. Some may realize that the pattern isn't in the list and leave it at that. Others might enter the command a few more times before giving up. Some users might even seek you out and report an error with `phfind1`. Let's face it. You shouldn't expect a user who needs an interface like `phfind1` to be able to figure out what is going on when it isn't obvious.

Instead of relying on the user to deduce what `phfind1`'s silence means, you should have the script announce when it can't find the entered pattern.

```
$ phfind1 Swartz
Swartz not found in the phone list
$
```

This message makes it clear that the pattern is not in the list.

There is no option that tells `grep` to print a message when it doesn't find a match. However, `grep` does provide information the shell can use to determine whether it found a match. To understand all this requires a closer look at how UNIX executes commands.

How Commands Are Executed

Most everything done on a UNIX System is done by a process. When you enter a command line into the shell, the shell scans it, interprets any metacharacters, and then creates a process to execute the resulting command line.*

Let's look at how the `phfind1` command is run. First, a user enters the command, `phfind1 Swartz`. The shell looks for and doesn't find any metacharacters, so then it creates a new shell process, called a *child* process, to run `phfind1`. The original (*parent*) shell goes to sleep, waiting for the child process to finish. The process executing `phfind1` reads the command line in the `phfind1` file, executes the `case` command for one argument, substitutes `Swartz` for the $1 in the line `grep "$1" phone.list`, and then creates a grandchild process to run the `grep` command. Then the child process running `phfind1` goes to sleep, waiting for the `grep` process to finish. Figure 13.1 shows how `phfind1` is executed.

When `grep` finishes and its process terminates, the shell running `phfind1` wakes up and immediately terminates because it has no more commands to execute. When the child shell terminates, the parent shell process wakes up and prints a $ prompt to tell the user it's ready for the next command (see figure 13.2).

Exit Status

When a process terminates, it passes back an *exit status* to its parent process (the one that invoked it). An exit status is actually a number from 0 to 255. The shell stores the last exit status it received in the $? metacharacter.

---

*The shell executes certain commands directly—such as `cd` and `echo`—without creating a new process. Check the documentation for the shell (`sh`) for a list of built-in shell commands.

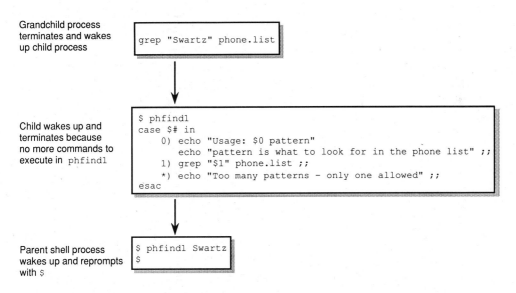

Parent shell reads line creating child; parent process goes to sleep

```
$ phfind1 Swartz
```

Child process reads `phfind1` command lines and creates grandchild process to run `grep`; child process goes to sleep

```
case $# in
    0) echo "Usage: $0 pattern"
       echo "pattern is what to look for in the phone list" ;;
    1) grep "$1" phone.list ;;
    *) echo "Too many patterns - only one allowed" ;;
esac
```

Grandchild process executes `grep` command

```
grep "Swartz" phone.list
```

Fig. 13.1. *Creating processes to execute* phfind1.

Grandchild process terminates and wakes up child process

```
grep "Swartz" phone.list
```

Child wakes up and terminates because no more commands to execute in `phfind1`

```
$ phfind1
case $# in
    0) echo "Usage: $0 pattern"
       echo "pattern is what to look for in the phone list" ;;
    1) grep "$1" phone.list ;;
    *) echo "Too many patterns - only one allowed" ;;
esac
```

Parent shell process wakes up and reprompts with `$`

```
$ phfind1 Swartz
$
```

Fig. 13.2. *How processes are terminated.*

Getting the Exit Status

The shell distinguishes between those processes that succeed and those that fail based on their exit status. An exit status of 0 equates to success; any other value means failure. Some programs fail in a meaningful way. For example, the `grep` command fails (returns an exit status of 1) if it doesn't find a line that matches the pattern.

```
$ grep Swartz phone.list
$ echo $?
1
$ grep Smith phone.list
Smith, Terry    7-7989
$ echo $?
0
```

Another example of a well-behaved command is `mkdir`. It fails if it can't make the directory and succeeds if it can. The same is true of the `cd` command. If it can change to the listed directory, it succeeds. If it can't, for any reason, it fails.

If `grep` fails when it can't find a match, it makes sense that `sed` should fail when its edit command isn't performed. In the following example, `sed` is asked to delete a line it can't match. Although `sed` can't find a line that matches the pattern, it reports success (exit status of 0) anyway.

```
$ sed '/Swartz/d' phone.list
Smith, Terry    7-7989
Adams, Fran     2-3876
StClair, Pat    4-6122
Brown, Robin    1-3745
Stair, Chris    5-5972
Benson, Sam     4-5587
$ echo $?
0
```

`grep` (as well as `egrep` and `fgrep`) is unusual in that it returns an exit status based on the results of a search. The other filters fail only if an error occurs while executing the command. For example, although `sed` doesn't fail if it can't perform the requested edit, it does fail if the edit command is incorrect or if the user lacks read permission on the edit file. In this example, `sed` returns an exit status of 1 even though the command sent to it is nonsense.

```
$ sed 'kjasdhkasdk' phone.list
sed: Unrecognized command: kjasdhkasdh
$ echo $?
1
```

Hands-on Exercise 13.1

Under what conditions does the ls command fail?

True and False, Shell Style

In addition to storing the exit status, the shell can choose whether to execute a command based on an exit status. The shell is a command processor and has no concept of true and false. Instead, it equates execution success to true and execution failure to false. Thus, an exit status of zero is equivalent to true, and any other value is the same as false.

Logical Operators

The shell offers two *logical operators* that take advantage of the information provided by an exit status. An operator is simply a symbol that represents a defined operation. In this case, the defined operations are *logical or* and *logical and*.

In a sense, the shell's logical operators are like the semicolon metacharacter. That is, they connect two or more commands and perform a type of sequential execution. The semicolon tells the shell to run the commands one at a time as listed from left to right on the command line. The logical *and*, which is represented by two ampersands (&&), tells the shell to execute the commands from left to right, only as long as the commands succeed. When a process returns with a nonzero exit status, the shell terminates the logical *and* command line; it does not execute the remaining commands on the line.

For example, the command line cd Letters && ls executes the cd Letters command first. The cd command fails if it can't change to the listed directory. If cd succeeds (the current directory is changed to Letters), the shell then executes the ls command and lists the directory's contents.

The logical *or* works just like the logical *and*, with the exception that logical *or* command lines are executed from left to right only as long as the commands fail. When a command succeeds (returning a 0 exit status), the shell ignores the rest of the command line.

The main reason for all this discussion is to explain how to tell users when the pattern they are looking for isn't in the phone list. You can do this by taking advantage of grep's exit status, the logical *or*, and an echo statement. If grep fails, the pattern wasn't found and you want to echo a not found message. Thus, the echo statement is only executed if grep fails.

```
$ grep Swartz phone.list ¦¦ echo "Swartz not in list"
Swartz not in list
$ grep Smith phone.list ¦¦ echo "Smith not in list"
Smith, Terry    7-7989
```

This command line is easily integrated into phfind1. Now, after the user enters a pattern, the script prints either the line(s) it found or a not found message. The new script is called phfind2.

```
$ cat phfind2
case $# in
   0) echo "Usage: $0 pattern"
      echo "pattern is what to look for in the phone list" ;;
   1) grep "$1" phone.list ¦¦ echo "$1 not found in list" ;;
   *) echo "Too many patterns - only one allowed" ;;
esac
$ phfind2 Swartz
Swartz not found in the list
```

Pipelines That Succeed and Fail

So far, this chapter has dealt with the success and failure of single commands. What about pipelines? What determines the success and failure of a pipeline?

The exit status of a pipeline is the exit status of the last command in the pipeline.

For example, suppose you want to print any entries found in first name, last name order. This is easily done with awk.

```
1) grep "$1" phone.list ¦ awk '{print $2, $1 "<tab>" $3 }' ;;
```

The problem with this pipeline is that `awk` doesn't fail simply because it gets no input. Thus, although the pipeline works when lines matching the pattern are found, it won't fail when there is no match. The shell ignores `grep`'s failure and uses `awk`'s exit status instead. Because `awk` succeeds even if no match is found, the pipeline succeeds.

The correct way to write the pipeline is to pipe `awk`'s output into `grep`. Then, if the shell finds no match, the pipeline fails, and you can use the logical *or* to catch its failure.

```
1) awk '{print $2, $1 "<tab>" $3}' phone.list ¦
     grep "$1" ¦¦ echo "$1 not found in the list" ;;
```

The script will still tell the user when a pattern isn't found and will also change the format of those lines it does find.

```
$ cat phfind2.1
case $# in
    0) echo "Usage: $0 pattern"
       echo "pattern is what to look for in the phone list" ;;
    1) awk '{print $2, $1 "<tab>" $3}' phone.list ¦
       grep "$1" ¦¦ echo "$1 not found in the list" ;;
    *) echo "Too many patterns - only one allowed" ;;
esac
$ phfind2.1 Swartz
Swartz not found in the list
$ phfind2.1 Smith
Smith, Terry     7-7989
```

As another example of using a pipeline and logical *or*, let's write a script that reports whether a user is logged in. The user enters a log-in name as an argument, and `ison` either prints `who`'s output line or the message `$1 is not logged in`, where `$1` is replaced by the script's argument. Note that `who` lists the log-in names at the start of each output line.

```
$ cat ison
who ¦ grep "^$1" ¦¦ echo "$1 is not logged in"
$ ison ray
ray      console Sep 22 08:29
$ ison lee
lee is not logged in
```

In addition to executing commands based on the exit status of previous commands, the ¦¦ and && themselves either succeed or fail. The logical *or* fails if all its commands fail. It succeeds otherwise. Just the opposite is true of the logical *and*. It succeeds only if all its commands succeed. It fails otherwise.

The exit values of these operators are important when you combine the ¦¦ and && operators. Incidentally, it is best to use parentheses to ensure that the commands are executed in the proper order. For example, consider a modification to `ison` that doesn't print `who`'s output, but instead simply says the user is currently logged on. If the user is logged on, the `who ¦ grep` pipeline will succeed. If the pipeline is successful, you want the script to `echo "$1 is currently logged-on"`. This requires the use of the && operator.

```
who ¦ grep "^$1" && echo "$1 is currently logged on"
```

One problem with this pipeline is the output of the `grep` command. If the user is logged on, the line(s) in `who`'s output containing that user's name are sent to the standard output by `grep`, in addition to the line displayed by `echo`.

```
$ who ¦ grep "^ray" && echo "ray is currently logged on"
ray        console Sep 22 08:29
ray is currently logged on
```

There is a simple way around this problem. Every UNIX System offers a *null* device—a file that looks and acts like a device but isn't connected to anything. The pathname of this device is `/dev/null`. When the shell reads from `/dev/null`, an immediate end-of-file is returned. Anything written to `/dev/null` is discarded.

If the user isn't currently on the system, the `grep` command will fail and so will the &&. This is where the ¦¦ comes in. If the && fails, you want to execute `echo "$1 is not logged in"`.

```
$ cat ison.1
( who ¦ grep "^$1" > /dev/null &&
echo "$1 is currently logged on" ) ¦¦
echo "$1 is not logged in"
$ ison.1 ray
ray is currently logged on
$ ison.1 lee
lee is not logged in
```

What is the exit status of the `ison.1` script? It turns out that shell scripts return a status of 0 (success) unless explicitly told to send back a different exit status. To send back an exit status, use the `exit` command. `exit` terminates a script, and, if sent an argument, returns an exit status. For example, the command `exit 1` terminates the script and, by returning an exit status of 1, tells the shell that it failed. It makes sense that `ison.1` should fail if its argument doesn't match a log-in name currently on the system. This is done by extending the second half of the ¦¦ operator.

```
$ cat ison.2
( who ¦ grep "^$1" > /dev/null &&
echo "$1 is currently logged on" ) ¦¦
( echo "$1 is not logged in"; exit 1 )
```

Hands-on Exercise 13.2

As currently written, `ison.2` prints a nonsense response if no arguments are passed to it. Rewrite the `ison.2` script to handle zero or more than one argument the way `phfind` does.

Hands-on Exercise 13.3

Write an `isused` script that checks whether a terminal is in use. Note that `who`'s output lists the currently active terminals in the second field.

Hands-on Exercise 13.4

One problem with the `cat` command that often plagues UNIX beginners is that `cat` is a filter. This means that `cat` reads the standard input if no file name is listed on the command line. Write a script called `look` that does one of three things:

- If no arguments are passed, `look` prints a usage message.
- If a single argument is sent, `look` checks whether the file exists and, if so, prints it out.
- If more than one file name is sent as an argument, `look` prints an error

---

Hands-on Exercise 13.5

Modify `phfind2` to fail if the user enters zero, if there are too many arguments, or if the pattern isn't found in the list.

Summary

When a process terminates, it passes back an exit status (a number from 0 to 255) to the parent process that invoked it. The shell stores exit status of the last command in the $? metacharacter.

The shell distinguishes between processes that succeed and ones that fail based on their exit status. An exit status of 0 equates to success; any other value means failure. Two logical operators let the shell execute commands based on the exit status of previous commands: logical *or* (|¦) and logical *and* (&&). The logical *or* fails if all its commands fail. It succeeds otherwise. Just the opposite is true of the logical *and*.

Using Shell Variables

In addition to matching patterns and testing an exit status, the shell also provides a way to store information for use later by supplying *variables*. Virtually all programming languages have variables. A variable is simply a name given to data. The key feature of a variable is that the variable's name doesn't change but the data stored in it can.

Consider a variable called `username`, whose purpose is to hold the name of the person currently using an application. Although you don't know the name of each user who might use the script, you do know that each user's name has been stored in the variable `username`. Thus, whenever you want to address the user by name, you just print whatever is stored in `username`. How do you get the person's name in the first place? You could ask each user to enter it when the application starts.

Naming Variables

Before you can use a variable to store information, you first have to give the variable a name. A variable's name must begin with an alphabetic character (either upper- or lowercase) or an underscore (_) and can contain additional alphanumeric (A-Z, a-z, 0-9) or underscore characters. For example, the following are legal variable names:

```
Username
search_pattern
_123
```

The following are illegal names:

`%age`	*(Names can't start with a %)*
`Grand.total`	*(Periods are not allowed)*

Note specifically that the shell is case-sensitive. Thus, the variable USERNAME is distinct from `username` due to the different case of the characters used.

Assigning Information

Another common programming feature employed by the shell is using the = character to assign information to a variable. For example, to assign Ray to the variable `username`, you would execute

```
$ username=Ray
```

Carefully note the syntax of the previous command. Specifically, observe that there are no spaces between the variable name, the = sign, and the data being stored. If any spaces appear in a variable assignment command, the shell won't recognize it and, instead, will think it is a command to execute. The following example shows inappropriate spaces in the assignment command being interpreted as an executable command by the shell.

```
$ username = Ray
username: not found
```

If the data itself contains spaces, the entire data string must be quoted.

```
$ username="Ray Swartz"
```

In addition to double quotes, you can use single quotes or a backslash (in front of the space).

The shell lets you assign several variables on the same command line. The only requirement is that the assignments be separated by one or more whitespace characters. The author's full name could be set up using

```
$ fname=Raymond   mname=Joel   lname=Swartz
```

Shell variables can handle only one kind of data: character strings. The shell has no concept of numbers. Although numbers can be stored in shell variables, such data is viewed as a series of characters. Because all shell variables store the same kind of data, there is no need to declare a variable before you use it, as is required in most programming languages. Instead, the shell creates the variable the first time you store something in it.

Retrieving Data from Variables

How do you tell the shell to retrieve what is stored in a variable? Not surprisingly, the shell provides a metacharacter to do the job. The metacharacter is the dollar sign placed at the front of a variable name. Thus, if `username` stores the user's name, the shell will substitute the actual user's name when it sees `$username`.

```
$ username=Ray
$ echo $username
Ray
```

You've used the dollar sign before with command-line arguments (for example, `$1` and `$2`). Variable names have all the same characteristics and can be used in the same ways as command-line arguments. In fact, there are only two differences between `$1` and `$username`. First, the shell assigns `$1` a value from the command line, where `username` requires an explicit assignment using =. Second, what's stored in `username` can be changed by simply assigning something else to it. However, `$1` cannot be changed with an assignment.

You may recall that the whole purpose of double quotes is to let the shell see certain metacharacters while ignoring others. The metacharacters seen inside double quotes are the dollar sign (`$`) and the backquote (`'`). Thus, `echo $username` and `echo "$username"` print the same thing.

Using Variables

A variable can be used anywhere you would use the string stored in that variable. You've already seen a variable's value used as an argument to an `echo` command. In addition, variable values can be assigned to other variables, either directly or as part of a larger string.

```
$ username=Ray
$ greeting="Hello, $username"
$ echo $greeting
Hello, Ray
```

Variables aren't created until you put something in them, so what happens if you ask the shell to print a variable's value that doesn't exist? No problem, the shell simply prints an *empty string*, which is a string that contains no characters.

```
$ echo "The variable junk: $junk."
The variable junk: .
```

The empty string (i.e., nothing) was substituted for $junk. The space after the colon was in the original argument list sent to echo.

Take a closer look at the previous echo command. Note that $junk is followed by a period. The shell doesn't view the variable's name as "junk" followed by a period (junk.). Instead, the shell tries to substitute for $junk and then puts a period after whatever $junk becomes. Because a shell variable name can consist of only alphabetic and numeric characters and the underscore, the shell sees $junk. as the variable junk followed by a period. Note that the period often $junk is not required. A period was used here for demonstration purposes only.

What happens if you try to add some characters to the end of a variable's value? For example, suppose a file name consists of the user's name and the number 1. Given that the user's name is stored in the variable username, it would appear that the file name could be created with $username1.

```
$ echo $username
Ray
$ echo $username1
                Blank line printed
```

Why doesn't $username1 work? The shell sees username1 as a legal variable name and assumes that you want what's stored in it. Because you haven't assigned anything to it, the echo command prints an empty string.

The shell looks for the longest name possible when dealing with variables. To identify only part of a string as a variable name, use braces after the dollar sign. When braces are combined with a dollar sign, the shell treats only the name inside the braces as the variable name and adds the other characters to the end of the variable's value. Thus, to create a file name that combines whatever is stored in `username` and a 1, use `${username}1`.

```
$ echo $username
Ray
$ echo ${username}1
Ray1
```

Variables come in very handy by letting you generalize your scripts. Instead of "hard-coding" information into a script, you can use variables that are easily changed. Most of your scripts will use variables.

The current phone list searching script, `phfind2`, refers only to the phone list file in the current directory. This means that users must have a phone list file in their current directory before they can run `phfind2`. This is a poor design for a multiuser system. A better idea is to have a single phone list file on the system and have everyone access that one file. Let's say the phone list file is stored in the `/usr/data` directory.

You could go ahead and put the path name `/usr/data/phone.list` into `phfind2`. However, hard-coding full path names into a script is not a good idea either. A better approach is to store the path name of the data file in a variable, which is easily changed, and then to use the variable's value to identify the data file. For example, you can use the variable `phonefile` to hold the name of the phone list file.

```
$ cat phfind2.general
phonefile=/usr/data/phone.list
case $# in
  0) echo "Usage: $0 pattern"
     echo "pattern is what to look for in the phone list" ;;
  1) grep "$1" $phonefile || echo "$1 not found in list" ;;
  *) echo "Too many patterns - only one allowed" ;;
esac
```

Now if you want to change the name of the phone list file, you simply assign a different file name to `phonefile`.

Hands-on Exercise 14.1

Modify `phfind2` to search for the entered pattern in the phone list file in the current directory. If the pattern isn't found there, search `/usr/data/phone.list`. If you don't find it in either file, print out a `not found` message. *Note*: If `grep` can't open a file, it will print an error message (to the standard error) and then fail.

Reading Data into Variables

Using *read*

In addition to assigning variables a value with the =, you also can store characters read from the standard input. You can read the standard input with the `read` command. When `read` is executed, the shell waits until you enter a line of text on the standard input. The shell then stores the entered text into the variable(s) listed after `read` on the command line. Input is terminated when the user presses Return.

```
$ read name
Ray Swartz
$ echo $name
Ray Swartz
```

If only one variable is listed in a `read` command, everything entered is stored in that variable. If more than one variable is listed, the shell breaks the input at whitespace, putting one "word" in each variable. If the shell runs out of variables before it runs out of entered words, the rest of the text is stored in the last variable on the line.

```
$ read fname lname
Ray J. Swartz
$ echo $fname
Ray
$ echo $lname
J. Swartz
```

If the opposite occurs and there are more variables than words, the remaining variables remain unassigned.

```
$ read fname lname
Ray
$ echo $fname
Ray
$ echo $lname
```
            Blank line printed

To break the input into words at whitespace, the shell must process the entered text. Does the shell recognize any other meta-characters when it is processing `read`'s input? First, the shell ignores any extra whitespace between words, such as leading blanks or several tabs, treating them simply as a single delimiter.

```
$ read fname lname
<tab> Ray <tab> <tab> Swartz
$ echo "$fname"
Ray
$ echo "$lname"
Swartz
```

In addition, the shell looks for and removes any backslashes in the input, preserving whatever is quoted by them.

```
$ read fname lname
\<tab> Ray <tab> Swartz
$ echo "$fname"
<tab> Ray
$ echo "$lname"
Swartz
```

Incidentally, the `read` command succeeds as long as at least one character is entered. Thus, a `read` is successful if your only entry is a new line.

```
$ read name
```
            New line only
```
$ echo $?
0
```

Does `read` ever fail? Since `read` gets characters from the standard input, `read` will fail if it gets no input because the input stream is at the end of file. If the shell is reading characters from the keyboard, a Control-D signifies the end of the input stream.

```
$ read name
<Control-D>
$ echo $?
1
$ read $name
ray<Control-D>
$ echo $?
0
```

If the `read` finds the end of the input stream and fails, the input variable is assigned an empty string.

Combining *echo* with *read*

Because the `read` command waits for the user to enter something, the command is usually combined with `echo` to prompt the user for what you want entered. The `echo` command adds a new line to what it prints. Thus, the prompts are printed on one line and the data is entered on the next.

```
$ cat getname
echo "Enter your name:"
read name
echo "Hi there, $name"
$ getname
Enter your name:
Ray
Hi there, Ray
```

Some shell programmers (myself included) prefer to have the user respond on the same line as the prompt. That is, we don't want `echo` to add a new line at the end of our prompting message. `echo` won't add a new line if `\c` is put at the end of `echo`'s argument.*

```
$ cat getname1
echo "Enter your name: \c"
read name
echo "Hi there, $name"
$ getname
Enter your name: Ray
Hi there, Ray
```

---

*On Berkeley-based systems, use a `-n` option (placed before the argument to print) to inhibit new line printing.

The \c is called a *special character sequence*. echo understands several special character sequences. These are shown in table 14.1. All of these special characters can be used with echo. The following command prints four new lines (remember that echo adds one of its own).

```
$ echo '\n\n\n'
```

Table 14.1. echo*'s special character sequences.*

Character	echo prints
\b	Backspace
\f	Formfeed
\c	No new line
\n	New line
\r	Carriage return
\t	Tab
\\	Backslash
\0*nnn*	The ASCII character represented by the octal number *nnn*

For an example of using an ASCII number, you can make most terminals "beep" by sending them a Control-G. In ASCII, a Control-G is represented by **7**, which can be represented as \07. Thus, sending a \07 to echo makes the terminal beep (assuming the standard output is a terminal). Note the 0 after the backslash; it is required.

```
$ echo '\07'
<terminal beeps>
```

The latest phfind script, phfind2, prints a usage message if the user doesn't list any arguments on the command line. Let's take advantage of the read command to have the script ask the user for a search pattern, if one isn't specified. One way to write this new version of phfind2 is to extend the zero argument case to include a prompt, a read command, and the resulting grep command.

```
$ cat phfind2.read
phonefile=/usr/data/phone.list
case $# in
  0) echo "Pattern to search for: \c"
     read pattern
     grep "$pattern" $phonefile ¦¦
```

```
      echo "$pattern not found in the list" ;;
   1) grep "$1" $phonefile || echo "$1 not found in list" ;;
   *) echo "Too many patterns - only one allowed" ;;
esac
```

Note that the `grep || echo` command line is used in both the 0 and 1 argument cases.

Another way to write `phfind2.read` is to use the `case` options to set up the variable `pattern` and then to have only a single `grep` command that searches for `$pattern`.

```
$ cat phfind2.read1
phonefile=/usr/data/phone.list
case $# in
   0) echo "Pattern to search for: \c" ;;
      read pattern
   1) pattern="$1" ;;
   *) echo "Too many patterns - only one allowed"
      exit 1 ;;
esac
grep "$pattern" $phonefile ||
echo "$pattern not found in the list"
```

Both `phfind2.read` and `phfind2.read1` do the same thing only in different ways. It is worth spending a bit of time studying both approaches to be sure you understand how they work.

Hands-on Exercise 14.2

Make `phfind2` completely interactive by having it always prompt the user for the search string.

Hands-on Exercise 14.3

Extend the `phfind2.general` script to ask which phone list to use, the one in the current directory or the system phone list (`/usr/data/phone.list`).

Redirecting *read* to Take Input

The `read` command takes its input from the standard input. On some versions of UNIX, the `read` command can be redirected to take input from a file.* For example, I maintain two phone lists, one to store business numbers and the other to hold social, personal, and family phone numbers. To create an interface, I wrote the `phfind2.lists` script.

```
$ cat phfind.lists
echo "\n1) Search Business List"
echo "2) Search Personal List"
echo "\nEnter number of list to search: \c"
read choice
case $choice in
    1) phonefile=/usr/ray/bus.list ;;
    2) phonefile=/usr/ray/personal.list ;;
    *) echo "Invalid entry, script terminated"
       exit 1 ;;
esac
case $# in
    0) echo "Pattern to search for: \c"
       read pattern
       grep "$pattern" $phonefile ||
       echo "$pattern not found in the list" ;;
    1) grep "$1" $phonefile || echo "$1 not found in list" ;;
    *) echo "Too many patterns - only one allowed" ;;
esac
```

After using `phfind2.lists` for a while, I noticed that I tend to search the same list several times in a row. For example, if I just looked up a business associate, odds are the next record I search for will also be in the business phone list. To modify `phfind2.lists` to better suit my usage, I had the script store the path name of the last phone list searched in the file `/usr/ray/default.list`. I did this easily with the command

echo $phonefile > /usr/ray/default.list

Then I changed the script to read the name of the phone list file from `/usr/ray/default.list` if I enter any value besides 1 or 2 in response to the `Enter number of list to search` prompt. I read

---

*The `read` command can't be redirected on some BSD UNIX systems or on System V UNIX earlier than release 2 (V.2).

the file by using a redirected `read` command: `read phonefile < /usr/ray/default.list`.

```
$ cat phfind2.lists1
echo "\n1) Search Business List"
echo "2) Search Personal List"
echo "\nEnter number of list to search: \c"
read choice
case $choice in
   1) phonefile=/usr/ray/bus.list ;;
   2) phonefile=/usr/ray/personal.list ;;
   *) read phonefile < /usr/ray/default.list ;;
esac
echo $phonefile > /usr/ray/default.list
case $# in
   0) echo "Pattern to search for: \c"
      read pattern
      grep "$pattern" $phonefile ||
      echo "$pattern not found in the list" ;;
   1) grep "$1" $phonefile || echo "$1 not found in list" ;;
   *) echo "Too many patterns - only one allowed" ;;
esac
```

Manipulating Variable Values

In addition to assigning and recalling variable values, the shell also provides two commands to manipulate them. The `test` command performs logical tests. The `expr` command implements arithmetic and additional logical testing capabilities.

The `test` command evaluates its command-line arguments as a logical test. `test` succeeds if the test is true, and fails otherwise. `expr`'s arguments can be an arithmetic calculation or a logical test. Let's look at `test` first.

The *test* Command

The `test` command offers a set of logical tests, implemented as arguments on a command line, to test a logical statement. For example, to test whether the variable contains Ray, you can use =. The command is `test $name = Ray`. If the test is true, `test` terminates with an exit status of 0 (success). If the test is false, the exit status is 1.

```
$ name=Ray
$ test $name = Ray
$ echo $?
0
$ name=Tom
$ test $name = Ray
$ echo $?
1
```

The test *Command's Logical Tests*

The test command offers three kinds of logical tests: string, numeric, and file. The = is a string test, true only if all the characters in both strings sent as command-line arguments match exactly. Thus, the first test, $name = Ray, would have failed if name had been assigned the string Raybo, or RayS, or even ray. Table 14.2 shows the characters test uses to create various logical tests.

Table 14.2.   test*'s logical tests.*

String tests

Arguments passed	Test performed
a	Is *a* nonempty?
a = b	Does *a* match *b*?
a != b	Does *a* not match *b*?
-n *a*	Does *a* contain characters?
-z *a*	Is *a* empty?

Numeric (integer) tests

Arguments passed	Test performed
a -eq *b*	Is *a* equal to *b*?
a -ne *b*	Is *a* not equal to *b*?
a -lt *b*	Is *a* less than *b*?
a -le *b*	Is *a* less than or equal to *b*?
a -gt *b*	Is *a* greater than *b*?
a -ge *b*	Is *a* greater than or equal to *b*?

File tests

Arguments passed	Test performed
-b *filename*	Is *filename* a block special file?
-c *filename*	Is *filename* a character special file?
-d *filename*	Is *filename* a directory?

-f *filename*	Does *filename* exist?
-g *filename*	Does *filename* have set-group-id set?
-k *filename*	Does *filename* have sticky bit set?
-p *filename*	Is *filename* a named pipe?
-r *filename*	Is *filename* readable by this process?
-s *filename*	Does *filename* have a nonzero length?
-t *fd*	Is file descriptor *fd* associated with a terminal?
-u *filename*	Does *filename* have set-user-id set?
-w *filename*	Is *filename* writable by this process?
-x *filename*	Is *filename* executable by this process?

Table 14.2 presents a great deal of information. Let's review it a step at a time. First, the numeric tests can be performed only on integers, that is, variables that hold only numeric characters. Next, note that some of the tests require three arguments (all the numeric tests and the = and ! = string tests), and some use only two (all the file tests and the -n and -z string tests) after the test command name. If test is sent the wrong number of arguments, it prints an error message and fails.

```
$ test $name =
test: argument expected
```

Also, because test is a command, there must be whitespace separating each argument that makes up the logical test. Be careful; not sending test enough arguments is a common error.

Double Quotes with test *Variable Arguments*

test is a command that is invoked by the shell, although in recent versions of the Bourne shell the test command was built into the shell to increase processing speed. Thus, test's arguments will be interpreted by the shell. This allows you to test the values stored in variables. However, the shell will also remove unquoted, empty variables. This almost always leads to an error, especially with the -n and -z string tests. Unless you have a reason not to, it is best to put double quotes around all of test's variable arguments.

Here are some sample test commands:

Are there more than four command-line arguments?

```
test "$#" -gt 4
```

Does the variable `input` hold any characters (usually tested after a `read` command)?

```
test -n "$input"
```

Is the file whose name is stored in the variable `filename` readable by the user?

```
test -r "$filename"
```

If the logical test is true, the `test` command succeeds; otherwise, the command fails.

File Test Options

Several of the file tests involve features of the UNIX System that we haven't covered, namely the −b, −c, −g, −k, −p, and −u options. These are presented for completeness and will not be explained further.

However, one file test, the ˙−t, deserves additional explanation. Recall that the standard streams have associated "file numbers": 0 for standard input, 1 for standard output, and 2 for standard error. In UNIX lingo, a "file number" is called a *file descriptor* and is represented in table 14.2 as *fd*. The −t test enables you to test whether a character stream is connected to a terminal. By default, −t tests file descriptor 1 (the standard output).

Note the distinction between the −f and −s file tests. The −f test asks only if a file exists and is true of a file created by output redirection. The −s test asks if the file contains any characters and is true only after output is written to the file. For example, the command

```
grep "$pattern" "$filename" > output.file
```

creates `output.file` every time. However, the file contains output only if `grep` finds a match. Although this difference is subtle, it often is a significant one.

The test Command in Use

To demonstrate usage, the `test` command can be paired with the shell's logical operators to test for error conditions before executing a command. Exercise 13.4 asked you to provide an interface to `cat` that prevents the user from entering `cat` without a file name argument. This script was listed as the answer to exercise 13.4.

```
$ cat newcat
case $# in
    0) echo "Usage: $0 filename" ;;
    1) ( ls | grep "^$1$" && cat "$1" ) ||
       echo "$1 not found" ;;
    *) echo "Too many arguments -- only one allowed" ;;
esac
```

One of the errors left undetected by `newcat` occurs when users try to `cat` a file they don't have permission to read. If such a file name is sent to `newcat`, it fails with the `cat` error message, `cat:` cannot open *filename*: permission denied.* Now, you can verify that the user can read the file before executing the `cat` command by using `test -r "$1"`.

```
$ cat newcat.test
case $# in
    0) echo "Usage: $0 filename" ;;
    1) ( ls | grep "^$1$" && test -r "$1" && cat "$1" ) ||
       echo "$1 not readable" ;;
    *) echo "Too many arguments -- only one allowed" ;;
esac
```

Hands-on Exercise 14.4

Rewrite the `newcat` script to use `test` to determine whether the file being listed exists.

Hands-on Exercise 14.5

Although `newcat.test` now fails if the user doesn't have `read` permission on the file to be listed, the error message (`$1 not found`) is incorrect. Modify the `newcat.test` script to report `You don't have read permissions on` *filename* if the `test -r` command fails.

---

*The actual error message will vary among different UNIX implementations.

test *Operators*

In addition to the tests listed in table 14.2, there are three other `test` operators. Two of them enable you to create compound logical statements by putting together other logical tests. The third enables you to test the opposite (negation) of the stated test.

You can create compound logical statements though the use of the *logical and*, `-a`, and the *logical or*, `-o`, arguments. As before, each component of the test must be listed as a separate argument. This `test` command

```
test $# -gt 2 -a $# -lt 6
```

checks that there are between three (`$# -gt 2`) and five (`$# -lt 6`) command-line arguments. Note that both sides of the `-a` test are complete `test` statements. Specifically, `$#` was used in both tests.

Both `-a` and `-o` are compound tests; that is, they are built by combining other logical tests. A `-a` test is true only if all (there can be more than two) of the included tests are true. A `-o` test is true if only one of the tests is true.

The shell performs tests from left to right, with one exception. A `-a` operator has a higher precedence so the logical *and* test is performed before a logical `-o` test. To demonstrate, consider a script that tests for either of two conditions: that the first argument is either a `-b` or a `-c` and that the second argument is a file readable by the current process.

```
test "$1" = -b -o "$1" = -c -a -r "$2"
```

Unfortunately, because `-a` is done first, the tests are evaluated as "the first argument is a `-c` AND the second argument is a file readable by the current process OR the first argument is a `-b`." This approach is incorrect.

To change the default testing order, use parentheses to group the tests accordingly. Be careful here; parentheses are shell meta-characters (see Chapter 2) and will have to be quoted. The correct command is

```
test \( "$1" = -b -o "$1" = -c  \) -a -r "$2"
```

To perform an opposite test, add a ! to the front of a test. The ! is `test`'s negation operator. The negation operator makes true statements false and false statements true. To test whether a file is not a directory, you can use

```
test ! -d "$filename"
```

Hands-on Exercise 14.6

Create the appropriate `test` command:
a. Does the variable `file` hold the name of a file that is both readable and executable (the permissions required for a shell script)?
b. Is the variable `response` empty or does it hold the word "QUIT" or "quit"?

Hands-on Exercise 14.7

Modify `phfind2.read` to test whether there is a `phone.list` file in the current directory. If so, use it; otherwise, use `/usr/data/phone.list`.

Invoking test with Brackets

To make shell scripts resemble programs written in other more traditional programming languages, the shell offers a second way to invoke the `test` command. Instead of using `test`, you can put brackets around the logical tests. Thus, the test

```
test "$a" -gt 10
```

can also be written as

```
[ "$a" -gt 10 ]
```

Both are perfectly acceptable; however, the bracketed version is far and away the most popular. Note that you must use a pair of brackets, one at the beginning and one at the end of the logical test. Also, spaces are required between the brackets and the other arguments.*

---

*Not all versions of the Bourne shell let you substitute brackets for the `test` command. Be sure to check your system's documentation before depending on this.

A common error made by programmers new to shell programming is to use brackets with exit status tests. The test command is only used with logical tests constructed with its own arguments. It makes no sense, say, to try to test grep's exit status with a test command. Because the shell automatically evaluates grep's exit status for you, no additional effort or syntax is necessary on your part. The following test is an error:

```
[ grep "$pattern" "$filename" ]
```

Therefore, a shell script containing it will fail.

For now, the proper way to test the exit status of a grep command is

```
grep "$pattern" $filename
[ $? = 0 ]
```

The *expr* Command

The test command enables you to create logical tests only. If you want to perform a calculation or compare a string to a regular expression, you have to look to another command, expr. expr, like test, creates expressions through the use of command-line arguments. In addition, expr sends its results to the standard output.

Arithmetic Operators

expr can perform simple arithmetic calculations involving adding, subtracting, multiplying, or dividing integers (numbers without decimal points). expr can also return the remainder of an integer division. Table 14.3 shows the operators that expr uses to represent these operations.

Table 14.3. *expr's arithmetic operators.*

Operator	Function
+	Addition
–	Subtraction
*	Multiplication
/	Division
%	Remainder (modulo division)

The following commands demonstrate `expr` calculations.

```
$ expr 4 + 5
9
$ nbr=23
$ expr "$nbr" % 6
5
```

The other operators are used in a similar fashion. Note that each part of an expression is a separate argument, as it was with `test`.

One caution is necessary. One of `expr`'s five operators is also a shell metacharacter, the `*`. Because `expr` is executed by the shell, all of its arguments will be evaluated first by the shell. This is quite useful when you want to make variable values part of the calculation. However, if the shell sees an `*`, it will perform file substitution before executing `expr`, and the resulting command will be meaningless. You must quote the `*` in an `expr` expression.

```
$ expr 3 \* 6
18
```

`expr`'s exit status is based on the value of the expression being evaluated. `expr` returns 0 if the expression's value is nonzero and returns 1 if it is zero.

```
$ expr 4 - 2
2
$ echo $?
0
$ expr 4 - 4
0
$ echo $?
1
```

Comparison Operators

`expr` can test a number of things, some of which duplicate `test`'s capabilities. For example, `expr` offers the same tests as `test`, except `expr` uses math symbols (for example, `>` instead of `-gt`). These symbols are shown in Table 14.4.

Table 14.4. *expr comparison operators.*

Arguments passed	Test performed
a = b	Is a equal to b?
a != b	Is a not equal to b?
a < b	Is a less than b?
a <= b	Is a less than or equal to b?
a > b	Is a greater than b?
a >= b	Is a greater than or equal to b?

Obviously, you will have to quote the < and > when you use them.

expr performs both integer and string tests using the same operators. expr only tests integers if both of the arguments being tested are integers. Otherwise, expr compares them as strings. Thus,

```
expr $# \< 3
```

does a numeric comparison, whereas

```
expr "$1" = "-c"
```

is a string comparison.

When expr tests strings, it evaluates them character by character, comparing them according to the *collating* sequence used by the computer. In UNIX, this sequence is usually the ASCII character set, although other character sets may be used, especially in the international arena. In ASCII, control characters come first, then the space, then digits (0-9), followed by uppercase and then lowercase letters. Thus, with strings, greater than and less than refer to which character comes first according to their ASCII codes.

expr *Output*

expr always produces output. In a logical test, it prints 1 if the test is true and 0 if the test is false.* If you want to ignore expr's output, redirect it to /dev/null. This example asks whether the characters stored in str1 come before the characters stored in str2.

---

*This follows the conventions of the C programming language where 0 is false and 1 is true. Note that when a logical test causes an output of 1, the exit status is 0. When the output is 0, the exit status is 1. Consider this behavior another gift from the people who brought you UNIX.

```
expr "$str1" \> "$str2" > /dev/null
```

In addition to testing strings against one another, you can compare them to regular expression patterns using the colon (:) operator. The colon test requires a string on the left and a regular expression on the right. Depending on how you construct the regular expression, a : test either prints the actual characters or the number of characters matched.

If you list only a regular expression to the right of the colon, `expr` prints the number of characters that match the pattern. Thus, to determine the length of a variable's value, compare it to . *.

```
$ str=abcdefg
$ expr "$str" : ".*"
7
$ echo $?
0
```

As with the other `expr` tests, `expr` returns 0 when the expression prints a nonzero value. This means the previous test would have returned 1 if `teststr` were empty.

If you surround a portion of the regular expression pattern with quoted parentheses (i.e., use a bracketed regular expression), `expr` prints the characters that match the quoted part of the pattern. For example, suppose you have written a shell script that recognizes four options, denoted by -a, -c, -d, and -e. Using a quoted regular expression, you can test whether one of the options was entered and, if so, which one.

```
expr "$optstr" : "-\([ac-e]\)"
```

This expression prints the option character contained in `optstr` if the pattern is matched (exit status is 0); otherwise, only a new line is printed (exit status of 1).

Logical Operators

In addition to evaluating single expressions, `expr` offers a logical *and* and logical *or*. Logical *and* is represented by & and logical *or* by ¦. Because both of these are also shell metacharacters, they must be quoted.

Differentiating Test Characters from Argument Strings

One potential problem is that `expr` doesn't distinguish between operators and argument strings. Thus, whenever `expr` sees an =, it assumes you are asking for an equality test. However, if the character string you are testing happens to contain =, you are out of luck because

```
expr = = =
```

is an error. A common trick to get around this problem is to add a character to the test string. Thus, to test for a =, use

```
expr X= = X=
```

If you were testing a variable, the command would be

```
expr "X$str" = X=
```

Incidentally, `expr` assumes that all regular expressions are as you list them and not part of a larger string. As a result, you don't need to use the caret (^) to identify the beginning of a line. In fact, `expr` doesn't recognize a ^ as a special character.

Hands-on Exercise 14.8

Create the correct `expr` command.
a. Test that a string contains a capital letter followed by lowercase letters.
b. Test that a string is four letters long.
c. Test that a string contains the word "yes" with any combination of either upper- or lowercase.

Storing Output

Unlike the `test` command, which only succeeds or fails, `expr` prints output in addition to testing expressions. Often you will want to store the output of the `expr` command in a variable. This can be done by command substitution. Recall that the backquotes used with the construct tell the shell to execute the command inside the quotes and then to replace what's inside the quotes with the command's output. Thus, to add 1 to a variable's current value, use

```
nbr=`expr $nbr + 1`
```

Earlier, we saw an `expr` command that tested whether one of four options was stored in a string. If you want to assign the option letter found to a variable, you could use

```
option=`expr "$optstr" : "-\([ac-e]\)"`
```

Using the backquotes with the `expr` command is common.

The exit status of `expr` is preserved when the output of the command is stored in a variable using command substitution. Thus, not only can you store the output of an `expr` command, but you can test the exit status as well. For example, the previous `expr` command stored the output of a test for one of four command-line options. To test whether an option was found, you could use the ¦¦ operator.

```
option=`expr "$optstr" : "-\([ac-e]\)"` ¦¦
( echo "Command Option not found" ; exit 1 )
```

In addition to using `expr` with commands, programmers also combine backquotes and variable assignment. For example, suppose you want to save a phone list entry for use later. You can store the output of `grep` in a variable using backquotes.

```
$ phnbr = `grep Smith phone.list`
$ echo "$phnbr"
Smith, Terry    7-7989
```

Note that the tab between the first name and the phone number is stored in `phnbr`. However, the shell would have thrown it away if the double quotes had not been used in the `echo` command.

```
$ echo $phnbr
Smith, Terry 7-7989
```

Command Substitution and Standard Error

Because the output (obtained by command substitution) of shell scripts can be stored in a variable through the use of command substitution, you must be careful about where you send error messages. Otherwise, you may end up storing them, too.

```
$ phnbr=`phfind.general Swartz`
$ echo "$phnbr"
Swartz not found
```

Ideally, you want to send error messages to the standard error stream. However, `echo` prints its output to the standard output. The obvious solution is to redirect the output from the `echo` commands that print the error messages. If you always want them to go to the user's terminal, you can use a UNIX shorthand. The file `/dev/tty` identifies the user's current terminal. Thus, to keep output and error messages separate, use `echo "`*message*`" > /dev/tty`.

The problem with redirecting errors to `/dev/tty` is that errors go to the terminal regardless of where the actual standard error of the script points. Whenever a script is executed, the user has the ability to redirect standard error by using `2>`. Therefore, instead of sending error messages to `/dev/tty`, you should print them on the script's standard output, which will be the terminal, unless it has been redirected.

Although there is no way of determining the name of the standard error stream, you can identify where it points by using the `>&2` metacharacter sequence. Redirecting output to `>&2` will send it wherever the standard error of this process goes.

```
$ cat phfind2.error
phonefile=/usr/data/phone.list
case $# in
    0) echo "Usage: $0 pattern" >&2
       echo "pattern is what to look for in the phone list" >&2 ;;
    1) grep "$1" $phonefile || echo "$1 not found in list" >&2 ;;
    *) echo "Too many patterns - only one allowed" >&2 ;;
esac
```

The 2 in `>&2` refers to the standard error. You can use a 0 if you need to identify where the standard input points; a 1 refers to the standard output.

Parameter Substitutions

In addition to providing `test` and `expr`, the shell provides four retrieval options that combine some features of both the `test` command and variables. All four have the same format: a dollar sign, a set of braces, a variable, a colon, an option character, and a *word*. The option character determines what is done with the *word*.

A common shell programming need is to test whether a variable has been set to something. This is important after a `read` command, because if the user just pressed return, the variable is assigned an empty string. These four retrieval options perform differently depending on whether or not the variable being evaluated is empty. You must be aware of the distinction between *empty* variables, those that have been assigned an empty string, and *unset* variables, those that haven't yet been assigned a value.

The four options are specified by −, =, ? and +. The format of these options is

```
${parameter:-word}
```

where the − can be replaced by =, ?, or +. In all cases, the result of these four options is a string, just like the "regular" $. The option used and the current state of the tested variable will determine which string results.

$(parameter:-word}

According to the − retrieval option, if the listed variable is set and not empty, use its value; otherwise, if the variable is empty or unset, use *word*. In this context, *word* is a string of characters that don't contain any whitespace. Note that *word* can also be a quoted string. This option can be used to establish a default value for data entry. For example, you can use the system phone list (`/usr/data/phone.list`) as a default entry to the prompt `Which phone list file to use?`

```
echo "Which phone list file to use: \c"
read file
phonefile=${file:-/usr/data/phone.list}
```

When executed, these commands will prompt for and read the name of the phone list file and then either assign the name entered or, if the user entered a return only, the system phone list, which is the default.

$(parameter:+word}

The opposite of the − option is the + option, which evaluates to *word* if the variable isn't empty and does nothing otherwise. This option might be used to print a message only if something is found.

```
match=`grep "$pattern" $phonefile`
echo ${match:+"Found in $phonefile"}
echo "$match"
...
```

If the shell finds the pattern in the file, the message `Found in filename` is printed. If the shell does not find a match, the `echo` commands print blank lines. Note that the *word* in the retrieval option can be a quoted string and that it can contain shell metacharacters, such as the $, *, [...], ?, `... `, and the backslash.

$(parameter:=word}

The = option assigns a value to the variable if it is currently unset or empty; otherwise, the current variable's value results. In a previous example (the {:-} section), the variable `file` was used to hold the entered characters and the `phonefile` variable was then assigned either the enter file name or the default. The same thing can be accomplished without `file` using the = retrieval option.

```
echo "Which phone list file to use: \c"
read phonefile
: ${phonefile:=/usr/data/phone.list}
...
```

Now, if the user enters no characters (i.e., simply presses Return), the shell directly assigns the default value to `phonefile`. Remember that these retrieval options evaluate to some string of characters. If performed as the first (or only) argument on a command line, the shell will try to execute the value of the operation. In this case, you are interested in the result of the operation, not its value. You could `echo` the result to `/dev/null`. An easier way to ignore the value is to use the null command, represented by a `:`. The shell scans the line, evaluates the = retrieval option, and then executes the colon command, which it simply ignores. The purpose of the colon command is to make the shell evaluate the metacharacters without executing a command.

$(parameter:?word}

The ? option tests whether a variable has been assigned a value. If it has, the ? option evaluates to the variable's value. If the variable is unassigned or is empty, this option prints *word* and exits this script. If the option doesn't contain *word*, a preset message, `parameter null or not set`, is displayed.

For example, this option can be used to terminate a shell script if the user simply presses return in response to a `read` command.

```
echo "Which phone list file to use: \c" read phonefile
: ${phonefile:?"Must enter a file name"}
...
```

Now the user will see an error message if only Return is pressed.*

The *unset* Command

A shell variable stays in memory until one of two things happens—either the process terminates or the variable is erased with the `unset` command. To erase a variable, simply enter `unset` and the variables you want to erase.

```
$ name=Ray
$ echo $name
Ray
$ unset name
$ echo $name
```

Usually it is unnecessary to erase variables you've created, although because of their longevity, you occasionally need to `unset` variables in your login shell to prevent conflict with future commands.

Summary

Like other programming languages, the shell stores information in variables. UNIX also offers the `test` and `expr` commands to test and manipulate the values stored in variables. The shell provides additional operators that allow you to test whether a variable is set or not and to act accordingly.

---

*This description of what the ? option does is based on the UNIX manual. My own experience is that in addition to printing the error message if the variable is unset or empty, this option prints the name of the script file and the variable name, too. Check your own system and its documentation to see how it works.

15

The *for* Loop

In the last few chapters, we have taken a simple, one-line shell script and expanded it into a useful application that validates its input, responds to errors, and notifies the user if it is unsuccessful. Although the `phfind` script has come a long way, it still can be improved. A final enhancement is to make it handle multiple command-line arguments differently. At present, `phfind2`, the current version, prints an error message and terminates, without searching for anything.

```
$ phfind2 Smith Benson
Too many patterns - only one allowed
```

Handling Multiple Arguments

There are two ways for `phfind2` to view multiple arguments. One is that all the arguments identify a single person, as in `phfind2 Smith, Terry`. We already know how to treat all the arguments as a single pattern. Instead of using `$1` as `grep`'s pattern in `phfind2`, use `$*`, which represents all the command-line arguments. (See the solution to exercise 12.2.)

Another possibility is that each pattern specifies a different person, as in `phfind2 Smith Jones`. In this case, searching for all the patterns at once might mislead the user into thinking that none of the patterns were found in the list. Consider the previous `phfind2` example. Even if the script prints out `Smith Benson not found in the list` (indicating that both arguments were treated as a single pattern), it's still easy to think that the shell searched for both names individually.

The best solution is to treat each argument on the command line as a separate pattern. This approach guarantees that the name the user is looking for is found. If two command-line arguments are actually someone's first and last names (i.e., a single pattern), searching for them separately will, in fact, find the name the user wants. In this case, the script produces more output than necessary (all the names that match either pattern), but it finds the correct information, too.

The problem with implementing this directly is the `grep` command. There is no way to tell `grep` to search for more than one pattern in a file. You could use the `egrep` command, which can handle multiple patterns, but then the problem becomes creating the proper search pattern. The easiest solution to implement is searching for each argument individually with a separate `grep` command. If there are three patterns, three `grep` commands would be run.

Looping

In programming, *looping* is a set of commands that are repeated. The shell provides three looping statements as part of its command language. One of them, the `for` loop, uses patterns to control the number of iterations. The other two, the `while` and `until` loops, use a command's exit status and are discussed in Chapter 16.

The `for` loop is tailor-made for the `phfind2` script. It takes a list of words and executes a set of commands once for each word. In `phfind2`, the word list will be the command-line arguments, and the loop will execute a `grep` command for each word in the list.

Where do `grep`'s patterns come from? In addition to looping once for each word, the `for` loop also maintains a *loop variable* that is assigned a different word from the list for each loop iteration. Thus, the `grep` command will simply use the pattern supplied by the `for` loop, each loop will search for a different pattern.

The `for` loop's syntax contains three parts: the loop control statement, the keyword `do`, and the keyword `done`. The loop control statement is the first line in the loop, and it must start with the word `for` and be followed by the loop variable's name, the keyword `in`, and the word list. The `do` and `done` are used to mark where the commands begin and end.

```
for variable in word-list
do
     commands to execute
done
```

When the shell encounters a `for` loop, it scans *word-list* for certain shell metacharacters, expands those, and then breaks *word-list* into words, using whitespace as a delimiter. The shell then stores the first word in the loop variable and executes the commands between the `do` and `done`. After the commands are done for the first word, the shell assigns the second word to the loop variable and then repeats the loop commands. This continues until the shell executes the loop once for each word in *word-list*.

The shell performs file name matching and command substitution (backquotes) on the words in *word-list*. Also, positional parameters can (and often do) appear in a `for` loop's *word-list*. Here are some `for` loop examples.

This `for` loop uses the files in the current directory that start with `chapter.` (The word chapter followed by a period).

```
for cfile in chapter.*
do
     commands to execute
done
```

In this sample code, the loop variable is `cfile`.

This `for` loop uses the first two command-line arguments. Here, the loop variable is `arg`.

```
for arg in "$1" "$2"
do
     commands to execute
done
```

Note that the word list first undergoes shell metacharacter substitution and then is separated at whitespace. Thus, the same precautions need to be made with positional parameters in `for` loops as are made whenever the shell looks at an argument; namely, putting them inside double quotes.

This example is a bit more complicated because it uses command substitution to create the word list. This `for` loop uses `awk` to get only the last names in the phone list.

```
for lname in 'awk '{ print $1 }' phone.list'
do
     commands to execute
done
```

As a last example, you can loop a set number of times by using a *word-list* of counting numbers. This `for` loop loops ten times, printing the "loop iteration" number each time.

```
$ cat loop.count
for count in 1 2 3 4 5
do
     echo "loop iteration $count"
done
$ loop.count
loop iteration 1
loop iteration 2
loop iteration 3
loop iteration 4
loop iteration 5
```

Incidentally, the reason a different loop variable is used in each sample `for` loop is to demonstrate that you can use whatever variable name you want. No special variable name is required. However, it is best for variable names to describe what they hold.

Sending Arguments

`for` loop variables are just like any other shell variable except that they don't require an explicit assignment statement to take the value of the next word in the *word-list*.

The `for` loop in `phfind2` will be used to perform a separate search of the phone list for each command-line argument. To do this, the `for` loop needs to get all the command-line arguments as its *word-list*. This `for` loop will use `$*`, which represents all the command-line arguments, as its *word-list*. The commands executed by the `for` loop consist of a single command line that searches for `$pattern` (the loop variable) and prints a message if it does not find `$pattern`. The entire `for` loop looks like

```
for pattern in $*
do
    grep "$pattern" $phonefile ||
    echo "$pattern not found in list"
done
```

When this `for` loop is inserted into `phfind2`, the result is `phfind2.for`.

```
$ cat phfind2.for
phonefile=/usr/data/phone.list
case $# in
    0) echo "Usage: $0 pattern"
       echo "pattern is what to look for in the phone list" ;;
    1) grep "$1" $phonefile || echo "$1 not found in list" ;;
    *) for pattern in $*
       do
            grep "$pattern" $phonefile ||
            echo "$pattern not found in list"
       done ;;
esac
$ phfind2.for Smith Benson
Smith, Terry    7-7989
Benson, Sam     4-5587
```

Hands-on Exercise 15.1

Modify the `phfind2.for` script to number the searches with the title "The results of search number XX," where XX is the number of the `for` loop iteration.

If the shell passes only a single argument to `phfind2.for`, a single `grep` command is run. The `for` loop in `phfind2.for` handles two or more arguments by running a separate `grep` for each one. There is no difference between the command line executed for one argument and the command line executed by the `for` loop. In fact, the 1) option in the `case` statement is redundant; its work can be done by the `for` loop, which only loops once on a single argument. When you remove the 1) option, the result is the `phfind2.merged` script.

```
$ cat phfind2.merged
phonefile=/usr/data/phone.list
case $# in
    0) echo "Usage: $0 pattern"
       echo "pattern is what to look for in the phone list" ;;
    *) for pattern in $*
       do
            grep "$pattern" $phonefile ||
            echo "$pattern not found in list"
       done ;;
esac
```

Unfortunately, there is a problem with phfind2.merged, and it again involves our old friend, the quoted space. Note what happens if the user enters someone's full name.

```
$ phfind2.merged 'Smith, Terry'
Smith, Terry    7-7989
Smith, Terry    7-7989
```

The shell scans phfind2.merged's command-line arguments twice. The first time is when the single argument is assigned to $1 (and $*). In this scan, the shell quotes the space between the first and last names. The arguments are interpreted a second time when, after substituting for $*, the shell must break the for loop *word-list* into words. Because the space is no longer quoted, the for loop sees two words and searches for each one of them individually, finding the same name both times.

We solved a similar problem with phfind by quoting the argument with double quotes. In phfind2.merged, this would entail quoting the $* in the for loop.

```
$ cat phfind2.merged1
phonefile=/usr/data/phone.list
case $# in
    0) echo "Usage: $0 pattern"
       echo "pattern is what to look for in the phone list" ;;
    *) for pattern in "$*"
       do
            grep "$pattern" $phonefile ||
            echo "$pattern not found in list"
       done ;;
esac
```

Now the script works properly when the command-line arguments make up a single name.

```
$ phfind2.merged1 'Smith, Terry'
Smith, Terry    7-7989
```

Unfortunately, the script no longer looks for multiple arguments.

```
$ phfind2.merged1 Smith Benson
Smith Benson not found in list
```

The problem is caused by quoting the $*. Recall that the double quotes allow for parameter substitution but that the shell treats the resulting string as a *single* argument. As a result, the `for` loop in `phfind2.merged1` does only one search, regardless of the number of command-line arguments present.

Double quotes work for `grep`'s pattern when `grep` takes a single argument. The same approach works with `phfind2.merged1`, if you quote each argument individually. However, this requires a different command for every combination of arguments. For example, this code can handle up to three arguments, but no more.

```
phonefile=/usr/data/phone.list
case $# in
    0) echo "Usage: $0 pattern"
       echo "pattern is what to look for in the phone list" ;;
    1) grep "$1" $phonefile || echo "$1 not found in list" ;;
    2) grep "$1" $phonefile || echo "$1 not found in list"
       grep "$2" $phonefile || echo "$2 not found in list" ;;
    3) grep "$1" $phonefile || echo "$1 not found in list"
       grep "$2" $phonefile || echo "$2 not found in list"
       grep "$3" $phonefile || echo "$3 not found in list" ;;
    *) echo "Too many patterns -- up to three allowed" ;;
esac
```

It seems we're in a bind. Neither $* or "$*" works. What's left? As usual, the shell provides a metacharacter solution.

The $@ Metacharacter

What our script needs is a way to put double quotes around each positional parameter, without knowing in advance how many there are. This is the exact purpose of the $@ metacharacter. In reality, the $@ evaluates two different ways, depending on usage.

When used by itself, the $@ is another way to represent all the arguments on the command line. In other words, $@ is equivalent to $*. The distinction between them comes when $@ is enclosed in double quotes. The "$@" expands to all the positional parameters individually quoted with double quotes. For example, if there are two command-line arguments, then "$@" evaluates to "$1" "$2". The atsign.test script shows the $@ in action.

```
$ cat atsign.test
count=1
for arg in "$@"
do
    echo "Argument $count is $arg"
    count=`expr $count + 1`
done
$ atsign.test 'Smith, Terry' Benson, Sam
Argument 1 is Smith, Terry
Argument 2 is Benson,
Argument 3 is Sam
```

Incidentally, if no arguments are sent to atsign.test, the shell does not execute the for loop.

```
$ atsign.test
$
```

Replacing the "$*" with "$@" corrects the for loop so it works properly for arguments that contain quoted spaces. The result is the phone.find script.

```
$ cat phone.find
phonefile=/usr/data/phone.list
case $# in
    0) echo "Usage: $0 pattern"
       echo "pattern is what to look for in the phone list" ;;
    *) for pattern in "$@"
```

```
        do
            grep "$pattern" $phonefile ¦¦
            echo "$pattern not found in list"
        done ;;
esac
```

Now, both types of arguments, those that contain quoted spaces and those that don't, are handled successfully.

```
$ phone.find 'Smith, Terry' Benson Robin
Smith, Terry    7-7989
Benson, Sam     4-5587
Brown, Robin    1-3745
```

phone.find now offers all the functionality we're looking for. The script checks whether at least one argument was entered and prints a message if no arguments are found on the command line. This script tells the user when the pattern isn't found in the list. phone.find can also handle several arguments, searching for each one as a separate pattern in the phone list.

Hands-on Exercise 15.2

Create a script called phone.chg that takes two arguments and substitutes the second argument for the first, writing the resulting corrections back into the phone list. *Hint*: Use sed to make the changes and mv to update the list.

Hands-on Exercise 15.3

Write a script called add that sums its integer arguments.

The most common *word-list* sent to a for loop is the complete list of command-line arguments. It is so common, in fact, that the shell supplies a shorthand form of the for loop that defaults to a *word-list* of "$@". The shorthand is to leave off the "in *word-list*" part of the for loop. Thus,

```
for variable in "$@"
```

and

```
for variable
```

are completely equivalent. This means the `for` loop in `phone.find` can be written

```
for pattern
do
    grep "$pattern" $phonefile ¦¦
    echo "$pattern not found in list"
done
```

You might be wondering why the `do` is needed in the `for` loop. Since the keyword `for` denotes where the loop starts, what is the purpose of the `do`? The `do` is a delimiter that allows the *word-list* section of the `for` loop to span several lines, if necessary. This can easily happen if command substitution is used with a fairly long pipeline.

For example, suppose a `for` loop's *word-list* is to be the number of words in a set of files. You can use `wc` to count each file's words, but `wc`'s output includes the file's name, which you don't need for this application. To get rid of the file names, you can pipe `wc`'s output through `awk` to print only the word counts, `wc` *file-list* ¦ `awk` `'{print $1}'`.

A `for` loop that used this pipeline to generate its *word-list* might use two lines for the pipeline.

```
for count in ` wc chapter.1 figures book.t.of.c ¦
                awk '{print $1}' `
do
    commands to execute
done
```

The purpose of the do keyword should now be clear. Without a separate marker at the beginning of the command section, any *word-list* or command that generates a *word-list* would be limited to a single line.

Summary

phone.find is a robust shell script. It checks for arguments, handles whatever kind and number of arguments are sent to it, and tells the user if anything unexpected happens. Except for a few cosmetic changes, the development of this script is finished.

Writing Interactive Shell Scripts

Not every task performed on a UNIX System requires shell meta-characters, pipelines, and special programming commands. Often, users need only a simpler interface to accomplish the task at hand. One way to make things easier is to write interactive programs. By interactive, I mean a program that asks a question and waits for the user's response.

Interactive shell scripts are easy to create using `read` and `echo` statements. As an example, consider the problem of updating the phone list. The phone list file has a specific format, and you must ensure that users add new names properly. For this reason, it isn't a good idea to let someone directly edit the file. A better idea is to write a data entry shell script that prompts for and reads a name and phone number from the user and then writes the correctly formatted information into the file.

```
$ cat phadd
phonefile=/usr/data/phone.list
echo "\nFirst Name: \c"
read fname
echo "Last Name: \c"
read lname
echo  "$fname $lname's phone extension: \c"
read phnbr
echo "$lname, $fname <tab> $phnbr" >> $phonefile
```

When executed, `phadd` gets a name and a phone number from the standard input and then writes the name, properly formatted, to the end (note the >>) of the phone list file.

```
$ phadd
First Name: Ray
Last Name: Swartz
Ray Swartz's phone extension: 8-9708
$ cat /usr/data/phone.list
Smith, Terry    7-7989
Adams, Fran     2-3876
StClair, Pat    4-6122
Brown, Robin    1-3745
Stair, Chris    5-5972
Benson, Sam     4-5587
Swartz, Ray     8-9708
```

Hands-on Exercise 16.1

At present, phadd takes whatever is entered to be someone's phone extension. Modify phadd to verify that the extension entered is in the proper format (a number, followed by a dash, followed by four numbers). If it isn't in the proper format, the shell should print an error message and terminate the script without writing anything to the file.

Although the phadd script works, several enhancements are needed. First of all, the script makes no attempt to verify any of the data entered (see exercise 16.1). Is the name being entered already in the list? Did the user make any data entry errors that need to be corrected? Shouldn't the phone list be sorted after new names are entered? These questions will be answered in this chapter as more shell programming features are introduced.

The fact that phadd can add only a single entry when it runs is a problem and will quickly become a bother. In general, when phadd is run, there will be more than one name to enter. A much better design is to write phadd to continue reading names and phone numbers until the user says to stop.

Additional Loops

In addition to the for loop, the shell offers two others, the while and until loops. Unlike the for loop, which controls the number of iterations by counting words in a list, the while and until statements control looping based on the exit status of a loop control command. The `while` loop continues as long as the control command succeeds whereas the `until` loop repeats as long as the control command fails.

The *while* Loop

The syntax of the `while` loop is similar to that of the `for` loop, with one exception. Instead of a *word-list* to control the loop, a `while` statement executes a command and uses its exit status to control the loop. The loop continues as long as the control command succeeds.

```
while command
do
      commands to execute
done
```

The control command is executed each time through the loop. If the control command fails when it is first executed, the loop is not entered at all.

The most common `while` loop control command is `test`, and variable's value generally controls the `while` loop. As an example of usage, the `sumit` script sums the integers from one to the argument.

```
$ cat sumit
count=1
total=0
while [ $count -le "$1" ]
do
      total=`expr $count + $total`
      count=`expr $count + 1`
done
echo "The sum of the integers from 1 to $1 is $total"
$ sumit 5
The sum of the integers from 1 to 5 is 15
```

A `while` loop can make `phadd` more useful by looping until the user says to quit. The `phadd.while` reads someone's name and phone number from the user and then asks "Enter another name? (y/n)". If the response starts with a y, the loop continues and prompts the user for another name. If the response begins with an n, the loop terminates.

The controlling command of a `while` loop is executed *before* the `while` loop begins. Thus, to make `phadd.while` loop, you must establish a `while` loop test that succeeds the first time it is tested. In `phadd.while`, the loop will be controlled by the value stored in the variable `looptest`.

```
looptest=y
while [ $looptest = y ]
do
      commands to execute
done
```

The code executed by the `while` loop consists of two parts, the commands previously shown in `phadd` and the commands that ask whether the user wants to add more names. The only change to the original `phadd` code is that the `phonefile` variable is set outside the `while` loop since it needs to be assigned only once for the entire script.

```
$ cat phadd.while
phonefile=/usr/data/phone.list
looptest=y
while [ $looptest = y ]
do
      # phadd commands
      echo "\nFirst Name: \c"
      read fname
      echo "Last Name: \c"
      read lname
      echo  "$fname $lname's phone extension: \c"
      read phnbr
      echo "$lname, $fname <tab> $phnbr" >> $phonefile
      # loop control commands
      echo "\nEnter another name? (y/n) \c"
      read answer
      case $answer in
          [Yy]*) looptest=y ;;
          [Nn]*) looptest=n ;;
      esac
done
```

There is no real need to assign y to `looptest` if the user answers y (or any equivalent) to the Enter another name? prompt, since `looptest` was set to y originally. The script will run the same if an empty option is substituted for the statement `looptest=y`

```
case $answer in
    [Yy]*) ;;
    [Nn]*) looptest=n ;;
esac
```

or, for that matter, if that option is eliminated entirely

```
case $answer in
    [Nn]*) looptest=n ;;
esac
```

I prefer the first version containing the `[Yy]*` option and assigning y to `looptest` because it provides some documentation that shows how the script works.

Why bother putting the `case` statement in `phadd.while` at all? Can't the `while` loop simply test what's stored in `answer` directly? It can; however, the `test` command doesn't have the flexibility of the `case` statement. `test` requires explicit string comparisons since it doesn't offer any pattern matching. The two `case` options accept any string that starts with an upper- or lowercase y to mean "yes" and any string starting with n or N as "no." Using the `case` statement is easier and provides more flexibility.

To demonstrate different shell programming approaches, the `phadd.while` script has been written without the `case` statement. Although you can use the `test` command to control the `while` loop, it is easier to use the pattern-matching capabilities of `expr`. This script is shown as `phadd.expr`.

```
$ cat phadd.expr
phonefile=/usr/data/phone.list
answer=y
while expr "$answer" : "[Yy]*" > /dev/null
do
    # phadd commands
    echo "\nFirst Name: \c"
    read fname
    echo "Last Name: \c"
    read lname
    echo "$fname $lname's phone extension: \c"
```

```
        read phnbr
        echo "$lname, $fname <tab> $phnbr" >> $phonefile
        # loop control commands
        echo "\nEnter another name? (y/n) \c"
        read answer
done
```

Specifically note that there are no brackets around the `expr` command. Brackets are a shorthand for the `test` command. Since a `while` loop directly executes the control command, the `expr` command line is listed without brackets. The `test` command is not involved. The `while` loop tests the exit status of the `expr` commands. Recall that `expr` prints output in addition to returning the appropriate exit status. The redirection is needed to get rid of `expr`'s output, which would be sent to the standard output otherwise.

```
$ phadd.expr
First Name: Lee
Last Name: Wilson
Lee Wilson's phone extension: 7-3321


Enter another name? (y/n) n
```

Hands-on Exercise 16.2

Write a `phfind.while` script that prompts for a pattern to find in the phone list and then asks the user if there are more patterns to find.

Hands-on Exercise 16.3

In Chapter 14, the `phfind.lists` script was shown that searches for names in one of two lists, one that contains business names (`/usr/ray/bus.list`) and one for social, personal, and family phone numbers (`/usr/ray/personal.list`). Write a `phadd.lists` script that enables the user to enter names in either or both lists in a single session. The script should ask the user which list to use and then add names until the user has no more to add to that list. When name entry terminates, the script reprompts from the beginning, giving the user an opportunity to add names to other phone lists or terminate the script.

The *true* and *false* Commands

Often, programmers simply use a `while` loop to repeat a command continuously, without using the control command to terminate it. In programming, such loops are called *infinite* loops, since there is no obvious way for them to stop. A continuous `while` loop can be created by using [1 = 1] as the control command.

```
while [ 1 = 1 ]
do
     commands to execute
done
```

This loop executes until something unrelated to the `while` loop stops it. One way to end the loop is to `exit` the script from within the loop.

There are two alternatives to the [1 = 1] control command. We've already talked about one: the colon, or null, command. The exit status of the null command is 0 (success). The system provides the `true` command, which simply evaluates to an exit status of 0. `true`'s counterpart, the `false` command, always fails with an exit status of 1.

The current `phadd.while` script is not well written because it forces users to respond with a y every time they want to enter another name. This repetition quickly gets to be a bother. It is prone to entry errors. Eventually, a user will hit the Return key before y and someone will end up with a first name of y.

A better design is to have the script get names until the user enters "stop" for the first name. The `phadd.stop` script implements this design by having the `while` loop continue until the script exits when the user enters "stop".

```
$ cat phadd.stop
phonefile=/usr/data/phone.list
while true
do
     echo "\nFirst Name (stop to exit): \c"
     read fname
     case $fname in
         [Ss][Tt][Oo][Pp]) exit ;;
     esac
     echo "Last Name: \c"
```

```
        read lname
        echo  "$fname $lname's phone extension: \c"
        read phnbr
        echo "$lname, $fname <tab> $phnbr" >> $phonefile
done
```

Note that the single `case` option handles any combination of upper-
and lowercase characters that spell "stop".

The *until* Loop

The `until` loop is the converse of the `while` loop, in that the `until`
loop continues executing commands as long as the control command
fails. The syntax of the `until` loop is identical to the `while` loop.

```
until   command
do
        commands to execute
done
```

As with the `while` loop, the `until`'s control command is executed
each time through the loop. In addition, if the control command
succeeds the first time it is executed, the loop is not entered, and the
commands inside the loop are not run.

The `until` loop can help solve a problem with `phadd.stop`. At
present, there is no way for the user to correct any data entry mistakes.
If a name is mistyped or a key is pressed by mistake, the user can't do
anything to correct it. The only choices are to put the erroneous data
into the file and change it later or to interrupt the script before the
data is written to the file and start over—neither one is a very good
alternative.

The best solution is to provide the user with a way to edit each
entry before it is written to the phone list. The idea is to print what was
entered and to ask "Is this correct? (y/n)". If the user's response is
affirmative, the data is sent to the file. If there is an error, the user is
repeatedly asked which entry to fix. The corrections continue until the
user says the entry is correct.

The correction section of `phadd.stop` can be implemented as
an `until` loop. The section starts by printing the entered data on
separate lines. In addition, each entry is numbered so that if there is a
mistake, the user can refer to the data item by number. Then the script
asks the user if this is correct and then reads the response.

```
echo "1. $fname"
echo "2. $lname"
echo "3. $phnbr:
echo "\nIs this correct? (y/n) \c"
read answer
```

If the data are correct as entered, the script terminates the `until` loop by setting the loop control variable, `correct`, to y. If there is an error, the script asks the user to enter the number of the entry that must be corrected and prompts for the correct information.

```
correct=n
until [ $correct = y ]
do
      echo "\n1. $fname"
      echo "2. $lname"
      echo "3. $phnbr"
      echo "\nIs this correct? (y/n) \c"
      read answer
      case $answer in
          [Yy]*) correct=y ;;  # loop exit condition
             *) echo "\nNumber to correct: \c"
                read nbr
                case $nbr in
                   1) echo "First Name: \c"
                      read fname ;;
                   2) echo "Last Name: \c"
                      read lname ;;
                   3) echo "Phone Number: \c"
                      read phnbr ;;
                esac ;;
      esac
done
echo "$lname, $fname <tab> $phnbr" >> $phonefile
```

Note that the `echo` statement, which writes the entry into the phone list, is placed after the end of the correction loop.

When the data entry segment is combined with the correction section, the `phadd.verify` script results.

```
$ cat phadd.verify
phonefile=/usr/data/phone.list
while true
```

```
      do
          echo "\nFirst Name (stop to exit): \c"
          read fname
          case $fname in
              [Ss][Tt][Oo][Pp]) exit ;;
          esac
          echo "Last Name: \c"
          read lname
          echo  "$fname $lname's phone extension: \c"
          read phnbr
          correct=n
          until [ $correct = y ]
          do
              echo "\n1. $fname"
              echo "2. $lname"
              echo "3. $phnbr"
              echo "\nIs this correct? (y/n) \c"
              read answer
              case $answer in
                  [Yy]*) correct=y ;;   # loop exit condition
                  *) echo "\nNumber to correct: \c"
                     read nbr
                     case $nbr in
                         1) echo "First Name: \c"
                            read fname ;;
                         2) echo "Last Name: \c"
                            read lname ;;
                         3) echo "Phone Number: \c"
                            read phnbr ;;
                     esac ;;
              esac
          done  # end of until loop
          echo "$lname, $fname <tab> $phnbr" >> $phonefile
      done  # end of while loop
```

Here is `phadd.verify` in action.

```
$ phadd.verify
First Name (stop to exit): Ray
Last Name: Smartz
Ray Smartz's phone extension: 8-9708
1. Ray
2. Smartz
```

```
3. 8-9708
Is this correct? (y/n) n
Number to correct: 2
Last Name: Swartz
1. Ray
2. Swartz
3. 8-9708
Is this correct? (y/n) y
First Name (stop to exit): stop
```

The `phadd.verify` script is a bit longer than the other scripts we've written. What's more, it might seem like there are "better ways to do it" than what is shown. But, don't be alarmed by either of these observations.

First of all, shell scripts can get rather long—primarily due to the lack of certain features that make programming languages efficient. The tricks you might use to make a Pascal or C program concise are simply not available when you are writing shell scripts.

What's more, a shell script executes much more slowly than an equivalent program written in a compiled programming language. The advantage of shell scripts is not in execution speed but in how little time it takes to write a useful application. The key to effective shell scripting is solving the problem at hand as quickly as possible. Although programming style and efficiency are important, it is often better to solve a problem (at least initially) with a "brute force" method than to spend a good deal of time designing an elegant application.

Hands-on Exercise 16.4

The `phadd.verify` script assumes that any response besides y in response to the "Is this correct?" prompt is an error. Modify `phadd.verify` to enable the user to cancel a correction. As an additional task, have the script print an error message if the user enters an invalid response when correcting fields.

Hands-on Exercise 16.5

The `while` and `until` loops in `phadd.verify` are interchangeable; interchange them.

The *break* and *continue* Statements

Once the user enters the first name into `phadd.verify`, there is no way to cancel the current entry, except to terminate the script by using the interrupt key. Since your main objective is to keep the phone list current and correct, you want to give users every opportunity to correct a mistake. One such error might be starting to enter a name that, it turns out, shouldn't be entered.

What `phadd.verify` needs is an escape hatch that enables a user to cancel the entry of the current name and restart the entry loop. For example, if the user enters a special token, in our case "XX", the loop immediately restarts. This can be done with a `case` statement.

```
echo "Last Name: (XX to restart) \c"
read lname
case $lname in
    XX) ;;  # skip rest of loop
    *) echo "$fname $lname's phone extension: (XX to restart) \c"
       read phnbr
       case $phnbr in
           XX) ;; # skip rest of loop
           *) correction section and rest of script
```

Although this approach works, it is awkward. Implementing entry cancellation with `case` statements involves empty options and much indenting, making the resulting script complex and hard to read.

A better solution is to use the `continue` statement, a special shell programming command that restarts loops. When the shell encounters the `continue` statement in a loop, it immediately jumps to the beginning of the loop and starts executing. In a `while` or `until` loop, a `continue` causes the immediate execution of the loop-control command. In `for` loops, `continue` forces the assignment of the next word in the *word-list* to the loop's variable and then restarts the commands inside the loop. The `continue` statement can only appear in `for`, `while`, or `until` loops.

Although entry cancellation also requires `case` statements, the `continue` statement accomplishes the job in a more direct way. The `phadd.cancel` script implements entry cancellation.

```
$ cat phadd.cancel
phonefile=/usr/data/phone.list
while true
```

```
do
    echo "\nFirst Name (stop to exit): \c"
    read fname
    case $fname in
        [Ss][Tt][Oo][Pp]) exit ;;
    esac
    echo "Last Name (XX to restart): \c"
    read lname
    case $lname in
        XX) continue ;;  # skip rest of loop
    esac
    echo "$fname $lname's phone extension: (XX to restart) \c"
    read phnbr
    case $phnbr in
        XX) continue ;; # skip rest of loop
    esac
    correct=n
    until [ $correct = y ]
    do
        echo "\n1. $fname"
        echo "2. $lname"
        echo "3. $phnbr"
        echo "\nIs this correct? (y/n) \c"
        read answer
        case $answer in
            [Yy]*) correct=y ;;  # loop exit condition
            *) echo "\nNumber to correct: \c"
               read nbr
               case $nbr in
                   1) echo "First Name: \c"
                      read fname ;;
                   2) echo "Last Name: \c"
                      read lname ;;
                   3) echo "Phone Number: \c"
                      read phnbr ;;
               esac ;;
        esac
    done  # end of until loop
    echo "$lname, $fname <tab> $phnbr" >> $phonefile
done  # end of while loop
```

Note that the cancellation is not necessary for the first name, because it's at the start of the loop.

The shell command offers another loop command: break. The break command is similar in effect to continue. The only difference is that break terminates a loop, instead of skipping the rest of its commands. Like continue, break can only be used inside a loop.

At present, the current script, phadd.cancel, uses an exit command to quit the entry loop when the user enters stop. The problem with using exit is that the entire script has to be terminated to quit the loop. This will cause a problem if you need to do some more work after the data entry is finished. An obvious example is sorting the phone list after new names are entered.

To provide more flexibility in the script, you should use break, instead of exit, to terminate the loop. Thus, the fragment

```
echo "\nFirst Name (stop to exit): \c"
read fname
case $fname in
    [Ss][Tt][Oo][Pp]) exit ;;
esac
```

becomes

```
echo "\nFirst Name (stop to exit): \c"
read fname
case $fname in
    [Ss][Tt][Oo][Pp]) break ;;
esac
```

Hands-on Exercise 16.6

Rewrite the until loop that runs the correction section in phadd.cancel so that it is a continuous (infinite) loop that breaks when the user says the data is correct.

Both the break and continue commands have an interesting feature. By default, they work on the enclosing loop that contains them, restarting or terminating only the loop they are in. However, you often will write scripts that have loops inside of loops. phadd.cancel is a good example. The data-entry loop contains the data-correction loop.

The phadd.cancel script doesn't allow you to cancel an entry once the script enters the data-correction loop. To cancel an entry from inside the data-correction loop, you must break out of one loop and to restart another one. Note that breaking out of the data-correction loop won't work, because that would write the canceled entry to the file (the file-writing echo follows the data-correction loop).

You need to continue a loop beyond the current one, which can be done by adding an integer counter to the continue command. Thus, the command continue 2 says to restart the loop "two loops up from here." In phadd.cancel, executing continue 2 inside the data correction loop will restart the data entry loop. The same indexing can be done with the break command to exit several loops with one command. The phadd.cancel1 script demonstrates this new continue feature.

```
$ cat phadd.cancel1
phonefile=/usr/data/phone.list
while true
do
    echo "\nFirst Name (stop to exit): \c"
    read fname
    case $fname in
        [Ss][Tt][Oo][Pp]) exit ;;
    esac
    echo "Last Name: (XX to restart) \c"
    read lname
    case $lname in
        XX) continue ;;  # skip rest of loop
    esac
    echo "$fname $lname's phone extension: (XX to restart) \c"
    read phnbr
    case $phnbr in
        XX) continue ;; # skip rest of loop
    esac
    correct=n
    until [ $correct = y ]
    do
        echo "\n1. $fname"
        echo "2. $lname"
        echo "3. $phnbr"
        echo "\nIs this correct? (y/n) \c"
        read answer
```

```
        case $answer in
        [Yy]*) correct=y ;;  # loop exit condition
             *) echo "\nNumber to correct (0 to cancel entry): \c"
                read nbr
                case $nbr in
                    0) continue 2 ;;  # cancel entire entry
                    1) echo "First Name: \c"
                       read fname ;;
                    2) echo "Last Name: \c"
                       read lname ;;
                    3) echo "Phone Number: \c"
                       read phnbr ;;
                esac ;;
        esac
    done  # end of until loop
    echo "$lname, $fname <tab> $phnbr" >> $phonefile
done  # end of while loop
```

The *if* Statement

The main purpose for writing the `phadd` application is to give users an easy way to update the phone list, without having to worry about its format to use an editor. Most of the changes added to the original `phadd` script are designed to improve the script's data-entry correction capabilities. Although users can now correct an error or cancel an entry, there is one important problem not yet addressed by `phadd`: duplicating existing phone list entries.

Even if the name entered is correct, it is an error to put duplicated data into the phone list. What's worse is when the same number is incorrectly given to two different people or the same name is shown with different phone numbers. Although some people have several phone numbers and employees often share phones, entering data already in the phone list indicates a possible error condition that the user should be made aware of.

Checking for matching entries can be done with `grep`. The tough part is integrating such data checking into the `phadd.cancel` script. To determine whether the name or phone number being entered is already in the list, the script must run `grep` and then check its exit status. If `grep` succeeds, the data may be a duplicate. If `grep` fails, the name and phone numbers are not currently in the list.

You already know how to test the exit status of a command using the shell's logical operators. The problem with using logical operators to implement duplicate testing in phadd.cancel is complexity. The logical operators work best when a series of commands need to be executed conditionally. A good example is the grep and echo command line that prints a not found message in the phfind script developed earlier.

In phadd.cancel, if an entry is a duplicate, several commands will have to be executed. Adding code that performs a duplication test will get too complicated if you use logical operators. However, once again, the shell comes to your rescue with a command that does exactly what you need, the if command.

The if command implements conditional execution based on the exit status of a control command. The syntax of the minimal if command is

```
if    control-command
then
      commands to execute if control-command succeeds
fi
```

Note that an if command ends with the word fi, which is required. An execution error will result if you omit it.

A good example for using the if command is searching for duplicate names. The control command is grep, and if grep finds a match and succeeds, you want to tell the user that a duplicate has been found and prompt for how to continue. If the entry is a duplicate and the user wants to cancel it, you simply have to execute a continue to restart the data entry. Here is the code that does the duplicate testing.

```
if grep "$lname, $fname <tab>" $phonefile
then
    echo "\n$fname $lname is already in the list\n"
    echo "Cancel this entry? (y/n) \c"
    read answer
    case $answer in
        [Yy]*) continue ;;  # restart entry loop
    esac
fi
```

When grep finds a match, it produces output. Thus, this code prints all lines found by grep, tells the user these lines were found in the list,

and asks if the entry should be canceled. Adding this code to
`phadd.cancel` results in the `phadd.dup` script.

```
$ cat phadd.dup
phonefile=/usr/data/phone.list
while true
do
    echo "\nFirst Name (stop to exit): \c"
    read fname
    case $fname in
        [Ss][Tt][Oo][Pp]) break ;;
    esac
    echo "Last Name: (XX to restart) \c"
    read lname
    case $lname in
        XX) continue ;;  # skip rest of loop
    esac
    echo "$fname $lname's phone extension: (XX to restart) \c"
    read phnbr
    case $phnbr in
        XX) continue ;; # skip rest of loop
    esac
    if grep "$lname, $fname <tab>" $phonefile
    then
        echo "\nfound in the list"
        echo "\nCancel this entry? (y/n) \c"
        read answer
        case $answer in
            [Yy]*) continue ;;
        esac
    fi
    correct=n
    until [ $correct = y ]
    do
        echo "\n1. $fname"
        echo "2. $lname"
        echo "3. $phnbr"
        echo "\nIs this correct? (y/n) \c"
        read answer
        case $answer in
            [Yy]*) correct=y ;;  # loop exit condition
               *) echo "\nNumber to correct: \c"
                  read nbr
```

```
            case $nbr in
                1) echo "First Name: \c"
                    read fname ;;
                2) echo "Last Name: \c"
                    read lname ;;
                3) echo "Phone Number: \c"
                    read phnbr ;;
            esac ;;
        esac
    done  # end of until loop
    echo "$lname, $fname <tab> $phnbr" >> $phonefile
done  # end of while loop
```

Let's execute `phadd.dup` and try to add Terry Smith to demonstrate how the duplicate testing section works.

$ **phadd.dup**

```
First Name (stop to exit): Terry
Last Name (XX to restart): Smith
Terry Smith's phone extension (XX to restart): 7-7989
Smith, Terry  7-7989

Terry Smith is already in the list

Cancel this entry? (y/n) y
First name (stop to exit) stop
```

Although duplicate testing works for this simple case, there are two shortcomings. First, the duplicate checking section looks only for a "yes" response to the "Cancel this entry?" question. Second, the script looks only for matching names in the phone list.

It is a poor programming style to *assume* that people will respond in only the obvious ways. Thus, you shouldn't check for "yes" without also explicitly checking for both "no" and "neither." If neither "yes" nor "no" is entered, the script should continue to prompt until one of them is.

Although this additional check requires a few more commands, it is not difficult to do. The approach is to create a continuous loop that terminates only if the user enters "yes" or "no."

```
while true
do
    echo "\nCancel this entry? (y/n) \c"
    read answer
    case "$answer" in
        [Yy]*) cancel this entry ;;
        [Nn]*) resume data entry ;;
            *) echo "\nEnter Y or N only\n" ;;
    esac
done
```

Because you've added another loop, the `continue` command no
longer restarts data entry. Instead, you must use `continue 2` to get
back to the beginning of the data-entry loop. If the user enters "no,"
which means not to cancel the current entry, simply `break` out of this
loop and resume by prompting for the phone number.

```
while true
do
    echo "\nCancel this entry? (y/n) \c"
    read answer
    case "$answer" in
        [Yy]*) continue 2 ;;
        [Nn]*) break ;;
            *) echo "\nEnter Y or N only\n" ;;
    esac
done
```

The second problem is that the duplicate testing section in
`phadd.dup` checks only for phone list entries that match the name.
Since the phone number could also be a duplicate, `phadd.dup`
should check for that, too.

Recall that the `egrep` command can look for multiple patterns in
a file. To check for duplicate entries, use `egrep` to search for both
matching names and phone numbers at the same time. The search
command need use only `egrep` and the appropriate pattern.

```
if egrep "$lname, $fname <tab>¦<tab> $phnbr" $phonefile
then
    entry cancellation commands
fi
```

There are no spaces around the ¦ in egrep's pattern.

Using some of the more advanced programming features of the shell, we were able to expand a simple data-entry script into a fully featured application that lets the user correct data-entry errors and completely cancel incorrect entries and to check whether any entry duplicates existing data. When all these features are combined, the end result is the phone.add script.

```
$ cat phone.add
phonefile=/usr/data/phone.list
while true
do
    echo "\nFirst Name (stop to exit): \c"
    read fname
    case $fname in
        [Ss][Tt][Oo][Pp]) break ;;
    esac
    echo "Last Name: (XX to restart) \c"
    read lname
    case $lname in
        XX) continue ;;  # skip rest of loop
    esac
    echo "$fname $lname's phone extension: (XX to restart) \c"
    read phnbr
    case $phnbr in
        XX) continue ;; # skip rest of loop
    esac
    if egrep "$lname, $fname <tab>¦<tab> $phnbr" $phonefile
    then
        echo "\nDuplicates were found in the list"
        while true
        do
            echo "\nCancel this entry? (y/n) \c"
            read answer
            case "$answer" in
                [Yy]*) continue 2 ;;
                [Nn]*) break ;;
                *) echo "\nEnter Y or N only\n" ;;
            esac
        done
    fi
    correct=n
    until [ $correct = y ]
```

```
      do
          echo "\n1. $fname"
          echo "2. $lname"
          echo "3. $phnbr"
          echo "\nIs this correct? (y/n) \c"
          read answer
          case $answer in
              [Yy]*) correct=y ;;   # loop exit condition
              *) echo "\nNumber to correct: \c"
                 read nbr
                 case $nbr in
                     1) echo "First Name: \c"
                        read fname ;;
                     2) echo "Last Name: \c"
                        read lname ;;
                     3) echo "Phone Number: \c"
                        read phnbr ;;
                 esac ;;
          esac
     done  # end of until loop
     echo "$lname, $fname <tab> $phnbr" >> $phonefile
done  # end of while loop
```

Hands-on Exercise 16.7

Currently the data correction section of `phone.add` checks only for a "yes" response. Modify it to check for "yes," "no," or "neither."

The *else* and *elif* Commands

The `if` command contains two optional sections that provide a good deal of programming flexibility. The commands that appear after the `then` keyword are executed if the control command succeeds. By placing commands after the `else` keyword, you can also execute a set of commands if the control command fails.

```
if  control-command
then
    commands to execute if control-command succeeds
```

```
else
     commands to execute if control-command fails
fi
```

Note that then is not required after else and only one fi is required at the end of the entire command, whether or not an else is used.

To demonstrate the use of else, let's replace the case statement in the data correction section with an equivalent if test. After the entered data is printed, the script asks, "Is this correct? (y/n)". If the user enters a string starting with "y", the variable correct is set to "y". If the user enters something else, the script asks how to correct the entered data. In an if command, the "y"-action is performed in the then section and data correction occurs in the else section.

```
if expr "$answer" : "[Yy]*" > /dev/null
then
     correct=y ;;   # loop exit condition
else
     echo "\nNumber to correct: \c"
     read nbr
     case $nbr in
         1) echo "First Name: \c"
            read fname ;;
         2) echo "Last Name: \c"
            read lname ;;
         3) echo "Phone Number: \c"
            read phnbr ;;
     esac
fi
```

Another feature of the if command is its ability to test additional commands if the first control command fails. In other programming languages, this part of an if is called *else if*. Because spaces are command-line delimiters, the shell implements *else if* as elif. The syntax of the full if command is

```
if control-command1
then
     commands to execute if control-command1 succeeds
elif control-command2
then
     commands to execute if control-command1 fails
     and control-command2 succeeds
```

```
else
    commands to execute if both control-command1 and
    control-command2 fail
fi
```

Note that a `then` is required after an `elif`.

The `elif` enables you to handle several sequential tests, such as determining which entry is to be corrected. At present, this test is done with a `case` statement. It also provides a good example for demonstrating `elif`.

If the user has made a data entry error and wants to correct it, the script shows the three entered fields and asks which one to correct. The user's response needs to be tested for being a 1, 2, 3, or something else.

```
echo "\nNumber to correct: \c"
read nbr
if [ "$nbr" = 1 ]
then
    echo "First Name: \c"
    read fname
elif [ "$nbr" = 2 ]
then
    echo "Last Name: \c"
    read lname
elif [ "$nbr" = 3 ]
then
    echo "Phone Number: \c"
    read phnbr
else
    echo "Invalid entry"
fi
```

In this example, two `elif`'s are used. Although there can be only one `if` and one `else`, there is no limit to the number of `elif`s an `if` command can have.

In demonstrating both the `else` and `elif` features of the `if` command, we converted `case`s into `if`s. Since both perform conditional execution, there will be many times when you can use either an `if` or a `case` command. You will do fine if you stick to the rule that `case` is used when the conditional test can be handled by pattern matching and `if` is used when the condition depends on an exit status.

Hands-on Exercise 16.8

`phone.add` checks for duplicate names and phone numbers in the same command. This approach forces users to enter an entire entry before they discover that they have entered a duplicate name. Modify `phone.add` to test for a duplicate name after the first and last names are entered and to test for duplicate phone numbers after the phone number is entered. This way, users don't waste time entering a phone number for duplicated names.

Hands-on Exercise 16.9

To be complete, the script should also check for duplicates after one of the fields is corrected. Modify `phone.add`, or the solution to exercise 16.8, to check for duplicates when a field is changed.

Hands-on Exercise 16.10

The user may want to take a look at the current phone list before entering a name. Modify `phone.add` to print the entire phone list if the user enters ? in response to either the first name, last name, or phone number prompts.

Redirecting Shell Programming Commands

All of the shell programming commands—the `for`, `while`, and `until` loops and the `if` and `case` commands—can be redirected. When one of these programming commands is redirected, the redirection becomes effective for every command executed inside the loop, `if` command, or `case` command. A programming command is redirected after the ending keyword, be it `done`, `fi`, or `esac`. The following example shows how to redirect the output of a `while` loop. You can redirect the `for` and `until` loops the same way.

```
while control-command
do
     redirected commands to execute
done > output file
```

The following example is an input-redirected `case` statement.

```
case $answer in
    pattern1) redirected commands
    pattern2) redirected commands
esac < input file
```

The following example shows redirecting the standard error of an `if` command.

```
if control-command
then
    redirected commands to execute
fi 2 < error file
```

In the same way that these programming commands can be redirected, they also can be connected to a pipeline. For example, consider the `phsearch` command that reads a pattern from the redirected standard input, searches for it in the phone list, and keeps looping until there is no more input. `phsearch`'s first argument is a file that contains the search patterns.

```
$ cat phsearch
phonefile=/usr/data/phone.list
while read pattern
do
    grep "$pattern" $phonefile ¦¦
    echo "$pattern not found" >&2
done < $1
```

It is fairly common to use a `read` command to control a `while` loop. Recall that `read` fails when it reaches the end of the file. Thus, `phsearch` continues to get and search for patterns until the standard input reaches the end of the stream. Note that the `not found` message is sent to the script's standard error with >$2.

```
$ cat pattern.file
7--7989
6-
4-
$ phsearch pattern.file
Smith, Terry    7-7989
6- not found
```

```
StClair, Pat     4-6122
Benson, Sam      4-5587
```

The output of `phsearch` is a set of matched names and phone numbers (the error messages are going to the standard error). Instead of seeing the actual entries matched, you might want to know how many were found (this would provide you with a list of unused phone numbers). To count the number of matches, you can pipe the output of the `while` loop into a `wc -l` command, which counts lines from its standard input.

```
$ cat phsearch.count
phonefile=/usr/data/phone.list
while read pattern
do
      grep "$pattern" $phonefile ||
      echo "$pattern not found" >&2
done < $1 | wc -l
$ phsearch.count pattern.file
```

```
6- not found                  Error message
3                             wc's output
```

Redirected shell programming commands (loops, `if`, and `case`) are not executed directly by the shell (as the unredirected ones are). Instead, to implement the redirection, the shell creates a child process, sets up the redirection, and then executes the programming command—in this example, the entire `while` loop in that child process. This works well unless you change the value of a shell variable *inside* the redirected loop. Changes to shell variables are *local* to the shell where the change takes place.* Thus, a variable has the same value at the start of a redirected shell programming command as it does at the end of it, regardless of what happens inside the loop, `if`, or `case`.

The `phsearch.cnt1` script counts the number of patterns from the input file that actually are found in the phone list.

```
$ phsearch.cnt1
phonefile=/usr/data/phone.list
count=0
```

---

*How processes are executed and how data is stored are discussed in Chapter 17.

```
      while read pattern
  do
    if grep "$pattern" $phonefile
      then
         count=`expr $count + 1`
      else
         echo "$pattern not found" >&2
      fi
  done < $1 ¦ wc -l
  echo "\nMatched $count patterns"
  $ phsearch.cut1 pattern.file
  6- not found
  3              .
Matched 0 patterns
```

The number of matched patterns displayed is incorrect because the increment occurred inside a redirected `while` loop.

One-Line Programming

Up to now, the keywords in a shell programming command have been put on separate lines. However, you can put some or all of them on the same line by putting a semicolon between them. Thus, instead of

```
if command
then
    commands
fi
```

you can write

```
if command; then
    commands
fi
```

In fact, this is a convenient shorthand that you will see often. The same abbreviation can be done with `for`, `while`, and `until` loops and the `case` command.

Summary

You've now seen all of the shell's programming commands. These programming commands allow you to anticipate and solve potential problems a user may encounter when using a script. As this chapter demonstrated, shell scripts can get quite complicated when all facets of an application are accounted for.

The Process Environment

How Shell Variables Work

Up to now, I've discussed in vague terms about how commands get executed:

- Every commmand you enter is executed by a separate process.
- A child process is created by a parent process to execute a specific command.
- A child process returns an exit status to its parent process.

Processes are more than an executing program. As defined in Chapter 1, a process is an environment within which a program gets executed. What makes up a process? Where does this environment come from? How is it changed?

To be an effective shell script writer, you need to know how to use a process' environment. The focus of this chapter is UNIX processes: how they are created, their environment, and ways to take advantage of how they work.

Are variables assigned in one process available to another? A simple test will give us the answer. The `print.var` script does nothing more than print the value of the `phonefile` variable.

```
$ cat print.var
echo "The value of phonefile is $phonefile"
```

Now we'll assign `phonefile`, a value in the interactive shell, execute `print.var`, and see whether it gets to `print.var`.

```
$ phonefile=/usr/data/phone.list
$ print.var
$ The value of phonefile is
$ echo $phonefile
/usr/data/phone.list
```

As you can see, `phonefile` has a value in the current shell, but the value of `phonefile` isn't available to `print.var`. Why not? The answer lies in how UNIX executes commands and how processes work.

Command Execution

On the UNIX System, the shell executes a command in two stages. First it creates a process to run the command. Processes are created by making a copy of the current process. Thus, all commands executed by the shell start off as a copy of the current shell's process. Creating a new process by copying the current one is called `forking` a process. The original shell is called the parent process and the newly created process is called the child.

Once a new process exists, it has to be converted into a process executing the desired command. This conversion occurs when the new process tells UNIX to run the new command. This command exchange is called exec*ing a command.*

The key point is that a process is more than just a command, it is an environment within which a program executes. Thus, `forking` a process creates an environment while `execing` a command overwrites only the execution code. This means that a new command contains the environment of the process that created it. So why didn't the `phonefile` variable make it from the shell to the process running `print.var`?

Passing Information from Parent to Child

As it turns out, not everything in the environment is copied when a new process is `forked`. A process's environment consists of two parts, local and exported. The shell copies only the exported part of the environment during a `fork`. The `forking` (creating) process's local environment isn't copied. What gets copied by a `fork` is shown graphically in figure 17.1.

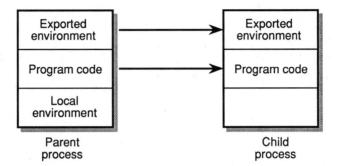

Parent process   Child process

Fig. 17.1.   *What* fork *copies.*

The reason `phonefile` has no value in `print.var` is that all shell variables are stored in the local environment. Because `phonefile` is in the local part of the environment, when a new process is `forked` to run `print.var`, the shell doesn't copy the current value of `phonefile`. Inside `print.var`, the `phonefile` is unassigned, so $phonefile evaluates to an empty string, which is what `print.var` prints.

Local Environment Is Private

Because a shell script is run by the newly created process (often referred to as a subshell), any changes made to shell variables are reflected only in the new process's local environment. Thus, if you modify `print.var` to assign a value to `phonefile` before printing it, you would expect `print.var` to notice it but for the value of `phonefile` to be unchanged in the parent process.

```
$ phonefile=/usr/data/phone.list
$ cat print.var1
phonefile=bus.list
echo "The value of phonefile is $phonefile"
$ print.var1
The value of phonefile is bus.list
$ echo $phonefile
/usr/data/phone.list
```

The assignment to `phonefile` inside `print.var1` affects only that shell script's local environment; it has no effect anywhere else.

This behavior is the reason that the shell does not see variables changed inside a redirected loop, or `if` or `case` command. To handle the redirected programming command, the shell `forks` a process, redirects the appropriate stream, and then executes the commands inside the loop, `if` or `case` command. Again, any changes made to variables are local to that child process, and the parent does not see them.

Contents of an Exported Environment

If shell variables aren't part of the exported environment, then what is? A process's exported environment comes in two sections. The first segment holds the user and group owner of this process, the current standard streams, the terminal it is connected to, any other open files, a unique ID number, the root and current directory, and other system information. The second section is nothing more than a list of shell variables that are sent to a new process when a `fork` occurs.

This is the tricky part. Even though variables are stored in the local environment, some of them are exported to new processes during a `fork`. Not surprisingly, variables that are exported to a new process are called *exported variables*. To see which variables are exported by the current process, run the `export` command.

```
$ export
export EDITOR
export SHELL
export TERM
export TZ
```

More will be said about the function of these and other exported variables later in this chapter.

Although the values of exported variables are stored in the processes' local environment, when this process `forks`, the shell copies these variables' values along with the rest of the exported environment to the child process. This is easily demonstrated with a simple shell script.

```
$ cat print.exp
echo "The value of EDITOR is $EDITOR"
$ export
export EDITOR
export SHELL
export TERM
export TZ
$ echo $EDITOR
/usr/ucb/vi
$ print.exp
The value of EDITOR is /usr/ucb/vi
```

The value of the variable EDITOR is available directly to print.exp without a local assignment.

How are variables made part of the exported environment? You simply export them with the export command. To export a variable, enter the command export variable into the shell. Here's an example of how exporting a variable changes the environment.

```
$ export
export EDITOR
export SHELL
export TERM
export TZ
$ realname="Ray Swartz"
$ export realname
$ export
export EDITOR
export SHELL
export TERM
export TZ
export realname
```

Note that the shell exports the name of the variable (realname), not its value ($realname).

Now that realname is part of the exported environment, it is available to all processes created by this shell. This, too, is easily demonstrated.

```
$ cat prname
echo "realname is $realname"
$ prname
realname is Ray Swartz
```

Exported variables are not required to have only uppercase characters in their names. However, using uppercase characters makes the distinction between exported and local varables much more obvious. It is a shell programming convention that we follow throughout the rest of this book.

A distinction must be made between the output of the `export` command and what variables are actually exported into a new process. `export` shows you only the variables marked for export by this process; that is, it shows only variables for which the command `export` *variable* was executed in the current process.

The `env` command shows you all the variables passed by the current process to the next one, not just those exported by the current process. The environment contains all the variables ever exported to this process.

```
$ export
export EDITOR
export SHELL
export TERM
export TZ
$ env
EDITOR=/usr/ucb/vi
HOME=/home/ray
LOGNAME=ray
PATH=/bin:/usr/ucb:/usr/bin:.
SHELL=/bin/sh
TERM=ansi
TZ=PST8PDT
```

The difference in the output of `export` and `env` shows that the variables `PATH`, `HOME`, and `LOGNAME` are part of the environment but were not exported by this process. They were put into the environment by a process that is an earlier ancestor. Also, note that `export` reports the exported variable names, but `env` shows both their names and values.

After a variable is exported, it is exported from every process derived from the current one. This means that every command executed by the current shell will be sent the value of the exported `realname`. For example, consider `run.prname`, which prints the value of `realname` and then runs `prname`.

```
$ cat run.prname
echo "In run.prname, realname is $realname"
prname
$ run.prname
In run.prname, realname is Ray Swartz
realname is Ray Swartz
```

realname was not only exported by the shell to run.prname, but also by run.prname to prname.

Modifying an Exported Variable

What happens if a child process changes the value of an exported variable? After a child process is forked, it runs independently of its parent. Therefore, any changes made to an exported variable are made in the exporting process's local environment. As a result, any changes made to an exported variable are local to that process only. Altering run.prname shows an example.

```
$ cat run.prname.chg
realname="Enzo Bernardi"
echo "In run.prname.chg, realname is $realname"
prname
$ run.prname.chg
In run.prname.chg, realname is Enzo Bernardi
realname is Ray Swartz
```

The value of realname changed inside run.prname.chg only. In prname, realname reverted to its exported value. Figure 17.2 shows how run.prname.chg works.

The value of an exported variable is the value assigned to the variable by the last process that exported it. This means that the changes made in run.prname.chg can be exported to prname by having run.prname.chg export realname.

```
$ cat run.prname.exp
realname="Enzo Bernardi"
export realname
echo "In run.prname.chg, realname is $realname"
prname
```

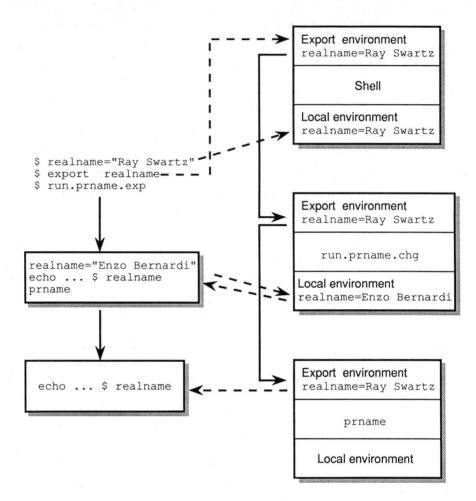

Fig. 17.2. *A local change to an exported variable.*

```
$ run.prname.exp
In run.prname.exp, realname is Enzo Bernardi
realname is Enzo Bernardi
$ echo $realname
Ray Swartz
```

There is nothing a child process can do to change the environment of its parent. Changing directories or redirecting standard streams will affect the current process's environment, as well as any process forked from it, but the parent won't notice these changes.

Because the run.prname.exp is run by a child of the current process, there is nothing run.prname.exp can do to affect the environment of the current process. A process's environment can only be changed by a parent process. This is why the environment of `prname` is affected by the export in `run.prname.exp`. Figure 17.3 shows how `run.prname.exp` changes an exported variable.

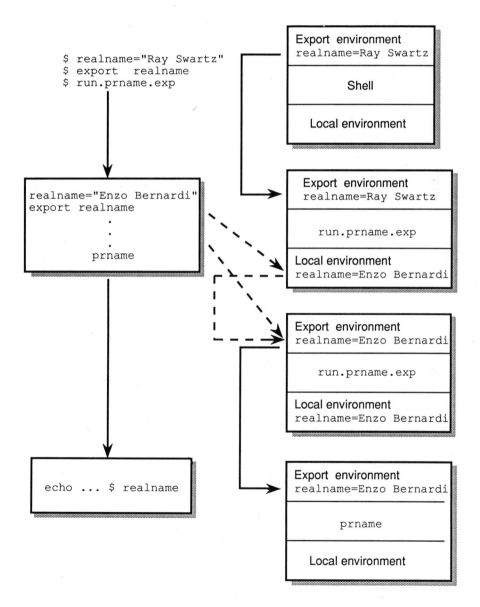

Fig. 17.3.   *Changing an exported variable.*

A process can designate a variable to be `readonly`. The shell will not allow `readonly` variables to be changed. Unfortunately, `readonly` limitations apply only to the current process, even on exported variables. Thus, an exported `readonly` variable cannot be changed by the current shell before it is exported. However, once a new process is `forked`, the `readonly` limitation goes away.

Review of Shell Variables

Since it is important to know how shell variables work, let's review this material.

1. Commands are executed in two steps. First, a process is created (`forked`), and then its command segment is replaced with the desired command (`exec`ed).

2. When a new command is executed, it inherits the environment of the process that spawned it.

3. Shell variables are stored in the local part of a process's environment and are not passed to a new process unless that variable has been explicitly exported either in the current process or in one of its parents.

4. The environment that is passed from one process to another consists of some system information related to the process and a set of variables marked for export.

5. Once a variable is exported, its (current) value is sent to every child process. This includes grandchild processes, which are processes created by a child process.

6. Changes made to inherited exported variables are not seen in child processes unless the variable is re-marked for export by the current process.

7. There is no way that a child process can change the environment of its parent.

8. A variable can be made `readonly` so that it cannot be changed. However, the `readonly` limitation holds only in the current process. A child process can modify a `readonly` exported variable.

There is only one exception to these rules. If one or more variables are assigned a value on the command line before the command name, those variables are created in the child process's local environment `fork`ed to run the command. For example, recall the `prname` script:

```
$ cat prname
echo "realname is $realname"
```

To assign `realname` a value within `prname`, you can assign it one on `prname`'s command line:

```
$ realname="Enzo Bernardi" prname
realname is Enzo Bernardi
```

Commands Built into the Shell

If a process executes every command on the UNIX System and a child process cannot modify its parent's environment, how does `cd` work to change the listed directory? If a separate process executes `cd`, it will change the directory of that new process and have no effect on the current shell. Since `cd` does change the directory of the current process, `cd` must be executed by the current process, but not a child process.

For `cd` to work, it has to be built into the shell, so that a new process isn't required to execute it. Such commands are called *built-in* shell commands. Other commands directly interact with the current process's environment, and they too must be executed without `fork`ing a new process. Variable assignment is one such command. The `export` command is another.

Table 17.1 lists commands we've covered so far that are built into the Bourne shell. Note that some commands are built into the shell to make them run more quickly. The `echo` and `test` commands are examples.

To *fork* or Not to *fork*

The shell provides three metacharacters that affect how a command is executed. We've already covered one of them, the parentheses, which group commands. Because parentheses group commands by execut-

Table 17.1.   *Commands built into the Bourne shell.*

Command	Meaning
:	Null command
cd	Change directory
echo	Send arguments to standard output
export	Mark a variable for export
pwd	Print the path name of the current directory
read	Read input from the standard input
readonly	Make variable read-only
test	Evaluate arguments as a logical test

ing them all in a subshell (child process), anything done inside parentheses has no effect on the parent shell.

For example, if you want to change temporarily to another directory and execute a command without affecting the current environment, you can use parentheses.

```
$ pwd
/usr/ray/Unix.book
$ ( cd /usr/data; cat phone.list )
Adams, Fran     2-3876
Smith, Terry    7-7989
StClair, Pat    4-6122
Brown, Robin    1-3745
Stair, Chris    5-5972
Benson, Sam     4-5587
$ pwd
/usr/ray/Unix.book      Directory unchanged
```

Because the command (cd /usr/data; cat phone.list) is enclosed in parentheses, the shell forks a new process to execute it. It is this child process whose current directory is changed. Note that the original shell's directory remains the same after the cd command within parentheses.

Two other shell execution metacharacters tell the shell not to fork a new process and, instead, tells the shell to run the listed commands as part of the current shell. One of these is a grouping command, the other executes the contents of a command file. The grouping command is braces ({ }). The main difference between parentheses and braces is that commands enclosed in braces are executed by the current process. Thus, changes made to brace-enclosed commands are reflected in the current process's environment.

To contrast braces and parentheses, note the effect of executing `cd /usr/data; cat phone.list` inside braces.

```
$ pwd
/usr/ray/Unix.book
$ { cd /usr/data; cat phone.list; }
Adams, Fran      2-3876
Smith, Terry     7-7989
StClair, Pat     4-6122
Brown, Robin     1-3745
Stair, Chris     5-5972
Benson, Sam      4-5587
$ pwd
/usr/data       Directory changed
```

Note the ending semicolon inside the braces. If the commands inside braces are all on one line, then a semicolon must appear after the last command.

Parentheses and braces are grouping commands. You can execute the commands stored in a file in the current process using the dot command. The dot command is represented by a period and tells the shell to run the commands in a file, as part of the current process.

For an example of how the dot command works, consider the `setvars` script, which contains a set of variables that you want to assign before you run a certain command.

```
$ cat setvars
phonefile=/usr/data/phone.list
realname="Ray Swartz"
printer=/dev/prt1
```

If `setvars` is executed as a shell script, the variables will be set in a new child process and will not be in the current shell. However, if `setvars` is executed by the dot command, the variables are set in the current shell.

```
$ echo $phonefile $realname $printer
                         Variables currently unset
```

```
$ . setvars
$ echo $phonefile $realname $printer
/usr/data/phone.list Ray Swartz /dev/prt1
```

Because the dot command causes commands to be executed by the current process, it must be built into the shell, which it is.

Important Environment Variables

The *HOME, MAIL, TERM,* and *LOGNAME* Variables

Not surprisingly, the shell uses several environment variables to hold important information. One key piece of information is the path name of your home directory. The path to your home directory is needed to ensure that the shell knows where to go if cd is invoked without an argument. When you log in, your home directory's path name is put in the exported variable HOME.

```
$ pwd
/usr/ray/Unix.book
$ cd                     Return to HOME directory
$ pwd
/usr/ray
$ echo $HOME
/usr/ray
```

Incidentally, HOME is assigned by the shell when you log in.

The MAIL variable works like HOME except that MAIL holds the name of the file where your electronic mail messages are sent. The shell periodically* checks the MAIL file to see whether any new mail has arrived. If it has, the shell notifies you with the message you have mail.

Several UNIX commands need to know what kind of terminal you are using. This information is stored in the TERM variable and then exported into the environment. The shell does not actually maintain TERM. Usually it is exported when a user logs in (exporting variables when you log in is discussed in detail later in this chapter).

---

*The shell checks for the arrival of new mail every 600 seconds unless a different value is stored in MAILCHECK. If MAILCHECK is set to 0, the shell checks for mail before issuing each prompt.

The SHELL variable holds the path name of the log-in shell. If you are using the Bourne shell, it is /bin/sh.

The LOGNAME variable holds your log-in name.

The *PATH* Variable

How does the shell know where to find the executable files for the commands that you enter? For example, the cat command is stored in the /bin directory, so why don't you have to enter /bin/cat to execute it? The reason lies with the exported variable PATH. PATH holds a list of colon-separated directories that the shell searches for any commands you enter. If it can't locate a command in one of those directories, it prints the error message *command*: not found. This is why the directories identified by PATH are called the *search path*.

As you can see, one of the directories (the first one in this case) stored in PATH is /bin:

```
$ echo $paTH
PATH=/bin:/usr/ucb:/usr/bin:
```

Thus, when you enter cat, the shell starts looking for the cat command file in /bin, finds it, and executes it. Note that the search path ends with a colon. This isn't a mistake. It is a shorthand way of saying, "if you haven't found it yet, check the current directory." The same thing works at the beginning of the search path.* You also can use an explicit period (.), if you like.

As with TERM, the shell does not maintain PATH. Instead, when you log in, it is assigned and exported in your log-in shell. An improper PATH variable can easily cause confusion because common commands can no longer be executed (found).

The *CDPATH* Variable

There are two ways to change to another directory: You can start at the top of the directory tree and use an absolute path name, or you can start at the current directory and use a relative path name.

---

*It is best not to place your current directory at the front of your search path. This can cause security problems since name conflicts between files in the current directory and UNIX commands can result in the wrong (insecure) program being executed.

However, if you are taking full advantage of the organizational capabilities of the UNIX file system hierarchy, you might have a large number of directories. For instance, I have more than a hundred subdirectories in my home directory tree. This leads to long cd commands whether you use relative or absolute path names. As an example, moving from the directory holding this chapter to where the course materials for my three-day System V shell programming course are stored requires a long path name.

```
$ pwd
/usr/ray/Unix.book/Chapter.17
$ cd ../../Classes/3dayshell.prog
$ pwd
/usr/ray/Classes/3dayshell.prog
```

To help make moving around in the file system easier, the shell provides another path variable, CDPATH. CDPATH works much like the PATH variable with the exception that CDPATH supplies a set of search directories for the cd command. Once the shell assigns CDPATH a set of colon-separated path names, the cd command will search them for a relative directory name.

```
$ echo $CDPATH
:/usr/ray:/usr/ray/Classes:/usr/ray/Unix.book
$ pwd
/usr/ray/Unix.book/Chapter.17
$ cd 3dayshell.prog
/usr/ray/Classes/3dayshell.prog
$ pwd
/usr/ray/Classes/3dayshell.prog
```

The cd 3dayshell.prog command tells cd to search the current directory (as with PATH, an empty first or last directory is seen as the current directory), then my home directory, then the Classes directory (where the directory I'm changing to is found), and finally the Unix.book directory. If the desired directory isn't found in one of them, the shell reports bad directory.

Note that cd printed the name of the new current directory after it moved to the shell. This happened because the new directory is not relative to the original directory. CDPATH isn't used if the argument passed to cd is an absolute path name.

The *TZ* Variable

Because UNIX is a portable operating system, it is liable to be used anywhere in the world. As a result, making sure your machine knows the correct time is a bit of a challenge. To help UNIX tell time, the TZ (Time Zone) variable is exported into the environment. TZ holds three pieces of data: the current time zone, the number of hours this time zone is before Universal Coordinated Time (the new name for Greenwich Mean Time), and the daylight savings time zone. Both time zones are abbreviated with the standard three character time zone names. Table 17.2 shows the relevant time zone names for the United States. If you are outside the U.S., check your system documentation for the appropriate TZ setting.

Table 17.2.   *Time zone names.*

Abbreviation	Zone
PST	Pacific Standard Time (8 hours before UCT)
PDT	Pacific Daylight Time
MST	Mountain Standard Time (7 hours before UCT)
MDT	Mountain Daylight Time
CST	Central Standard Time (6 hours before UCT)
CDT	Central Daylight Time
EST	Eastern Standard Time (5 hours before UCT)
EDT	Eastern Daylight Time

Typically (some places don't use daylight savings time), the ''ST'' names are paired up with the same zone's ''DT'' names. In California, where this book is being written, the TZ variable is assigned PST8PDT. This TZ value says that the time should be calculated according to Pacific Standard Time, which is eight hours before Universal Coordinated Time and which turns into Pacific Daylight Time in certain parts of the year.

PS1 and *PS2*

The Bourne shell's command prompts are stored as part of the shell's environment, which means you can change them if you want. PS1 holds the primary prompt, which is the dollar sign followed by a space. PS2 stores the secondary prompt, which is the greater-than symbol (>) followed by a space. To change them, simply assign them a value. They do not have to be exported because the shell directly manages `PS1` and `PS2`.

```
$ PS1="What can I do for you? "
What can I do for you? PS2="There's more to this? "
What can I do for you? echo "A two line command
There's more to this? to show the two prompts"
A two line command
to show the two prompts
```

Note that a space was left at the end of both new prompts. If you don't insert that space, there won't be one before your cursor and after the shell prompt.

```
What can I do for you? PS1="$"
$PS1="$ "                           No space after $
$ PS2="> "                          That's better
```

The variables listed here are summarized in table 17.3.

Table 17.3. *Commonly used Bourne shell environment variables.*

Variable	Meaning
CDPATH	Your cd search path
HOME	Your home directory
LOGNAME	Your log-in name
MAIL	The file that holds your electronic mail
PATH	Your command search path
PS1	The shell's primary prompt
PS2	The shell's secondary prompt
SHELL	The path name of your default shell
TERM	Your terminal type

Your shell environment may not use all of these variables and, most likely, will hold others not described here. Check your system documentation for what these other variables represent.

The *.profile* File

Where do these variables get set in the first place? Some of them are set by the shell: HOME, MAIL, PS1, PS2, SHELL, and LOGNAME. The others—PATH, CDPATH, TERM, and TZ—you must set and export yourself.

In addition to assigning a value to and exporting certain variables, you might want to do other things before your log-in shell begins accepting commands. You might want to assign and export other variables, run certain commands, or do other tasks.

To make it easy for you to do all your set-up work, the Bourne shell executes a special file for you when you log in, .profile. The commands in the .profile file in your home directory are executed by your log-in shell before it issues a command prompt. Put all of your initializing commands in .profile.

```
$ cat $HOME/.profile
EDITOR=/usr/ucb/vi
PATH=/bin:/usr/ucb:/usr/bin:
CDPATH=:/usr/ray:/usr/ray/Classes:/usr/ray/Unix.book
TERM=ansi
TZ=PST8PDT
export PATH EDITOR TERM TZ CDPATH
if mailx -e  # succeeds if there is mail
then
     mailx
fi
date
```

In my .profile, I set the listed variables, export them, check whether there is any new mail to read (mailx -e succeeds if there is mail to read; otherwise, it fails), and then print the current date and time.

The $$ Variable

One piece of information stored in each process's environment is a unique process ID number, often referred to as the *PID*. The PID has to be unique because UNIX uses it to identify a process. The PID is used by kill to terminate a process, and it is the value displayed by the shell when a command is run in the background. The $$ variable holds the PID of the current process.

```
$ echo $$
249        This process's PID
```

Because the PID is guaranteed to be unique, you can use it to generate unique names for temporary files. Because $$ is a number unique to this process, `tmp$$` creates a file name that only this process knows. Using the above PID, such a temporary file would be called `tmp249`. In general, PIDs are no larger than five-digit numbers.

Passing Information Through the Environment

Now that you understand what constitutes a process's environment and how parts of that environment are shared with other processes, let's develop an application that demonstrates its use. In previous chapters, we created two scripts, `phone.add` and `phone.find`, to help maintain a company's phone list. However, using either the `phone.add` or `phone.find` scripts or accessing the phone list file directly requires interaction with the UNIX System and the shell. For some people, even this much contact with UNIX is undesirable.

To make the phone list system easy for everyone to use, you need to provide a simple interface that hides UNIX and the shell completely. One easy interface to understand is a *menu*. A menu program gives the user a list of options from which to choose and then executes the appropriate set of commands to fulfill the option chosen.

Most people who use computers are familiar with menu interfaces. Further, menus are easy to implement as shell scripts. However, before we start, let's set some ground rules. A menu should

- Display all possible options
- Specifically prompt for needed information
- Provide help if the user makes an error
- Accept only "correct" information (i.e., accept only y or n if it is a yes/no question)
- Be consistent
- Provide a straightforward user interface

A menu shell script consists of these parts: displaying the menu, prompting for user input, getting the user's response, and processing the user's choice.

What options should this menu offer? Two obvious ones are searching the phone list and adding names to it. In this menu, we will offer two other functions, printing the entire list and sorting it by last name.

You can display the menu with a series of `echo` commands, by using `cat` with in-line redirection, or by printing the contents of a file. For this script, we will use `echo` commands. We will get the user's response with `read`.

```
echo "\n\n"
echo "A - Add a name to the Phone List"
echo "L - Look for information in Phone List"
echo "P - Print the Phone List"
echo "S - Sort the Phone List by Last Name"
echo "\nEnter choice and press <RETURN> \c"
read choice
```

Processing the user's entry is done with a single `case` command. You can implement the A, P, and S options by calling a single command for each one. Option A runs `phone.add`; option P uses `cat` (or `more` or `pg`); option S runs `sort`. The L option executes `phone.find`. However, `phone.find` requires a search pattern as an argument. Thus, handling an L entry involves prompting for and reading a search pattern, which is then passed to `phone.find`. Here are the commands that implement the user's selection:

```
case $choice in
    [Aa]) phone.add ;;
    [Pp]) cat $phonefile ;;
    [Ll]) echo "\nSearch pattern? \c"
          read pattern
          phone.find "$pattern" ;;
    [Ss]) sort $phonefile -o $phonefile ;;
    *) echo "Invalid Entry" ;;
esac
```

Note that the S option sorts the file in place, that is, the sorted output is put back into the `phone list`.

If you assembled these two parts, you would have a usable menu script. However, it would enable a user to make only a single entry. The menu should continue to prompt until the user chooses the quit option. You can accomplish the looping with a `while` command.

```
$ cat phmenu
phonefile=/usr/data/phone.list
looptest=y
while [ "$looptest" = y ]
do
    echo "\n\n"
    echo "A - Add a name to the Phone List"
    echo "L - Look for information in Phone List"
    echo "P - Print the Phone List"
    echo "S - Sort the Phone List by Last Name"
    echo "\nQ - Quit the menu"
    echo "\nEnter letter of choice and press <RETURN> \c"
    read choice ¦¦ continue
    case $choice in
        [Aa]) phone.add ;;
        [Pp]) cat $phonefile ;;
        [Ll]) echo "\nSearch pattern? \c"
              read pattern  ¦¦ continue
              phone.find "$pattern" ;;
        [Ss]) sort $phonefile -o $phonefile ;;
        [Qq]) looptest=n ;;
        *) echo "Invalid Entry" ;;
    esac
done
```

Recall that the read command fails if it tries to read past the end of the stream (a Control-D from a terminal). Because a failed read results in empty variables, if either of phmenu's read commands fails, the continue statement restarts the menu.

When executed, phmenu provides a simple, yet effective phone list interface.

```
$ phmenu
A - Add a name to the Phone List
L - Look for information in Phone List
P - Print the Phone List
S - Sort the Phone List by Last Name

Q - Quit the menu

Enter choice and press <RETURN> L
```

```
Search pattern? Smith
Smith, Terry    7-7989


A - Add a name to the Phone List
L - Look for information in Phone List
P - Print the Phone List
S - Sort the Phone List by Last Name


Q - Quit the menu

Enter choice and press <RETURN> P
Adams, Fran     2-3876
Smith, Terry    7-7989
StClair, Pat    4-6122
Brown, Robin    1-3745
Stair, Chris    5-5972
Benson, Sam     4-5587


A - Add a name to the Phone List
L - Look for information in Phone List
P - Print the Phone List
S - Sort the Phone List by Last Name


Q - Quit the menu

Enter choice and press <RETURN> Q
```

Hands-on Exercise 17.1

In phmenu, the only search option is to look for a *single* pattern. Add an M option that enables a user to repeatedly search for patterns in the phone list. The searching loop terminates when the user enters "stop" as the search pattern.

Hands-on Exercise 17.2

phmenu's P option prints the phone list on the standard output. Extend phmenu or the answer to exercise 17.1, to display a submenu when a user chooses the P option, which provides three output destinations: a file, the terminal (/dev/tty), or the printer (use lp). If the user chooses output to a file, be sure to test whether the file (whose name the user enters) currently exists before writing to it.

The `phmenu` application involves three shell scripts: `phmenu`, `phone.add`, and `phone.find`. All three of them use the `phonefile` variable to hold the path name of the phone list file. It clearly makes no sense to have all three use the same local variable to hold exactly the same data. A much better design is to use a single exported variable. This approach guarantees that all the phone list scripts use the same data file.

Before going into how `PHONEFILE` (it's been capitalized because it will be an environment variable) is exported, you need to modify `phone.add` and `phone.find` to access `PHONEFILE` from the environment. The required changes are slight. Both `phone.add` and `phone.find` assign the phone list's path name to a local variable, `phonefile`. The scripts can continue to use the local variable; you simply need to assign to the local `phonefile` the value of the exported `PHONEFILE`. Just to be tidy, you should use a default if `PHONEFILE` is unassigned.

```
phonefile=${PHONEFILE:-/usr/data/phone.list}
```

This new assignment uses the `:-` operator, which says to set `phonefile` to the value of `PHONEFILE`, unless `PHONEFILE` is empty, in which case `phonefile` is set to `/usr/data/phone.list`. Note that this new assignment doesn't change how the scripts work. It's the process's environment that determines which data file is used. To save space, the new versions of `phone.add` and `phone.find` aren't shown.

There are two ways to export `PHONEFILE`. First, you can export it from the shell, either directly at the command line or in your `.profile`. Second, you can `export` it from `phmenu`. Wherever the `export` occurs, these two statements are required to do it.

```
PHONEFILE=/usr/data/phone.list
export PHONEFILE
```

To document our script more clearly, let's export `PHONEFILE` in `phmenu`.

```
$ cat phmenu.exp
PHONEFILE=/usr/data/phone.list
export PHONEFILE
phonefile=$phONEFILE
looptest=y
while [ "$looptest" = y ]
```

```
do
    echo "\n\n"
    echo "A - Add a name to the Phone List"
    echo "L - Look for information in Phone List"
    echo "P - Print the Phone List"
    echo "S - Sort the Phone List by Last Name"
    echo "\nQ - Quit the menu"
    echo "\nEnter letter of choice and press <RETURN> \c"
    read choice ¦¦ continue
    case $choice in
        [Aa]) phone.add ;;
        [Pp]) cat $phonefile ;;
        [Ll]) echo "\nSearch pattern? \c"
              read pattern  ¦¦ continue
              phone.find "$pattern" ;;
        [Ss]) sort $phonefile -o $phonefile ;;
        [Qq]) looptest=n ;;
        *) echo "Invalid Entry" ;;
    esac
done
```

Hands-on Exercise 17.3

Extend `phmenu.exp` to give users a choice of working with either their own personal phone list (`/usr/data/$LOGNAME.list`) or the company's phone list (`/usr/data/phone.list`). The menu options remain the same.

Signals and the *trap* Command

As you probably know, when you interrupt a process, it terminates. On most UNIX Systems, an interrupt is generated by pressing the Delete, Break, or Control-C keys (only one works on a specific system). Although this makes sense from the user's perspective, how does an interrupt, entered on the keyboard, terminate a process? Recall that a process doesn't talk to the terminal. The process thinks it is working with a file. It's the UNIX kernel that knows how to handle individual devices.

The kernel, not the process, is notified when the user presses the interrupt key on the keyboard. UNIX then sends a signal to the process telling it that an interrupt has occurred. By default, the process terminates in response to this signal, though other actions are possible, as are discussed in this section.

Several different events can cause the kernel to send a process a signal. Because different events produce signals, each signal is numbered to identify the event that caused it. Table 17.4 shows the signals of interest to shell programmers.

Table 17.4. *Signal numbers.*

Number	Name	Generated by
0	exit	Shell exit
1	hangup	Losing terminal connection
2	interrupt	Pressing the interrupt key
3	quit	Pressing the quit key
9	kill	The `kill -9` command
15	terminator	The `kill` command

When a shell script exits, it sends itself a shell exit signal (0). Signal 1, called the hangup signal, is used to tell a process that the system has lost connection to its terminal. This signal is caused by turning your terminal off or by unplugging the cord that runs from the computer to the terminal or when the system loses your modem connection. The hangup signal is what causes you to be logged out on some UNIX Systems if you turn your terminal off. Signal 3, called the quit signal, is generated from the keyboard by pressing Control\ (backslash). This signal causes the process to "core dump" before it terminates. Signals 9 and 15 are sent by the `kill` command. 15 is the default signal sent by `kill`; 9 is a special signal that is sent only if the `-9` argument is passed to `kill`.

Using the *trap* Command

The default action taken by a process when it receives a signal is immediate termination. However, the shell provides a command, called `trap`, that enables you to handle signals in other ways. Instead of immediately terminating, a process can ignore a signal or perform a specified set of commands when it receives a certain signal. Both of these responses are set up by the `trap` command.

A `trap` command has two parts: what signals are being trapped and what to do if the trapped signal is received. The format of a `trap` command is

```
trap 'commands to execute' signals to catch
```

Note that the commands to execute are quoted. The commands to be executed are sent to `trap` as a single argument. Because the commands to execute are quoted, they can span several lines. Also, several signals can be trapped with a single `trap` command.

For example, the command

```
trap 'echo "Terminated by a signal";
        exit' 1 15
```

will execute the `echo` command and then terminate if a signal 1 (hangup) or 15 (terminate) is received.

If the commands-to-execute argument is an empty string, `trap` instructs the process to ignore signals 1 and 15.

```
trap '' 1 15
```

or

```
trap "" 1 15
```

Now, if the script receives a signal 1 or 15, the script continues to execute without interruption, ignoring the signal entirely.

A `trap` command sets a flag in the process environment that tells the kernel what to do if this process receives a signal. If the flag is set and the signal arrives, the process stops what it is doing and immediately executes the commands listed in the `trap`. When the `trap` commands are finished, the script continues where it left off. This is why an `exit` is added to the `echo` in this `trap` command.

```
trap 'echo "Terminated by a signal"; exit' 1 15
```

Without the `exit`, the process would print `Terminated by a signal` and then continue executing where it left off, which makes no sense.

A signal isn't trapped by a script until after the `trap` is executed by that script. As a rule, `trap` commands are the first ones listed in a shell script. A `trap` is active until the script terminates or another `trap` for that signal is executed. There is no limit to the number of `trap` commands a script can execute.

To reset a signal to the default handling after it has been trapped or ignored, list the signal numbers to reset and `trap` without a command argument. This command,

```
trap 1 15
```

resets signals 1 and 15 to terminate the script. Note the distinction between ignoring a set of signals

```
trap '' 1 15
```

and resetting them.

```
trap 1 15
```

When ignoring a signal, you send `trap` an empty first argument. When resetting a signal, you omit the first argument entirely.

Getting Signals from the Menu

The `phmenu.exp` script terminates if a user presses the interrupt key. Recall that the whole purpose of the phone menu was to make it easy for users to access the phone list without having to deal with UNIX or the shell. If `phmenu.exp` is interrupted, the user ends up in the shell, which defeats the purpose for which `phmenu.exp` was written in the first place.

It might seem unlikely that people who need to use `phmenu.exp` because they don't know anything about UNIX would know about the interrupt key. However, novice users are often told how to "get out" of a command by using the interrupt key. This saves them from having to ask someone every time they get stuck. It is for precisely this reason that `phmenu.exp` needs to be protected from an unexpected interrupt signal.

What should `phmenu.exp` do if it receives an interrupt signal? There are two choices. One is to simply ignore it (`trap '' 2`). Another is to tell the user to `Use the Q option to quit` and then continue the menu. The phone menu script, now called `phone.menu`, will use the second method, telling users to `Use the Q option to quit`.

```
$ cat phone.menu
trap 'echo "Use the Q option to quit" ' 1 2 3 15
PHONEFILE=/usr/data/phone.list
export PHONEFILE
phonefile=$PHONEFILE
looptest=y
while [ "$looptest" = y ]
do
    echo "\n\n"
    echo "A - Add a name to the Phone List"
    echo "L - Look for information in Phone List"
    echo "P - Print the Phone List"
    echo "S - Sort the Phone List by Last Name"
    echo "\nQ - Quit the menu"
    echo "\nEnter letter of choice and press <RETURN> \c"
    read choice ¦¦ continue
    case $choice in
        [Aa]) phone.add ;;
        [Pp]) cat $phonefile ;;
        [Ll]) echo "\nSearch pattern? \c"
              read pattern  ¦¦ continue
              phone.find "$pattern" ;;
        [Ss]) sort $phonefile -o $phonefile ;;
        [Qq]) looptest=n ;;
        *) echo "Invalid Entry" ;;
    esac
done
```

Note that all signals that a user can generate, except 9, are trapped. Signal 9 cannot be trapped by a process. This guarantees that there always is at least one way to kill a process.

When you send an interrupt to phone.menu, an unexpected result occurs.

```
$ phone.menu


A - Add a name to the Phone List
L - Look for information in Phone List
P - Print the Phone List
S - Sort the Phone List by Last Name
```

```
Q - Quit the menu

Enter letter of choice and press <RETURN> interrupt
Use the Q option to quit
Invalid entry



A - Add a name to the Phone List
L - Look for information in Phone List
P - Print the Phone List
S - Sort the Phone List by Last Name

Q - Quit the menu

Enter letter of choice and press <RETURN> Q
```

The menu did what it was supposed to if it received an interrupt, that is, print Use the Q option to quit. But, why did it then print Invalid entry? and continue the menu display? If after a trap it is supposed to start where it left off, why didn't it just keep waiting for the user to respond?

The answer has to do with how the UNIX kernel executes the read command. The kernel doesn't restart a read command after its execution is interrupted. The interrupt sent to phone.menu was done at a read command. Thus, the trap message is printed, and the read can't restart, leaving its variable empty. After the shell executes the echo in the trap, the script picks up after the read, and the case statement chooses the option that prints Invalid entry.

Although the read command can't be restarted, other built-in shell commands such as echo and test can be. For example, consider the ignore.intr script.

```
$ cat ignore.intr
trap 'echo Interrupt ignored' 2
while true
do
     echo 1
     echo 2
     echo 3
     echo 4
     echo 5
```

```
    echo 6
    echo 7
    echo 8
done
```

This script loops, continuously printing one to eight. Note that the script doesn't terminate.

```
$ ignore.intr
1
2
3
4
5
6
<Control-c>          Interrupt key pressed
Interrupt ignored
7
8
1
2
3
4
^\                   Untrapped quit signal terminates
```

Note that after the interrupt is entered and handled by `trap`, the loop continues at the next `echo` statement, printing 7 after the interrupt.

What happens if a script receives a signal while a child process is executing a command? First of all, signals generated from a terminal (hangup, interrupt, and quit) are sent to all processes connected to that terminal. This doesn't include background processes because they are "disconnected" from the terminal when they are put in the background. This is why, assuming default signal handling, an entire shell script, child processes and all, terminates when the user presses the interrupt key.

How a child process handles signals depends on how the parent process is trapping signals. If a parent ignores a signal, all child processes will also ignore it. If a parent process has set commands to be executed if a signal is received, then all child processes have default signal handling set and will terminate if a signal is generated while they are executing.

For example, if the user presses the interrupt key while
`phone.menu` is executing `phone.add`, `phone.add` terminates and
`phone.menu` prints `Use the Q option to quit`. This happens
because `phone.menu` has trapped the interrupt signal to run the echo
statement that prints this message. Remember that a child process
uses default signal handling if its parent sets a `trap` that executes
commands if a signal is caught. Thus, `phone.add` has default signal
handling.

The commands executed by `trap` when a specified signal is
received are actually interpreted twice by the shell: once when the
`trap` is set and a second time when the shell receives the signal and
runs the `trap`'s commands. The only time this double interpretation
is important is when your `trap` commands contain shell variables.

For example, suppose that one of the scripts run by `phone.menu`
creates a temporary file. This might be required by a deletion or
modification script, because `sed` doesn't have an overwrite option.
Now, if the script receives a signal, the script needs to clean up by
removing the no longer useful, temporary file before it exits. Consider
this `trap` command.

```
trap "rm $tempfile; exit" 1 2 3 15
```

Because the `trap` command argument is in double quotes, the shell
interprets `$tempfile` when the `trap` is set. If the `tempfile` variable
hasn't been set yet, the `trap`'s `rm` command will fail when one of the
signals arrives because `rm` will have no argument.

The proper `trap` command puts the `rm` inside single quotes.

```
trap 'rm $tempfile; exit' 1 2 3 15
```

Then, when the `trap` is set, the single quotes come off, but
`$tempfile` hasn't been interpreted yet. It isn't until the signal is
caught that the shell interprets `$tempfile`.

As a final note, regardless of when `$tempfile` is interpreted, it
still may be unassigned when it receives one of the signals. In this case,
`trap`'s `rm` command fails, sending a meaningless (from the user's
viewpoint) error message to the standard error. When cleaning up
temporary files, it is best to discard them:

```
trap 'rm $tempfile 2> /dev/null; exit' 1 2 3 15
```

Hands-on Exercise 17.4

Modify the `phone.add` script to make a copy of the current phone list before the data entry loop begins. Any new names should be added to this phone list copy. When the user terminates the loop, move the file copy over the actual data file. Now, if the script receives a signal 1, 2, 3, or 15, you can erase the temporary copy, leaving the phone list unchanged.

Summary

A process's environment contains a number of useful constructs that can help you in creating applications. Keep in mind that shell scripts tend to change over time. If your scripts rely on the environment to pass information and control interrupts, modifications will be easier to make in the future.

Additional Features

The purpose of this chapter is to describe a few more Bourne shell capabilities that haven't yet been covered in the previous chapters. Don't think that a feature isn't useful just because it appears in this chapter and not somewhere else. The sole determinant for chapter content was preserving what I feel is the logical presentation of the material.

It is important for you to become familiar with the commands described in this chapter. Your ability to create a shell script application will depend on how much you know about the UNIX System, UNIX tools, and the shell. What's more, it's often the tricks, represented by some of the commands in this chapter, that enable you to solve problems and avoid mistakes.

The *shift* Command

It makes sense that $10 identifies the tenth command-line argument. However, another way to interpret $10 is the first argument followed by a zero. How does the shell distinguish between the two? It doesn't. The shell treats $10 as the first argument followed by a zero. There is no shell metacharacter to retrieve the tenth argument. For example, show.arg prints the value of $10. When sent ten arguments, it prints the first one with a zero added to the end.

```
$ cat show.arg
echo $10
$ show.arg one 2 3 4 5 6 7 8 9 10
one0
```

Is there anything you can do if you need to handle more than nine command-line arguments? Although there is no way to identify the tenth argument directly, the shell does provide the `shift` command. The `shift` command discards the first argument and then moves the rest of them down one. After a `shift`, the second argument becomes the first, the third argument becomes the second, and so on. To identify the tenth argument, do a `shift` and `$9` now evaluates to the tenth argument. This is demonstrated by show.tenth.

```
$ cat show.tenth
shift
echo $9
$ show.tenth one 2 3 4 5 6 7 8 9 10
10
```

A common technique is to evaluate and store the first argument before the shift is done.

In addition to changing the positional paramenters, `shift` reduces the value stored in `$#` by 1. One method of handling arguments is to `shift` through them until `$#` equals 0.

```
while [ $# -gt 0 ]
do
    case $1 in
            process argument
    esac
    shift
done
```

This approach works well if your script accepts options. As soon as one argument doesn't match an option, you process the rest of the command line as data. Note that `$#` can be greater than 10, even though there is no direct way to get at arguments beyond the ninth one.

For example, `phone.find` assumes that all its arguments represent individual patterns. An obvious modification is to have it accept an option, `-1` in the following example, that says all the listed arguments make up a single pattern. `shift` can be used to implement a `-1` option for `phone.list`. As with most UNIX commands, the `-1` must be the first argument on the command line.

Once you've determined there is at least one command-line argument, the approach is to check whether the first argument is a `-1`. If it is, then `shift` to get rid of it and search for `$*`. If it is not, have the script process the argument list one at a time.

```
$ cat phone.find.all
phonefile=/usr/data/phone.list
case $# in
    0) echo "Usage: $0 pattern"
       echo "pattern is what to look for in the phone list" ;;
    *) case "$1" in
        -1) shift
            grep "$*" $phonefile ¦¦
            echo "$* not found in list" ;;
         *) for pattern in "$@"
            do
                grep "$pattern" $phonefile ¦¦
                echo "$pattern not found in list"
            done ;;
        esac;;
esac
$ phone.find Smith, Terry
Smith, Terry    7-7989
Smith, Terry    7-7989
$ phone.find.all -1 Smith, Terry
Smith, Terry    7-7989
```

Additional Shell Metacharacters

There are three metacharacters that haven't yet been discussed. One of them deals with redirection, and the other two store information about the shell.

Closing Standard Streams

One common use of `trap` commands is to remove temporary files if a script gets interrupted. One problem caused by using `rm` in a `trap` command is that `rm` will print an error message if it can't find the file to erase. This situation occurs if the script receives an interrupt before it can create the temporary file.

To prevent `rm` from delivering meaningless error messages to the terminal, `rm`'s standard error is usually redirected to `/dev/null`. While this approach works, there is another solution to the problem. Using shell metacharacters, you can close a process's standard streams. Sending output to or reading input from a closed stream is the same as reading or writing `/dev/null`. To close the standard input, use `<&-`. To close the standard output stream, use `>&-`. `2>&-` closes the standard error. Here is another way to eliminate `rm`'s error messages in a `trap` command:

```
trap 'rm $tempfile 2>&-' 1 2 3 15
```

Extending In-Line Input Redirection

In the `phone.menu` script, the menu was printed with a series of `echo` statements. As was mentioned at the time, the menu can also be displayed using in-line input redirection and the `cat` command.

```
phonefile=/usr/data/phone.list
looptest=y
while [ "$looptest" = y ]
do
    cat << MENU
    A - Add a name to the Phone List"
    L - Look for information in Phone List"
    P - Print the Phone List"
    S - Sort the Phone List by Last Name"
MENU
    echo "Enter choice and press <RETURN> \c"
    read choice
    rest of menu
```

The text printed by `cat` isn't indented like the rest of the commands in the `while` loop because the in-line input redirection would send the characters, including the indented spaces, to `cat`. As a result, the menu "looks funny."

```
$ phmenu.cat
```

```
        A - Add a name to the Phone List"
        L - Look for information in Phone List"
        P - Print the Phone List"
        S - Sort the Phone List by Last Name"
Enter choice and press <RETURN>
```

Because indenting commands is a common programming style, the shell provides an additional in-line input redirection directive that tells the shell to ignore tabs (but not spaces) preceding input text. The metacharacter is <<-, the regular in-line input redirection with a dash added to it. Using the <<- enables you to indent the input text without having the indenting tabs appear in the input stream.

```
phonefile=/usr/data/phone.list
looptest=y
while [ "$looptest" = y ]
do
    cat <<- MENU
     A - Add a name to the Phone List"
     L - Look for information in Phone List"
     P - Print the Phone List"
     S - Sort the Phone List by Last Name"

MENU
echo "Enter letter of choice and press <RETURN> \c"
read choice
rest of menu
```

One feature of in-line input redirection is that the shell will scan the input for shell metacharacters. If you don't want the shell to scan the input, use the <<\ redirection metacharacter, which is the regular in-line input redirection metacharacter with a backslash appended to it.

```
$ name=Ray
$ cat <<\ XX
> My name is $name
> Today's date is `date`
> XX
My name is $name
Today's date is `date`
```

The Background PID

When a process is executed in the background using the ampersand (&), the shell displays the PID of the background process. The shell also stores this PID in the $! variable.

```
$ sort big.list -o big.list &
4562
$ echo $!
4562
```

Note that $! holds the last process put into the background by this shell.

The *exec* Command

In Chapter 17, the UNIX process creation mechanism was described as consisting of two steps. First, a copy of the current process is forked. Then the new process overwrites the command portion of the process by execing a command.

Any process can exec a new command. However, once a command is execed from a process, the execing process begins running the execed command, because the previous command's code has been overwritten by the exec. Thus, when the new command terminates, so does the process.

When the shell executes a command, it forks and then the new process execs the command. You can exec commands directly from the current process, in essence substituting one command for another, using the exec command. Be careful when using exec. If you exec a command from your log-in shell, you will be logged out (your log-in shell process will terminate) when the execed command is finished.

```
$ exec date
Fri Dec 29 09:45:18 PST 1989

login:
```

When date was execed, the current process's command area (that was running the shell) was overwritten with date's executable code.

After `date` prints the current date and time, it terminates, ending your log-in session, which is why you see the `login` prompt after the date.

The `exec` command invokes programs more quickly because it doesn't involve the overhead of creating (forking) a new process to run the command. However, `exec` is of limited usefulness because there is no way to continue after an `exec`ed command terminates. To successfully use `exec` in a shell script requires that a string of processes `exec` one another, thereby executing a series of commands using a single process. In practice, this is usually too hard to do properly.

The `exec` command has a second capability, which enables you to change the current process's standard streams. When `exec` is sent a redirection without a command name, it performs the redirection on the current process. The command `exec < phone.list` modifies the current process so that it now takes input from the file `phone.list`. The same can be done for the standard output and error streams.

While the shell enables you to redirect its programming commands (the `for`, `while`, and `until` loops and the `if` and `case` commands), it `fork`s another process to do so. Because changes to variables are local to the process where the change occurs, the modifications made to a variable inside a redirected programming command are not seen outside the command.

This anomaly was demonstrated in Chapter 16 with the `phsearch.cnt1` script. The following version has been slightly modified by removing the pipeline to `wc -l` to make the example more useful.

```
$ cat phsearch.cnt1
phonefile=/usr/data/phone.list
count=0
while read pattern
do
    if grep "$pattern" $phonelist
    then
        count=`expr $count + 1`
    else
        echo "$pattern not found" >&2
    fi
done < $1
echo "\nMatched $count patterns"
$ cat pattern.file
7-7989
```

```
6-
4-
$ phsearch.exec pattern.file
Smith, Terry     7-7989
6- not found
StClair, Pat     4-6122
Benson, Sam      4-5587

Matched 0 patterns
```

The problem with `phsearch.cnt1` is that the value stored in `count` isn't available outside the `while` loop because the loop's run by a subshell.

If you use `exec` to redirect the script's input, the shell can execute the script directly, making the value stored in `count` available to the current shell.

```
$ phsearch.exec
phonefile=/usr/data/phone.list
count=0
exec < $1      # read from file on command line\4
while read pattern
do
    if grep "$pattern" $phonelist
    then
        count=`expr $count + 1`
    else
        echo "$pattern not found" >&2
    fi
done
echo "\nMatched $count patterns"
```

Now the script can tell you how many patterns were matched.

```
$ phsearch.exec pattern.file
Smith, Terry     7-7989
6- not found
StClair, Pat     4-6122
Benson, Sam      4-5587

Matched 2 patterns
```

The *hash* Command

Before the shell can execute a command, it must locate its command file. The purpose of the PATH variable is to provide a list of directories to search for a command file and the order in which these directories are searched. The shell would waste a lot of time if it had to repeatedly search these same directories every time a command was entered.

To increase efficiency, the shell remembers a command path name found in the search path. The next time a "found" command is run, the shell knows where to find it. If you want to see the command path names currently stored by the shell, use the hash command.

```
$ hash
hits     cost      command
2        1         /bin/ls
1        1         /bin/cat
1        3         /usr/ucb/vi
1*       5         ./phsearch.exec
$ echo $PATH
/bin:/usr/bin:/usr/ucb:/usr/ray:.
```

The hits column shows how many times that command has been executed. The cost column shows which PATH directory holds this command. To find vi, the shell had to search three directories. Commands found in /bin have a "cost" of 1, because it is the first directory listed in PATH.

The asterisk next to the hits entry for ./phsearch.exec means that the remembered path name is a relative one (the cost is 5 because the current directory is the last one in the PATH). The shell has to recalculate this path if the current directory is changed.

Sometimes the same file name will identify different shell scripts in different directories. For example, if you have several scripts named phsearch.exec, you might not want the shell to remember where the last phsearch.exec executed is located. Otherwise, if you move to another directory and execute phsearch.exec, the shell will run the wrong script. To remove a path name from the shell's memory, use hash -r *path name*, where *command* is the name repeated by the hash command without agreements.

You also can load path names into the shell's memory by using the hash command. This doesn't execute the commands. The shell simply searches for them and loads their path names into the hashed command list.

The *type* Command

The search path tells the shell where to look for commands you execute. To find out the actual path name of an executable command, use `type`. The `type` command searches the directories in `PATH` and displays the path names of the command to, run if you enter `type`'s arguments as commands. `type` also identifies files that are built into the shell.

```
$ type cat
cat is /bin/cat
$ type cd
cd is a shell builtin
$ type junk
junk not found
```

The *wait* Command

When a process is run in the background, the shell doesn't wait for it to finish but instead lets you continue executing commands (in the foreground). Sometimes you have other tasks to perform while waiting for the background process to finish. When you complete those additional tasks, you may still need to wait for the background process to finish. How will you know when it is done? Aside from running `ps` every 10 seconds or so, you won't.

The shell provides the `wait` command as a way to tell the shell not to do anything until a specific background process terminates. You need to tell the `wait` command the PID of the process it is to wait for. If you want to `wait` for the process most recently put in the background, use `$!`.

```
$ sort big.list -o big.list &
9274
run some commands
$ wait 9274              could use $! here, too
```

If `wait` is executed without arguments, the shell waits for all child processes to finish.

Shell Functions

In addition to executing commands interactively and putting a set of commands in a shell script, the shell provides another way to run commands, *shell functions*. A shell function is like a combination of an interactive command and a shell script. A function is like an interactive command because the shell executes it directly, and a function is like a shell script because it consists of commands that are run when the function's name is entered.

You must define a shell function before you can use it. Defining a shell function requires a specific syntax. A function definition consists of a function name (same name conventions as a shell variable), a set of parentheses, an opening brace, the function's commands, and a closing brace.

```
$ name ()
{
    commands to execute
}
```

If any of these pieces is left out, an error results.

For example, the `hls` function, defined in the following text, lists the files in your home directory.

```
$ hls ()
> {
> ls $HOME
> }
```

`hls` can also be defined on a single line. However, for single-line function definitions, the shell requires that at least one space or tab appear between the opening brace ({) and the first command in the function, and that a semicolon separate the last command from the closing brace. (A space is optional but improves readability.)

```
$ hls () {  ls $HOME;   }
```

Once `hls` is defined, the shell executes the `ls $HOME` command when you enter `hls`.

```
$ hls
files in home directory
```

There are two important distinctions between shell scripts and shell functions. First, a shell script is stored in a file. A shell function is stored in the shell's local environment. Thus, you must redefine a function every time you run a new shell or log in. For this reason, most users define functions in their `.profile` file.

The second difference is that a function is executed by the current shell, whereas a shell script is run in a child process. Thus, any changes made to the environment by a function are made to the current shell's environment and will remain after the function has terminated. A shell script's changes are made to the environment of the child process and have no effect on the current shell's environment.

Functions are stored in a process's local environment. Thus, a function only exists in the process where it is defined. Shell functions cannot be exported from one process to another.

One important similarity between functions and shell scripts is that functions can access the command-line arguments via the shell positional parameters. For example, shell scripts need to have execute permission before they will run. To change a file's permissions requires a one-line `chmod` command. This is a good candidate for a function. Here is a function named `chx` that adds execute permissions for its argument(s).

```
$ chx () {   chmod +x $*;   }
```

Note the use of `$*`. All the arguments sent to `chx` are delivered to `chmod`.

Hands-on Exercise 18.1

Write a function called `mkscript` that runs `vi` on the function's one argument and then adds execute permissions to this edited file.

When the shell executes a function, it replaces the command line with what is inside the function's braces. Thus, if the function definition doesn't contain command-line arguments, the shell ignores any arguments listed with the function's name on the command line. For example, if you are accustomed to using `dir` to list the files in a directory, you might want to create a `dir` function that does nothing more than substitute `ls` for `dir`.

```
$ dir () { ls; }
```

Since no positional parameters are listed inside `dir`'s definition, the shell ignores any arguments listed with `dir`. Thus, the command `dir chapter.*` simply runs `ls`, as if no arguments had been entered.

Another pitfall with functions is that the shell searches for functions when it executes a command line, including those commands inside the function. Thus, you can easily define functions that get into a *function loop*. A function loop occurs when a function refers to itself, causing the shell to repeatedly substitute the function into the function—in essence, chasing its own tail.

An example will help illustrate the point. Suppose that you want `ls` to display its output in several columns, instead of a single column. You might create this function:

```
$ ls () { ls -C $*; }
```

The idea is that whenever you enter `ls`, you want `ls -C` to run. The problem is that `ls -C $A` is repeatedly substituted for the `ls` in the function. As a result, the shell keeps expanding the command line until something forces it to quit, generally an *interrupt* from the keyboard.

There are two ways to create functions that refer to a command of the same name. One is to choose a different name for the function. Why not use `l` or `lc` instead of `ls` as the function name for creating a columnar listing? Another solution is to put the full path name of the command in the function definition. In the case of `ls`, use `/bin/ls` instead of just `ls`.

```
$ ls () { /bin/ls -C $*; }
```

This last strategy won't work with built-in commands like `cd` because they have no absolute path name.

Normally, functions return a value equal to the exit status of the last command executed (in the function). To return a preset value, use the `return` command, which is like a function's `exit` command. A function's exit status is listed after `return`.

Another feature common to both functions and shell scripts is their capability to use shell programming commands. Thus, you can put loops, `ifs`, and `cases` inside a function. In fact, you can even include function calls inside your shell scripts.

One main advantage of shell functions is that you can execute them quickly. The shell doesn't have to look through your search path or create a new process to run them. Just remember that functions exist only in the shell where they are defined. What some users do is to store all of their functions in a separate file and then use the dot (.) command to load them into their current shell.

```
$ cat funct.file
hls() { ls $HOME; }
x () { chmod +x $*; }
ls () { /bin/ls -C $*; }
$ . funct.file          Loads function into shell
```

As a detailed example of what can be done with functions, let's extend the cd command to handle patterns. One of the nice features of the UNIX System is the directory file system. Unfortunately, there is a trade-off to using lots of directories: the absolute path names of files grow longer and longer. Thus, it becomes harder to move from one to the other without a lot of typing.

Although you can list all your favorite directories in CDPATH, such lists become cumbersome to deal with every time you add or delete a directory. A better solution is to create a file, let's call it dirs, that contains the absolute path names of all the directories in your home directory tree.

```
$ cat dirs
/usr/ray/Uw
/usr/ray/Book
/usr/ray/C
/usr/ray/Letters
/usr/ray/Classes
/usr/ray/Video
/usr/ray/Unix
/usr/ray/Acct
/usr/ray/Expertips
/usr/ray/Invoices
/usr/ray/Unix.book
```

To change to another directory, use grep and a pattern to search the dirs file for the desired directory. Use the output of grep as the argument to cd. For example, the text of this book is stored in the Unix.book directory. To move to that directory from anywhere in my directory tree, I can use the command

```
$ cd `grep Unix.book $HOME/dirs`
```

It takes more effort to enter this `cd` command than to type the absolute path name of the `Unix.book` directory. To avoid typing the entire command line, you can create a shell function. Because `cd` is a shell built-in command, you can't name the function `cd`. Let's use `ncd`, for new `cd`, instead.

```
ncd ()
{
    cd `grep "$1" $HOME/dirs`
}
```

Incidentally, because the current shell executes `ncd`, the `cd` command will change directories for the current shell.

Now that we have defined the function, we need to clean it up a bit. First, `ncd` should act like `cd`. If no arguments are passed to it, it should change to your home directory. This can be implemented with a `case` command.

```
ncd ()
{
    case $# in
        0) cd ;;
        *) cd `grep "$1" $HOME/dirs` ;;
    esac
}
```

Note that `ncd` uses only the first argument even if more than one argument is passed to it. Also, if the `grep` fails to find a match, it has no output, and `ncd` changes to the home directory.

The `ncd` function works if one match or no match is found, but what if `grep` finds several matches? One solution is to take only the first one by piping `grep`'s output to `sed -n 1p`.

```
ncd ()
{
    case "$#" in
        0) cd ;;
        *) cd `grep "$1" $HOME/dirs | sed -n 1p` ;;
    esac
}
```

Hands-on Exercise 18.2

Because the `ncd` function moves to the first directory `grep` finds, it will always change to the same directory, given the same pattern (i.e., the first directory found in `dirs`). Extend `ncd` to print a menu of directories found and allow the user to choose the appropriate directory.

Hands-on Exercise 18.3

Write a `mkdir` function that adds a new directory to the `dirs` file.

Hands-on Exercise 18.4

Write a `rmdir` function that deletes the removed directory to the `dirs` file.

Bourne Shell Options

The shell assumes that its first argument is a command file to read and execute and that additional arguments are positional parameters passed to the command file. Like most UNIX commands, the shell also recognizes options in the form of a dash followed by a single character. Table 18.1 lists these options. The shell provides a variable ($-) that holds the command options set for the current shell.

You can watch a script run by executing it in a shell with the -x option set.

```
$ sh -x phone.find Smith Jones
phonefile=phone.list
+ grep Smith phone.list
Smith, Terry    7-7989
+ grep Jones phone.list
+ echo Jones not found in list
Jones not found in list
```

Table 18.1. *Bourne shell command options.*

Option	Function
a	Automatically export any variable that is modified or created
c *str*	Take commands from *str*
e	Exit immediately if a command fails (has a nonzero exit status)
f	Disable interpretation of file name metacharacters
h	Locate the commands inside a function definition when a function is defined (normally the commands aren't located until the function is executed)
i	Ignores *interrupts* (interrupt, quit, and terminate signals); the shell is interactive
k	Allow variables assigned anywhere on a command line to be passed to a new process, not just those before the command name
n	Read commands but do not execute them (good for checking syntax)
p	Don't set the effective user and group IDs to the real uses and group IDs (System V3.2 and later)
r	Start a restricted shell
s	Read commands from the standard input; treat command-line arguments as positional parameters to the shell
t	Exit after reading and executing one command
u	Make evaluating an unset variable an error
v	Print input as the shell reads it
x	Print command lines as they are executed
-	Arguments beginning with - are not seen as options

The lines beginning with a plus (+) show the commands executed by the shell (the assignment doesn't get a +). A new shell (sh) is run so that −x is set just for the duration of phone.fwd.

If the shell is run with an exec and the first character of the command name is a dash (that is, exec −sh), the shell executes the start-up files /etc/profile and .profile in your current directory. Note that sh can't be done from the command line; it can only be done with exec.

The *set* Command

The set command enables you to change the command-line settings for the current shell. Except for the c, i, and s options, you can set any shell option listed in table 18.1. If you want to remove an option previously set, use + instead of −. Thus, `set -a` turns option `a` on and `set +a` turns it off.

Another very useful feature of `set` is that it can change the current positional parameters.

```
$ echo $1                    Shell's first argument
                             is empty
$ echo $#
0
$ set Ray Swartz
$ echo $1
Ray
$ echo $#
2
```

Previously we used `awk` or `cut` to split lines into fields. For example, to extract the first name from an entry in the phone list, you might use `awk` this way:

```
$ grep Smith /usr/data/phone.list ¦
> awk '{ print $2 }'
Terry
```

You can do the same thing with `set`.

```
$ set `grep Smith /usr/data/phone.list`
$ echo $2
Terry
```

If the `grep` command doesn't find a `Smith` in the phone list, `set` gets no argument. When `set` is called without arguments, it lists all the current shell variables and their values. To prevent this variable listing, use `set --`. The `--` tells `set` not to interpret anything following the `--` as an option. If nothing follows `--` (say, the `grep` has no output), `set` has no output.

The IFS Variable

There are several times when the shell parses a line into "words": reading data from the standard input, assigning values to variables, substituting the output of a command with command substitution, getting words from a `for` command's *word-list*, and other instances. When the shell parses a+ line, it separates the line into arguments at whitespace characters, which are the space, tab, and newline characters, by default.

The shell's whitespace characters are not hard-coded into the shell. The contents of the IFS variable controls which characters the shell uses to separate arguments. IFS stands for Internal Field Separator, and it holds the shell's current delimiters.

Because spaces, tabs, and newlines are not "printable" characters, it is difficult to see what's stored in IFS.

```
$ echo "$IFS"
```

A better way to view what's in IFS is to use the `od` command. `od` is a filter that prints the individual characters. Depending on the option chosen, `od` displays its input as characters (-c) or in octal (default), hexadecimal (-x), decimal (-d), or other values.

```
$ echo "$IFS" | od -c
0000000        \t  \n  \n
0000004
```

As `od` shows, IFS contains three characters, a space, tab, and newline. The second newline `od` found was added by `echo`. Incidentally, the seven digits you see at the beginning of each line of `od`'s output are the character offset in the stream where `od` began printing characters.

To extract someone's last name from the phone list, you can add a comma to IFS and let `set` parse the line.

```
$ grep Smith /usr/data/phone.list
Smith, Terry    7-7989
$ IFS="$IFS,"
$ echo "$IFS" | od -c
0000000        \t  \n  ,  \n
0000005
$ set `grep Smith /usr/data/phone.list`
$ echo $1
Smith
```

The shell uses the IFS characters for every command. As a result, it is important to put IFS "back the way you found it."

```
$ IFS='            Space, tab, and newline entered
'
$ echo"IFS ¦ od -c
0000000       \t  \n  \n
0000004
```

One problem with resetting IFS is that you don't know if it was set to space, tab, and newline or to something else. Usually the solution is to store current IFS values in another shell variable and, when you're done using the modified IFS, reassign it to its previous characters.

```
$ OLDIFS="$IFS"
$ IFS="$IFS,"      Add a comma to IFS commands using new IFS
Commands needing comma in IFS
$ IFS="$OLDIFS"
```

A common setting for IFS is just newline.

```
$ IFS='            Newline entered only
'
```

Now arguments can be separated only by newlines.

```
$ read str
      This       string     has      lots of spaces
$ echo $str
      This       string     has      lots of spaces
```

Because the shell is no longer parsing on spaces, the spaces are stored into `str` along with the other characters entered. Also, note that `$str` isn't quoted. With IFS set to just a newline, it is no longer necessary to protect the spaces stored in `str`.

Hands-on Exercise 18.5

Set the IFS variable in such a way that `set` can extract both the area code and the first three digits from a phone number in the format `(408) 458-9708`.

Hands-on Exercise 18.6

Write a script to read in a date in the format `MM/DD/YY` and then to verify that this date is valid.

Shell Interpretation Sequence

Command lines are not interpreted by the shell all at once. Instead, the shell follows a well-defined order for evaluating them. The first thing the shell does is to read a command line and parse it into words using spaces and tabs as delimiters (IFS is used later). Note that the shell stops reading if it hits any command-line "dividing" characters, such as semicolons (`;`), ampersands (`&`), double ampersands (`&&`), and double pipe symbols (`||`). If the `-v` (verbose) command option is set, the shell displays the line just read, on the standard error. Any quotes in front of or around metacharacters are interpreted and removed here.

After the shell parses the line into words, it does parameter substitution. Parameter substitution includes positional parameters, variables, and other expressions that start with a dollar sign.

After performing parameter substitution, the shell does command substitution, represented by commands inside backquotes. It executes the command line in backquotes and substitutes the command's output for the original quoted command line. The executed command is subject to this same interpretation sequence.

Next the shell implements redirection. If the redirected file cannot be opened, the shell prints an error message and terminates its evaluation. If the redirection is successful, the shell removes the redirection characters from the line.

Because the characters on the command line may now be different from the ones originally entered (due to parameter or command substitution), the shell reparses the command line using the contents of IFS. If IFS characters are found, the shell removes them from the line and replaces them with a space. Note that consecutive IFS characters are replaced with a single space.

The shell then does file name matching. If there is a match to a file name metacharacter, the shell substitutes all the files that match for the metacharacter expression, separated by spaces. If it finds no match, the metacharacters are left as is.

If the -x (execution trace) option is set, the shell displays the current state of the command line. Because this is the last step before actual command execution, you see the command line that is actually run by the shell. The shell adds a plus to the traced lines printed by -x, with the exception of variable assignments.

The shell now has a command line to execute. If the command line is a variable assignment, the shell implements it now. If not, the shell searches for the command, first in its internal tables and then by looking through the PATH directories.

To demonstrate how the shell command interpretation sequence works, consider what happens when a command is put inside a shell variable and then that variable's contants are "executed."

```
$ cmd='date'
$ $cmd
Wed Jan 3  09:34:04 PST 1990
```

Because the shell performs parameter substitution before executing the command, $cmd is converted to date, which is then executed.

However, because parameter substitution occurs after the shell has parsed the line the first time, certain metacharacters are not "seen" if they are stored inside a variable whose contents are executed.

```
$ cmd='date > time.file'
$ $cmd
usage: date [mmddhhmm[yy]]  [+format]
```

In this case, the shell ignores the redirection and instead, passes date the > as an argument, which is why it fails. Not interpreting the redirection metacharacter is contrary to the stated interpretation sequence. After all, redirection occurs after parameter substitution. It seems that the shell should turn $cmd into date > time.file and then, at the redirection step, see the > and interpret it properly. The reason the shell doesn't see the > is because the shell doesn't reparse the command line between the time a parameter substitution occurs and the time redirection is implemented. In essence, the shell doesn't know that $cmd has added a metacharacter to the command line.

The shell can't recognize additional metacharacters until it reparses the line. Recall that the shell does parse the command line a second time after parameter and command substitution and implementing redirection, but before file name matching. Thus, a file name matching metacharacter stored in a variable whose contents are then executed will be interpreted properly by the shell.

```
cmd='ls *.17'
$cmd
chapter.17
examples.17
```

If the command is a shell built-in, the current shell executes the command. Otherwise, the shell determines whether the command is directly executable or a shell script. If the command is an executable (i.e., a compiled program), the shell forks a new process and execs the command file. If the command is a shell script, the shell forks a process and then execs sh *script-file* to run the script.

When two or more metacharacters are to be evaluated at the same step, the shell interprets them left to right. Thus, in the command line echo $3 $2 the shell interprets $3 before $2.

Knowing the shell's order of execution can often help explain why a command line failed and how to make it do what you want. For example, can you store a file name in a variable and then use the variable's value as the file name in a redirection?

```
$ filename=junk
$ echo "This is a test" > $filename
$ cat junk
This is a test
```

Because redirection takes place after parameter substitution, it works fine.

However, identifying the file name in a redirection using file name matching metacharacters won't work. Because redirection is set up *before* the shell interprets file name metacharacters, the redirection tries to use the file name as is (before expansion).

```
$ cat < ch*.17
ch*.17: No such file or directory
```

One way to make the shell see file name matching metacharacters is to use a metacharacter interpreted before redirection to do the file name matching for you. In this case, command substitution works.

```
$ cat < `echo ch*.17`
contents of chapter.17
```

Now the command substitution occurs first, so that the matched file name is what the redirection sees.

The *eval* Command

The shell provides an easier solution to the "out-of-order metacharacter evaluation" problem, the `eval` command. The `eval` command tells the shell to perform all its evaluation steps on `eval`'s arguments and then to execute the result as if it were a standard shell command line. In the case of the redirection and the file name matching metacharacters, `eval` would work, too.

```
$ eval cat \< ch*17
contents of chapter.17
```

`eval` causes the command `cat < ch*17` to be evaluated by the shell twice: once when `eval` is executed and once by the shell when the result of the `eval` command is executed. Note that the backslash is required to quote the `<` to prevent the shell from viewing the `<` as redirecting the input of the `eval` command. The first evaluation changes `ch*17` into `chapter.17` and removes the backslash from in front of the `<`. Now, when the shell executes the resulting command line, it looks like `cat < chapter.17`, which works fine.

As an example of using the power of `eval`, you can set up "numbered" variables using `eval`. In other programming languages, a numbered variable is called an array. However, the Bourne shell doesn't have many of the data-handling capabilities of other languages and doesn't offer arrays.

The problem with using numbered variables is the shell's evaluation order.

```
$ count=1
$ prompt1="Sort list"
$ echo $prompt$count
1
$ echo $prompt1
Sort list
```

Why doesn't `$prompt$count` evaluate to `Sort list`? Since the shell evaluates equivalent metacharacters from left to right, it evaluates `$prompt$count` as `$prompt` and then `$count`. Because `prompt` is unset, the only output from `$prompt$count` is 1, the value of `$count`.

You can fix this by using `eval` and a prudently placed backslash (\). Because a command line passed through `eval` is evaluated twice, a backslash can delay parameter substitution. To get the value of prompt, use

```
$ eval echo "\$prompt$count"
Sort list
```

Because the dollar sign in front of prompt is quoted, eval ignores it, removing the backslash. The dollar sign does, however, convert $count into 1. Thus, eval turns eval echo "\$prompt$count" into the command line echo $prompt1, which provides the correct prompt.

Summary

This concludes Part 3 of this book. In the first eighteen chapters of this book, you've learned how to use shell metacharacters, UNIX tools, pipelines, shell programming commands, a process's environment, and additional aspects of the Bourne shell. In Part 4, you will see how to combine these features to create truly useful UNIX applications.

## Part Four

CREATING APPLICATIONS WITH UNIX TOOLS

Now that you have covered the major features of the UNIX System, you can combine them together to create applications that solve everyday problems.

The purpose of this part is to show you how to design, write, and implement UNIX solutions using UNIX commands, filters, and shell programming.

In this part, each chapter is a separate application example. The purpose of these examples is to demonstrate the flexibility of the UNIX System and to describe the methods used. These examples are not intended to repeat information presented earlier and do not contain detailed explanations of previously described topics.

19

The *awk* Programming Language

In addition to shell programming, UNIX offers another programming language, the one supplied by `awk`.

Chapter 7 explained how the `awk` program worked as a filter. The examples in that chapter employed the `print` command and used both search patterns and logical tests to select text lines. In addition to those capabilities, `awk` also provides a complete programming language. This chapter provides second look at `awk` to reveal some of its programming power.

`awk`'s language closely resembles the C programming language. In fact, `awk` has been described as C wrapped inside a filter. Although it isn't necessary to know C in order to understand `awk`'s language, the more experience you have with computer (or shell) programming, the easier it will be to create `awk` programs.

You can use `awk`'s programming language to do many things; however, this chapter covers only those features that enable you to have more control of the formatting in your shell scripts.

awk Variables and Expressions

One feature that virtually all programming languages share is the capability to store information. Like most programming languages, `awk` provides variable names to refer to stored data. `awk`'s variable names have the same characteristics as shell variables. The name must start with an upper- or lowercase letter or an underscore (_), which can be followed by letters, the digits 0 through 9, or underscores.

An `awk` variable can store either character or numeric data. How `awk` treats a variable's data depends on how it is used. If you use a variable in a place where a numeric value is expected, `awk` treats the variable as numeric. `awk` will view the same variable as a character string if that's how it is used.

`awk` manipulates variables, like C does, using operators. Table 19.1 lists the arithmetic operators that `awk` recognizes.

Table 19.1. *awk's arithmetic operators.*

Arithmetic operator	Function
+	Addition
−	Subtraction
*	Multiplication
/	Division
%	Modulo division (remainder)
=	Assignment

To assign a value to a variable, use =.

```
count = 1
```

`awk`'s operators can be used together. This statement

```
count = count + 4
```

adds 4 to the existing value of `count`, assigning the sum back into `count`. Unlike the shell, `awk` does not require a dollar sign to extract the value from a variable. Whether you are assigning a value to a variable or referring to the value stored in it, use only its name.

In `awk`, dollar signs are used to identify fields in the current input line only. If you use a dollar sign with a variable, `awk` assumes that you want to refer to the field number represented by the value stored in the variable. Thus, if `count` holds 6, then `$count` evaluates to the contents of the sixth field of the input line.

`awk` doesn't require that variables be defined before they are used, and all variables are initialized to empty. Thus, the statement

```
count = count + 4
```

works the first time because `count` starts empty (which numerically is seen as 0).

As an example of awk's programming power, the number of words in a file can be totaled with this simple statement:

```
wcount = wcount + NF
```

Recall that the built-in variable NF holds the number of fields in the current line. Using the default field separators (spaces and tabs), a field is equal to a single word.

```
$ awk '{wcount = wcount + NF
> print wcount}' phone.list
3
6
9
12
15
18
```

Because each line in the phone list contains a last name, first name, and phone number, it isn't surprising that a total of 18 words were found. While the same answer could have been found using wc, the purpose of this example is to show how easy it is to get answers using awk.

awk provides an additional set of assignment operators that enables you to combine the value currently stored in a variable with the result of an arithmetic operation. (This is what happens to wcount in the previous awk command.) NF increases the current value of wcount. Another way to write this is to use the += operator, which says to add what's on the right of the operator to the value of the variable on the left and to store the result back into that variable. Thus,

```
wcount = wcount + NF
```

can also be written

```
wcount += NF
```

Note that any arithmetic expression can be placed to the right of one of these "new" assignment operators. Table 19.2 lists these additional operators.

Table 19.2. *awk's assignment operators.*

Assignment operator	Function
+=	Addition and assignment
-=	Subtraction and assignment
*=	Multiplication and assignment
/=	Division and assignment
%=	Modulo (remainder) division and assignment

To extend our previous example, you can also count the number of lines and calculate the average number of words in a line. First, awk keeps track of the number of lines read with NR. By dividing wcount by NR, you get the average words per line.

```
$ awk '{wcount += NF
> print NR, wcount, wcount / NR}' phone.list
1 3 3
2 6 3
3 9 3
4 12 3
5 15 3
6 18 3
```

The + operator works with numeric values only and cannot be used to concatenate (put together) two strings. Instead, awk concatenates two string variables if they are placed on a line together with only whitespace between them. For example, to create a full name from $1 (last name) and $2 (first name) in the phone list, use

```
name = $2 $1
```

This expression stores the first name followed by the last name (and a comma) in the variable name. Note that the first and last name will not be separated by a space. To add a space, you must concatenate these three strings:

```
name = $2 " " $1
```

BEGIN and *END* Processing

The previous awk command example has a major shortcoming. The output isn't labeled. To understand what each number in the output represents, you have to refer to the awk programming statements themselves. A title should be displayed *before* the first line is read.

As you recall, awk commands generally consist of two parts: a pattern to match and an action to perform on the lines that match the pattern.

To initialize values and print titles, awk reserves the pattern BEGIN to mean "Do these commands before you read input." Thus, anything specified as a BEGIN action is done first. You can use a BEGIN action to print a title for the output of the word count program.

```
$ awk 'BEGIN { print "Lines\tWords\tAverage"}
> { wcount += NF
> print NR, "\t", wcount, "\t", wcount / NR}' phone.list
Lines    Words    Average
1        3        3
2        6        3
3        9        3
4        12       3
5        15       3
6        18       3
```

Now that you have a heading, there is another obvious problem: too much output. Instead of getting the output for each input line, you really need only the totals for the entire file. awk reserves another pattern to handle termination statements, those statements that need to be performed after awk has finished reading its input. awk executes any statements following an END pattern after it reads all of its input.

To print only the output for the last line, you still have to count the number of words in each line. Thus, the next version of our example, named awc (for average word count), contains a BEGIN action to print a title, an action without a pattern to count the words in each input line, and an END action to print the accumulated totals. Because awc is a useful tool, I put it in a shell command file that takes the file to analyze off the command line as $1.

```
$ cat awc
awk 'BEGIN { print "Lines\tWords\tAverage" }
{ wcount += NF }
END {print NR, "\t", wcount, "\t", wcount / NR}' $1
$ awc phone.list
Lines   Words   Average
6        18       3
```

You can achieve the same output without a BEGIN action by printing the title in the END action.

```
awk '{ wcount += NF }
END {print "Lines\tWords\tAverage"
print NR, "\t", wcount, "\t", wcount / NR}' $1
```

In addition to counting words, you can use END actions to print other totals. Consider the owed.to.us file, which contains a list of companies that have outstanding bills due.

```
$ cat owed.to.us
Acme       234.98
Bestco     3456.98
Crompco    33.89
Dross      342.12
```

To determine the amount you are owed, total each line's second field and then print the total in an END action.

```
$ awk '{total += $2}
> END {print "Total <tab>",total}' owed.to.us
Total     4067.97
```

Note that this awk program assumes that companies that owe you money have one-word names.

Formatted Output with *printf*

Up to now, you've used only the print command to get output from awk, but awk offers another more capable printing command, printf.

awk's `printf` command is based directly on C's `printf()` function and uses almost the same system. The `print` command (introduced previously) displays only what's sent to it, either variables or quoted strings. `printf` works differently from `print`, because it uses a format string to specify what to display.

Because awk variables can hold either character strings or numbers, `printf`'s format string uses *format specifiers* to identify what type of value to insert into the format string and where to insert it. The format specifiers all start with a percent sign (%). Table 19.3 shows `printf` format specifiers.

Table 19.3.   printf *format specifiers.*

Format specifier	Function
%d	Integer (no decimal point)
%f	Decimal value (decimal point)
%o	Octal value
%x	Hexadecimal value
%s	String
%%	Percent sign

The `print` command adds a new line at the end of what it prints, but `printf` doesn't. If you want `printf` to add a new line, you must specify where it goes with \n. Table 19.4 shows other special character sequences you can use with `printf`.

Table 19.4.   printf *special character sequences.*

Special character sequences	Function
\n	Newline
\t	Tab
\f	Formfeed
\"	Double quote

If the format string doesn't contain any format specifiers, `printf` prints the format string as is. Thus, the `printf` command

```
printf "Lines\tWords\tAverage\n"
```

does the same thing as the following `print` command

```
print "Lines\tWords\tAverage"
```

Note the \n in the `printf` command. Without it, `awk` does not print a new line, and the next piece of output is placed right after the last "e" in `Average`.

Replacing Format Specifiers in a Format String

`printf`'s arguments replace the format specifiers listed in the format string. To print the phone list names in first name, last name order, you can use `printf` as follows:

```
$ awk '{printf "%s %s\t%s\n", $2, $1, $3}' phone.list
Terry Smith,    7-7989
Fran Adams,     2-3876
Pat StClair,    4-6122
Robin Brown,    1-3745
Chris Stair,    5-5972
Sam Benson,     4-5587
```

The `%s` format specifier is used because all three fields are characters strings. The `\t` in the format specifier string says to separate the second and third strings by a tab.

Printing Numbers

To print numbers, use either `%d` to print integers or `%f` for floating-point numbers (contain a decimal point). The contents and total of `owed.to.us` can be displayed with `printf`.

```
$ awk '{printf "%s\t%f\n", $1, $2
> total += $2}
> END {printf "\nTotal\t%f\n",total}' owed.to.us
Acme      234.980000
Bestco    3456.980000
Crompco   33.890000
Dross     342.120000

Total     4067.970000
```

`printf`'s output looks different than you might expect. The reason for all the trailing zeros is that, by default, `printf` displays six decimal places when %f is used. To change that, you can specify the exact number of decimal places to be printed by adding a decimal point and the number of decimal places to print in the %f directive. For example, %.2f tells printf to put exactly two decimal places in this number, even if it's zero. Note that printf rounds in the last decimal place, if necessary. Using %.2f makes the owed.to.us output less confusing.

```
$ awk '{printf "%s\t%.2f\n", $1, $2
> total += $2}
> END {printf "\nTotal\t%.2f\n",total}' owed.to.us
Acme        234.98
Bestco      3456.98
Crompco     33.89
Dross       342.12

Total       4067.97
```

Now, the numbers look better, but they still don't line up on the decimal points, which would be a nice touch. In addition to specifying the number of decimal places to print, you also can define each variable's print width.

The print width states the minimum number of characters printf uses for display. The print width specifier goes after the percent sign (%). Thus the format specifier %7.2f says to print a minimum of seven characters for this value. Note that because .2 was specified, three of the seven characters have already been allocated (a decimal point followed by two digits). Thus, %7.2f describes the format ####.##; the # to the left of the decimal point represents a space or a digit, and to the right of the decimal point it represents a digit only. Note how the numbers line up when a print width specifier is used:

```
$ awk '{printf "%s\t%7.2f\n", $1, $2
> total += $2}
> END {printf "\nTotal\t%7.2f\n",total}' owed.to.us
Acme        234.98
Bestco      3456.98
Crompco      33.89
Dross       342.12

Total       4067.97
```

If the value to print takes up less than the number of characters specified for the print width, `printf` pads the output with spaces on the left.

If the value requires more than the specified number of characters, `awk` ignores the print width and uses however many characters are required to print the full value. For example, note how the output changes when `%6.2f` is used to print the contents of `owed.to.us`.

```
$ awk '{printf "%s\t%6.2f\n", $1, $2
> total += $2}
> END {printf "\nTotal\t%6.2f\n",total}' owed.to.us
Acme      234.98
Bestco    3456.98
Crompco   33.89
Dross     342.12

Total     4067.97
```

Now the decimal points don't line up because the values greater than 999.99 are extended out to the right.

Adjusting Print Width for Strings

The print width works the same way with strings. Suppose that the Gizmotech Corporation buys some of your products. Now the output changes because the length of "Gizmotech" extends beyond the tab stop used by the other company names.

```
$ awk '{printf "%s\t%7.2f\n", $1, $2
> total += $2}
> END {printf "\nTotal\t%7.2f\n",total}' owed.to.us
Acme         234.98
Bestco       3456.98
Crompco      33.89
Dross        342.12
Gizmotech         398.09

Total      4466.06
```

It seems like this problem is easily solved by simply adding a print width to the `%s` format specifier. Let's try 20.

```
$ awk '{printf "%20s\t%7.2f\n", $1, $2
> total += $2}
> END {printf "\nTotal\t%7.2f\n",total}' owed.to.us
                Acme        234.98
              Bestco       3456.98
             Crompco         33.89
               Dross        342.12
           Gizmotech        398.09

    Total    4466.06
```

This is not exactly what we had in mind. There are two problems here. First, `printf` adds extra spaces to the left of (right-justifies) a value, which results in a strange look. Second, the last line doesn't line up with the previous ones.

The first problem is easily solved by telling `printf` to add the extra spaces on the right side of the value (left-justifying) by putting a dash (–) after the `%` in the format specifier. Thus, `%-20s` tells `printf` to left-justify its output.

The last line will be treated the same as the others if its format is the same. To print the word "Total" in a left-justified, 20-character print width, put it inside double quotes and make it an argument. This command has been stored in a file named `total.owed`.

```
$ cat total.owed
awk '{printf "%-20s\t%7.2f\n", $1, $2
    total += $2}
    END {printf "\n%-20s\t%7.2f\n","Total",total}' owed.to.us
$ total.owed
Acme                    234.98
Bestco                 3456.98
Crompco                  33.89
Dross                   342.12
Gizmotech               398.09

Total                  4466.06
```

When all you want to do is print a value, use `print`. It is easier to work with because it doesn't require a separate format string. However, when you want the output to look a certain way, use `printf`.

Redirecting Output of Single *print* or *printf* Statements

One last thing about printing. You can redirect output of a single print or printf statement by using a > or >> metacharacter inside an awk command. These redirection characters act the same as the shell's redirection metacharacters that they mimic. The name of the output file must be enclosed inside double quotes, because otherwise the filename is considered to be an uninitialized variable.

For example, suppose you want to track the amount you are owed throughout the year. Thus, in addition to displaying each line of the owed.to.us file and a total, you want to print the total to the owed.for.year file.

Printing to the summary file is done with

```
print "Total", total >> "owed.for.year"
```

To make the application complete, you would also want to print the current date into the owed.for.year file. This has been implemented in the owed.rept shell script, which prints the current date and then runs the total.owed.1 command.

```
$ cat owed.rept
echo "`date +%D` \c" >> owed.for.year
total.owed.1
$ owed.rept
Acme                    234.98
Bestco                 3456.98
Crompco                  33.89
Dross                   342.12
Gizmotech               398.09

Total                  4466.06
$ cat owed.for.year
01/03/90 Total 2765.98
02/06/90 Total 3243.91
03/11/90 Total 4466.06
```

The date +%D command prints the date in MM/DD/YY format. The \c is used to stop echo from printing a newline after the date so the date and total are put on the same line.

Inserting Commas into Numbers

`printf` can handle numbers with decimal points, but it cannot insert commas into values. To print the value 4466.06 as 4,466.06, you must take the number apart and reassemble it with a comma in the right spot.

To simplify this task, assume that you have no need to print values greater than one billion. Or, put another way, your code will have to insert no more than two commas into a number. The key idea involves separating a number into two parts: what's to the left of a comma and what's to the right.

Start by adding commas to a number in the thousands. The thousands can be identified by dividing by 1000 and extracting the integer part of the division, in essence getting rid of anything to the right of the decimal point. To demonstrate,

```
4466.06 / 1000
```

evaluates to 4.46606. Chopping off the fraction results in 4, which is the number of thousands in 4466.06. To "chop off the fraction," which is known as truncating, use awk's built-in `int()` arithmetic. The statement

```
int(4466.06 / 1000)
```

evaluates to 4. The rest of the number can be determined by subtracting the thousands from the original number. The expression

```
4466.06 - 4 * 1000
```

results in 466.06. Now that you have the number separated, put a comma in the middle.

The `add.comma.1st` awk program prints a simple prompt, with a `BEGIN` action; reads numbers from the standard input; and then prints those numbers with a comma in the appropriate spot.

```
$ cat add.comma.1st
awk 'BEGIN { print "Enter numbers over a thousand"}
    { thousands = int($1/1000)
      rest = $1 - thousands * 1000
      printf "%d,%.2f\n", thousands, rest
    }'
```

```
$ add.comma.1st
Enter numbers over a thousand
4466.06
4,466.06
234345.99
234,345.99
<Control-D>
```

add.comma.1st works as long as the numbers entered are over 1000. If they aren't, add.comma.1st inserts a comma anyway.

```
$ add.comma.1st
Enter numbers over a thousand
476.98
0,479.98
<Control-D>
```

The zero is printed because that is the value of the variable thousands. The problem arises because add.comma.1st converts every number it reads, regardless of its value. Clearly, you want to insert commas only if the number entered is over one thousand.

The *if* Statement

awk provides an if statement to solve just these kinds of problems. awk's if statement resembles the shell's if command, in that it selects a set of statements based on the outcome of a test expression. In awk, the if statement evaluates a logical comparison test. If it is true, awk executes the statements enclosed in braces. If the test is false, awk ignores them.

```
if ( logical test) {
    Statement(s) executed only if test is true
}
```

Note that the logical test is enclosed in parentheses and that the statements to be executed if the test is true are enclosed in braces.

The comparison test operators were first listed in Chapter 7 and are repeated in table 19.5.

Table 19.5. awk*'s comparison operators.*

Comparison operator	Meaning
==	Equal to
!=	Not equal to
<	Less than
<=	Less than or equal to
>	Greater than
>=	Greater than or equal to
~	Matches a regular expression
!~	Doesn't match a regular expression
||	Logical *or*
&&	Logical *and*
!	Logical *not*

Identifying Values That Require Commas

You want to add commas to numbers greater than or equal to 1000 only, so you need to use the `if` test to identify the values that require commas. `add.comma.1st` has been modified to test the values of the numbers entered. The resulting script is stored in `add.comma.if`.

```
$ cat add.comma.if
awk 'BEGIN { print "Enter numbers:"}
{
    if ( $1 >= 1000) {
        thousands = int($1/1000)
        rest = $1 - thousands * 1000
        printf "%d,%.2f\n", thousands, rest
    }
}
$ add.comma.if
Enter numbers:
345
3456
3,456.00
<Control-D>
```

Now another problem exists. Numbers less than 1000 won't be printed at all. If the `if` test is false, nothing needs to be done to the value. It can be printed directly.

To handle any number between 0 and 1,000,000, the program must do one thing if the logical test is true and another if it is false.

awk's if statement contains an optional else section. If the logical test is false, awk executes statements listed after the keyword else. It ignores the else statements if the logical test is true.

```
if ( logical test) {
      Statement executed only if test is true
}
else {
      Statement executed only if test is false
}
```

The add.comma.else script works properly for values above and below 1000.

```
$ cat add.comma.else
awk 'BEGIN { print "Enter numbers:"}
{
    if ( $1 >= 1000) {
        thousands = int($1/1000)
        rest = $1 - thousands * 1000
        printf "%d,%.2f\n", thousands, rest
    }
    else
        printf "%.2f\n", $1
}'
$ add.comma.else
Enter numbers:
345
345.00
3456
3,456.00
<Control-D>
```

Note that braces are required around an if - else section only if there are two or more statements in that section. This is why braces aren't used in the else section in add.comma.else.

add.comma.else doesn't work correctly for numbers greater than or equal to 1,000,000.

```
$ add.comma.else
Enter numbers:
19564345
19564,345.00
<Control-D>
```

In the same way that a comma can be inserted for thousands, one can be added for millions.

```
millions = int ($1 / 1000000)
rest = $1 - millions * 1000000
thousands = int(rest/1000)
rest = rest - thousands * 1000
printf "%d,%d,%.2f\n", millions, thousands, rest
```

Now there are three different number ranges to process: millions, thousands, and hundreds. An if -else section can handle only two ranges.

Using *else if* Sections

To deal with additional tests, the if statement offers another optional section, the else if. An else if statement provides a secondary logical test. If the original if test is false (say, a test for millions), the else if allows a second test when the first test fails (say, a test for thousands). When the first test is false and the second test is true, the commands contained in braces following the else if are executed.

```
if (first logical test) {
    Statements executed only if test is true
}
else if (second logical test) {
    Statements executed only if first test is false
    and second test is true
}
else {
    Commands executed only if test is false}
```

There can be any number of else if tests. Note that else appears after else if. When all the tests are false, awk executes the commands in the else section. Remember, both the else if and else section are optional.

Handling Numbers With and Without Commas

The design of the add.comma program gets a bit more complicated when millions are taken into account because you must be able to handle numbers that require commas and those that don't. The straightforward approach is to have different sections for each value being printed, be it millions, thousands, or neither. This is how we will write add.comma.all.

Incidentally, the # character is how awk comments are identified.

```
$ cat add.comma.all
awk 'BEGIN { print "Enter numbers:"}
{
    #
    # Test for and format millions
    #
    if ( $1 >= 1000000) {
        millions = int ($1 / 1000000)
        value = $1 - millions * 1000000
        thousands = int(value/1000)
        rest = value - thousands * 1000
        printf "%d,%d,%.2f\n", millions, thousands, rest
    }
    #
    # Test for and format thousands
    #
    else if ( $1 >= 1000) {
        thousands = int($1/1000)
        rest = $1 - thousands * 1000
        printf "%d,%.2f\n", thousands, rest
    }
    #
    # Must be a number without commas
    #
    else
        printf "%.2f\n", $1
}'
$ add.comma.all
Enter numbers:
34876534.47
34,876,534.47
23984.8
23,984.80
```

```
18
18.00
<Control-D>
```

add.comma.all has a serious formatting problem. Note what happens if a number over 1,000,000 but without any thousands is formatted.

```
$ add.comma.all
Enter numbers:
34000534.47
34,0,534.47
<Control-D>
```

This is not quite what we had in mind. The same problem occurs for numbers with thousands but no hundreds.

```
$ add.comma.all
Enter numbers:
34005.47
34,5.47
<Control-D>
```

If a number is larger than 1,000,000, it must have three digits in the thousands section and three in the hundreds section. The current format for numbers over 1,000,000 is %d,%d,%.2f\. The %d that represents thousands doesn't specify a print width. Forcing a print width of three with %3d will help. Unfortunately, the number 005 prints as 5, with two leading spaces, using the %3d format.

To fix this problem, you again have to reach into printf's bag of tricks. By default, printf fills print fields with spaces. If you put a 0 after the %, it will fill with zeros. Thus, the format %03d prints the value 5 as 005.

You can use a similar solution to pad out the hundreds section with zeros, if necessary. However, hundreds are printed with a decimal point and two decimal places. To make sure that three digits are to the left of the decimal point requires %6.2f. To fill the printed value with zeros requires %06.2f. Thus, the format for millions needs to be changed to

```
printf "%d,%03d,%06.2f", millions, thousands, rest
```

and for thousands,

```
printf "%d,%06.2f", thousands, rest
```

Now, `add.comma.all` works as long as the input is a *number* less than a billion. However, what happens if the input is a character string?

```
$ add.comma.all
Enter numbers:
ray
  0,000,000.00
<Control-D>
```

`awk` treats all of its variables as character strings unless they are used where a number is expected. For example, a variable is considered a character string unless you manipulate it like a number by using one of the arithmetic operators. Thus, in

```
$1 > "1000000"
```

`awk` assumes the comparison is between two strings and compares them alphabetically. But, in

```
$1 + 0 > 1000000
```

`awk` treats the comparison as being between two numbers. If `$1` doesn't hold a number, then the result of

```
$1 + 0 == 0
```

is true. This provides the technique for handling character strings. This `if` statement prints `$1` if it is a character string.

```
if ($1 + 0 == 0)
    print $1
```

Note that this logical test is true for the value 0, as well. To handle zero requires another `if` test.

```
if ($1 == 0)
    print "0.00"
```

Combining the test for zero with the test for a string completes the program.

```
if ($1 == 0)
   print "0.00"
else if ($1 + 0 == 0)
   print $1
```

Adding these statements to add.comma.all results in add.comma.str.

$ add.comma.str
```
awk 'BEGIN { print "Enter numbers:"}
{
    #
    # Test for zero
    #
    if ($1 == 0)
        print "0.00"
    #
    # Test for a character string
    #
    else if ($1 + 0 == 0)
        print $1
    #
    # Test for and format millions
    #
    else if ( $1 >= 1000000) {
        millions = int ($1 / 1000000)
        value = $1 - millions * 1000000
        thousands = int(value/1000)
        rest = value - thousands * 1000
        printf "%0d,%03d,%06.2f\n", millions, thousands, rest
    }
    #
    # Test for and format thousands
    #
    else if ( $1 >= 1000) {
        thousands = int($1/1000)
        rest = $1 - thousands * 1000
        printf "%d,%06.2f\n", thousands, rest
    }
    #
    # Must be a number without commas
    #
```

```
      else
          printf "%.2f\n", $1
}'
$ add.comma.str
Enter numbers:
ray
ray
0
0.00
<Control-D>
```

The *for* Loop

Now that you have a way to format numbers by adding commas, how can you use it? At present, add.comma.str can read only a single field from the standard input. A better idea is to modify add.comma.str to read through every field on the input line and to convert only those fields that are numbers. Any character strings would pass through the script unchanged.

To handle numbers on any field on the line, add.comma.str must be extended to check each field individually. awk's for loop can help here. The for loop repeats a set of statements until a logical test is false. With add.comma.str, you want awk to execute the formatting statements once for each field on the input line.

The for loop is controlled by three expressions that make up the for loop. The first one initializes the counter that will be used in the loop. The second expression is the logical loop test that determines when the loop is to terminate. The third expression tells the for how to increment the loop counter.

```
for (initialize; test; increment) {
    Statements to execute
}
```

Note that the control expressions in the for loop are separated by semicolons.

awk reads in a line of input, separates it into fields, and then sets the internal variable NF to the number of fields on the current line. To check whether every field is a number to format, you want to loop as long as a field counter is less than or equal to NF.

```
for (count = 1; count <=NF; count += 1) {
    Formatting statements
}
```

Formatting Each Field

Earlier we noted that a dollar sign is used only with a field number and that $count identifies the field number stored in the variable count. Thus, you can handle each field on a line individually by looping from one to NF (incrementing by one) and using $count to identify the field being formatted.

Since every field on a line is going to be passed through add.comma.for, the printf statements shouldn't print new lines after each field. Instead, the statements should print a new line at the end of the for loop. The resulting script is stored in add.comma.for.

```
$ add.comma.for
awk ' {
    for (count = 1; count <= NF; count += 1) {
        #
        # Test for zero
        #
        if ($count == 0)
            printf "0.00"
        #
        # Test for a character string
        #
        else if ($count + 0 == 0)
            printf "%s", $count
        #
        # Test for and format millions
        #
        else if ( $count >= 1000000) {
            millions = int ($count / 1000000)
            value = $count - millions * 1000000
            thousands = int(value/1000)
            rest = value - thousands * 1000
            printf "%d,%03d,%06.2f", millions, thousands, rest
        }
        #
        # Test for and format thousands
```

```
        #
        else if ( $count >= 1000) {
            thousands = int($count/1000)
            rest = $count - thousands * 1000
            printf "%d,%06.2f", thousands, rest
        }
        #
        # Must be a number without commas
        #
        else
            printf "%.2f", $count
    }  # end of for loop
    printf "\n"
}'
```

Basically, `add.comma.str` is a filter that adds commas to numbers and ignores nonnumeric fields. Since it is a filter, `add.comma.str` can be part of a pipeline. To demonstrate its usage, let's insert commas into `total.oweds` output.

```
$ total.owed
Acme                      234.98
Bestco                   3456.98
Crompco                    33.89
Dross                     342.12
Gizmotech                 398.09

Total                    4466.06
$ total.owed | add.comma.str
Acme234.98
Bestco3,456.98
Crompco33.89
Dross342.12
Gizmotech398.09

Total4,466.06
```

Formatting Columns

Although `add.comma.str` correctly formats the numbers, it doesn't provide any separation between the fields. Also, the numbers don't line up on their decimal points. You need `add.comma.str` to align the columns. To make things easier, `add.comma.str` will format columns this way: Strings will be left-justified in a 20-character field (`%-20s`) and numbers will be right-justified in a 14-character field.

Fourteen characters were chosen to match the largest number that the `add.comma` is prepared to handle (`###,###,###.##`). In addition, a space will be added between fields.

All the `printf` statements need to be changed in `add.comma.str`. The format for millions becomes `%3d,%03d,%06.2f`; for thousands the new format is `%7d,%06.2f`; and for smaller numbers, the format is `%14.2f`. Note that all of these formats result in a 14-character print width. Also, each field will be followed by a single space.

The final version of `add.comma` is here.

```
$ cat add.comma
awk ' {
    for (count = 1; count <= NF; count += 1) {
        #
        # Test for zero
        #
        if ($count == 0)
            printf "%14s ", "0.00"
        #
        # Test for a character string
        #
        else if ($count + 0 == 0)
            printf "%-20s ", $count
        #
        # Test for and format millions
        #
        else if ( $count >= 1000000) {
            millions = int ($count / 1000000)
            value = $count - millions * 1000000
            thousands = int(value/1000)
            rest = value - thousands * 1000
            printf "%3d,%03d,%06.2f ", millions, thousands, rest
        }
        #
        # Test for and format thousands
        #
```

```
            else if ( $count >= 1000) {
                thousands = int($count/1000)
                rest = $count - thousands * 1000
                printf "%7d,%06.2f ", thousands, rest
            }
            #
            # Must be a number without commas
            #
            else
                printf "%14.2f ", $count
        }   # end of for loop
        printf "\n"
}'
$ total.owed ¦ add.comma
Acme                        234.98
Bestco                    3,456.98
Crompco                      33.89
Dross                       342.12
Gizmotech                   398.09

Total                     4,466.06
```

Combining Command-Line Arguments and *awk* Programs

One of the more important features of awk is its capability to perform arithmetic. This is important because the shell's numeric capability is nil and expr must be use to perform arithmetic. awk often comes in handy just to add up a column of numbers. In fact, there are many times when it's nice to have a column-summing tool.

The tricky part is telling awk which column you want to sum. Put another way, how can you put a command-line argument into an awk program?

Getting awk to respond to a command-line argument requires some delicate work. The problem stems from the fact that an awk program is surrounded by single quotes. This means the shell has no way of inserting the command-line argument into awk's program.[*]

---

[*]The new version of awk, also called nawk, introduced as part of AT&T's System V Release 3.1, can read command-line arguments directly.

What's more, you can't just use double instead of single quotes around awk's program, because awk uses some of the same characters as the shell. One obvious example is $1. Since the shell looks inside double quotes for any shell variables, the shell might interfere with other parts of awk's program.

The key to having the shell insert command-line arguments into an awk program is to let the shell "see" certain parts of awk's program. Consider the insert.args script.

```
$ cat insert.args
echo '$# equals '$#' in this script'
$ insert.args 1 2 3
$# equals 3 in this script
```

We can't use double quotes around echo's argument because the shell would interpret both occurrences of $#. We want the shell to substitute only for the second one.

Note that there are two complete sets of single quotes in echo's argument. The first set goes from the beginning of the argument to just before the second dollar sign (the one you want the shell to "see"). The second set starts just after the second # and goes to the end of the argument.

```
echo '$# equals '$#' in this script'
     {            } {              }
         set 1          set 2
```

This means that the second $# is *unquoted*. When the shell scans echo's argument, it sees only the second $#, which it converts to the proper value.

After the shell substitutes a 3 for the $#, this line results:

```
echo '$# equals '3' in this script'
```

The two sets of single quotes prevent the shell from seeing any whitespace in echo's argument. Thus, the shell sees and interprets the unquoted $# and then treats what results as a single argument to echo.

This same technique can be used to insert command-line arguments into awk programs. For example, in the past, not all UNIX Systems supplied the cut command. A simple version of cut can be simulated by the cut.awk shell script. Note that the characters visible to the shell are in bold.

```
$ cat cut.awk
awk '{print $'$1'}' $2
$ cut.awk 2 phone.list
Terry
Fran
Pat
Robin
Chris
Sam
```

Note that the $1 is "outside" both sets of single quotes. Thus, the shell inserts the script's first argument (substituting 2 for $1) into the awk program. Then awk combines the dollar sign inside the single quotes with the first command-line argument (written by the shell) to tell awk which field to print.

The sumit script requires one argument. sumit is written as a filter, although a second argument is used as an input file name if one is listed on the command line. Again, the characters visible to the shell are shown in bold.

```
$$ cat sumit
awk '{ total += $'$1' }
END { printf "%.2f\n", total}' $2
$ sumit 2 owed.to.us
4466.06
```

To format sumit's output, pipe it to add.comma.

```
$ sumit 2 owed.to.us ¦ add.comma
4,466.06
```

Summary

The flexibility and power of awk's programming language combined with the shell's capability to insert virtually anything into the middle of an awk program provides a wide range of capabilities to serve your needs and stimulate your creativity. Furthermore, we haven't even explored all of awk's features since this chapter has introduced only those parts of the awk programming language that you are likely to use within a shell programming application.

The authors of the awk program have written a book that describes the awk programming language in complete detail. Titled

The AWK Programming Language, it was written by Alfred Aho, Peter Weinberger, and Brian Kernighan and published by Addison-Wesley (1988). This book is highly recommended to anyone interested in learning more about `awk`.

Mail Merge, UNIX Style

A common business and personal need is to create customized letters. These might be Christmas messages, direct mail sales letters, or invitations to a meeting or party. Whenever you want to create a set of individualized letters, it is useful to be able to combine an existing form letter with a list of names and addresses.

There are several word processing and database management programs that will merge a list of names and a form letter. However, you can handle the same task using the tools available on your UNIX system, without buying any additional software.

For example, suppose that people respond to a magazine advertisement that you recently ran in *MicroCompuTechnoWorld*. When you send the brochures they request, you want to include a personalized cover letter.

The letter you want to send simply thanks someone for responding to the advertisement and asks them to call you if they have any questions or would like to place an order. See figure 20.1.

The file `responses.ad` holds a list of names and addresses with seven tilde-separated fields. To keep our examples short, assume that this file contains only these two records.

```
Pat~Thomas~Acme Inc.~111 First St.~San Jose~CA~95131
Chris~Johnson~Lunar System~222 Second St.~Dallas~TX~75217
```

Thus, the first letter should be addressed to Pat Thomas, and the second letter goes to Chris Johnson.

The key component of this mail merge system is the UNIX formatting command, `nroff`. The `nroff` (or its typesetting relative `troff`) is

```
Date

Address

Dear First name,

Thank you for responding to our advertisement in
MicroCompuTechnoWorld. I have enclosed the
product information you requested.

If you would like to place an order or need more
information, please give me a call at (408) 555-9708.

                        Yours truly,


                        Terry Wilson
```

Fig. 20.1.   *A response form letter.*

described in most introductory UNIX books (see references in Appendix C) and is not covered in any detail here.

Briefly, `nroff` is a filter that interprets formatting codes embedded inside its input stream. The formatted result is sent to `nroff`'s standard output. The formatting codes are identified as lines that start with a dot. To format the letter in figure 20.1, the `nroff` input would be as shown in figure 20.2.

The program that merges the form letters with names and addresses must distinguish between those lines in the form letter template that will change for each individual's letter and those that won't. In this example, the lines that change are those for date, address, and first name. A special code will be used for these three: `~DATE` for the date, `~ADDRESS` for the person's address, and `~FNAME` for the salutation (the line that starts with "Dear").

Interpreting Code Words

To simplify the programming, all code words must start at the beginning of a line and be the only thing on that line. The nonchanging text and the code words form a template that has been stored in a file named `response.let`, and is shown in figure 20.3.

```
Date
.sp
Address
.sp
Dear First name,
.fi
.sp
Thank you for responding to our advertisement in
MicroCompuTechno World. I have enclosed the
product information you requested.
.sp
If you would like to place an order or need more
information, please give me a call at (408) 555-9708.
.sp
.ce 2
Yours truly,
.sp 2
Terry Wilson
```

Fig. 20.2. *A response form letter with* nroff *formatting commmands.*

```
~DATE
.sp
~ADDRESS
.sp
~FNAME
.fi
.sp
Thank you for responding to our advertisement in
MicroCompuTechno World. I have enclosed the
product information you requested.
.sp
If you would like to place an order or need more
information, please give me a call at (408) 555-9708.
.sp
.ce 2
Yours truly,
.sp 2
Terry Wilson
```

Fig. 20.3. *Template for a response form letter.*

The code words are easily processed using a `case` statement and a `while` loop redirected to read from the `response.let` file.

```
while read line
do
    case $line in
        "~DATE") print date ;;
        "~ADDRESS") print address ;;
        "~FNAME") print Dear first name ;;
        *) echo $line ;;
    esac
done < response.let
```

Printing the date can be done with the `date` command. In addition to displaying the current date and time in its default format:

```
$ date
Sun Feb 25 07:50:04 PST 1990
```

the `date` command recognizes simple formatting codes. You can create the date on the response letter by using the `date` command directly, assuming that you want a date in one of the formats it can use. For this example, the date will be in the U.S. format, MM/DD/YY. This can be printed with

```
$ date '+%D'
02/25/90
```

To insert the address and the first name into the letter, you must convert a line from the `responses.ad` name list file into separate fields. To do this, change the `IFS` shell variable to a tilde and then use the `set` command to assign the first seven tilde-separated fields in a line from `responses.ad` to the first seven positional parameters.

```
oldifs="$IFS"
while read name
do
    IFS='~'
    set $name
    IFS="$oldifs"
    rest of script
done < responses.ad
```

Remember that the IFS variable affects how the shell parses command lines and should be restored to its previous value immediately after the set command. The original IFS value was stored in oldifs for easy restoration.

After the fields in a line from responses.ad have been assigned to positional parameters, the fields can be referenced as shown:

```
$1    First Name
$2    Last Name
$3    Company Name
$4    Street Address
$5    City
$6    State
$7    Zipcode
```

Thus, the ~ADDRESS code word in the letter template is replaced by

```
echo $1 $2
echo $3
echo $4
echo $5, $6 $7
```

The ~FNAME salutation is inserted into the form letter with the following statement:

```
echo Dear $1,
```

The complete case statement that processes the form letter code words becomes:

```
while read line
do
    case $line in
        "~DATE") date '+%D' ;;
        "~ADDRESS") echo $1 $2
                    echo $3
                    echo $4
                    echo $5, $6 $7 ;;
        "~FNAME") echo Dear $1, ;;
        *) echo $line ;;
    esac
done < response.let
```

When the commands that process the entries in the `responses.ad` file are combined with the commands that generate the personalized letter, you get the following `mk.resp.let` script:

```
$ cat mk.resp.let
oldifs="$IFS"
while read name
do
    IFS='~'
    set $name
    IFS="$oldifs"
    while read line
    do
        case $line in
            "~DATE") date '+%D' ;;
            "~ADDRESS") echo $1 $2
                        echo $3
                        echo $4
                        echo $5, $6 $7 ;;
            "~FNAME") echo Dear $1, ;;
            *) echo $line ;;
        esac
    done < response.let
done < responses.ad
```

Since `mk.resp.let` outputs text with embedded `nroff` formatting commands, you can store the output in a file for formatting later or pipe it to `nroff` for immediate formatting. When run through `nroff`, the letter in figure 20.4 for Pat Thomas, the first name in the `responses.ad` file, is created.

As written, `mk.resp.let` reads names from the `responses.ad` file and the form letter templates from `response.let`. A better design is to take these file names off the command line. The only tricky part is that, because `set` is used in the script, the command-line arguments, which are placed in positional parameters, must be saved in user-defined variables before the positional parameters are overwritten by using `set` for the first time.

```
02/25/90

Jan Horner
333 Third St.
Sacramento
CA, 95818

Dear Jan,

Thank you for responding to our advertisement in
MicroCompuTechno World. I have enclosed the product
information you requested.

If you would like to place an order or need more
information, please give me a call at (408) 555-9708.

                    Yours truly,



                    Terry Wilson
```

Fig. 20.5.   *Letter generated for an entry with an empty field.*

can test whether an entry has a company name by testing whether the positional parameter $3 is a space.

```
if [ "$3" != ' ' ]
then
    echo $3
fi
```

This approach solves the "blank line" problem. Here is the final version of mk.resp.let:

```
case $# in
   2) letterfile="$1"
      namefile="$2" ;;
   *) echo "Usage: $0 letter-file namelist-file"
      exit 1 ;;
esac
oldifs="$IFS"
while read name
```

```
do
    IFS='~'
    set $name
    IFS="$oldifs"
    while read line
    do
        case $line in
            "~DATE") date '+%D' ;;
            "~ADDRESS") echo $1 $2
                            if [ "$3" != ' ' ]
                            then
                                echo $3
                            fi
                            echo $4
                            echo $5, $6 $7 ;;
            "~FNAME") echo Dear $1, ;;
            *) echo $line ;;
        esac
    done <$letterfile
done <$namefile
```

```
02/25/90

Jan Horner

333 Third St.
Sacramento, CA 95818

Dear Jan,

Thank you for responding to our advertisement in
MicroCompuTechno World. I have enclosed the product
information you requested.

If you would like to place an order or need more
information, please give me a call at (408) 555-9708.

                        Yours truly,



                        Terry Wilson
```

Fig. 20.6.   *Corrected letter generated for an entry with an empty field.*

Since the name list file has tilde-separated fields and space-separated tildes, it is best to provide a data entry script to ensure that the file is created properly. Thus, completing this application requires a data entry script that acts as the interface between the user and this oddly formatted data file. This script is patterned on the `phone.add` script written in Chapter 16.

Correcting Errors

Because this is intended to be a real application, you should enable the user to correct data entry errors. Thus, the `get.responses` entry script not only prompts for and reads the name and address fields, but it also gives the user a chance to correct errors.

Data verification is important because it enables the user to correct any mistakes made during entry. In this script, data is verified by printing the data as it is read and then asking whether it is correct. If it is, the data is written to the data file (named as the first command-line argument). If it isn't, the user is allowed to correct it, a field at a time.

Data is corrected with a large `case` statement. If the user says the data is incorrect, the script asks the number of the field to correct. (Note that the fields are printed with line numbers in the data verification loop.) A case statement then prints the appropriate prompt and reads in the proper variable. Although the implementation requires a good deal of code, it is straightforward.

Here is the `get.responses` script.

```
$ cat get.responses
if [ $# != 1 ]
then
    echo "Usage: $0 namelist-file"
    exit
fi
while true
do
    echo "Enter First Name [Enter stop to quit]: \c"
    read fname ¦¦ exit
    test "$fname" = 'stop' && exit
    echo "Enter Last Name: \c"
    read lname ¦¦ exit
    echo "Enter Company Name: \c"
```

```
read coname ¦¦ exit
#
# test if coname is empty
#
if [ -z "$coname" ]
then
     coname=" "
fi
echo "Enter Street Address: \c"
read straddr ¦¦ exit
echo "Enter City: \c"
read city ¦¦ exit
echo "Enter State: \c"
read state ¦¦ exit
echo "Enter Zipcode: \c"
read zip ¦¦ exit
#
# print the data and ask if correct
# verify is the loop control variable
#
verify='n'
while [ $verify = 'n' ]
do
    echo "\n1. First Name: $fname"
    echo "2. Last Name: $lname"
    echo "3. Company Name: $coname"
    echo "4. Street Address: $straddr"
    echo "5. City: $city"
    echo "6. State: $state"
    echo "7. ZIP code: $zip\n"
    echo "\nIs this correct? (y/n) \c"
    read entry
    case $entry in
       [Yy]) verify=y ;;
       [Nn]) echo "Number of entry to correct: \c"
             read nbr
             #
             # allow user to change on field
             # at a time
             #
             case $nbr in
               1) echo "Enter First Name: \c"
                  read fname ¦¦ exit ;;
```

```
        2)  echo "Enter Last Name: \c"
            read lname ¦¦ exit ;;
        3)  echo "Enter Company Name: \c"
            read coname ¦¦ exit
            if [ -z "$coname" ]
            then
                    coname=" "
            fi ;;
        4)  echo "Enter Street Address: \c"
            read straddr ¦¦ exit ;;
        5)  echo "Enter City: \c"
            read city ¦¦ exit ;;
        6)  echo "Enter State: \c"
            read state ¦¦ exit ;;
        7)  echo "Enter Zipcode: \c"
            read zip ¦¦ exit ;;
        esac ;;
    *)  echo "\nEnter y or n only\n" ;;
    esac
    done
    echo "$fname~$lname~$coname~$straddr~$city~$state~$zip" >> $1
done
```

Adding Extensions

The `mk.resp.let` script can be modified to perform a number of
related tasks. For example, by adding more code words, you can add
additional sentences, or even paragraphs, to a form letter. You can
even create custom invoices or other types of letters.

Since my company teaches public C and UNIX seminars, we use a
script like `mk.resp.let` to create student registration letters and
invoices. The main extension we made indicates that a student can be
registered in any of four or five classes, each with different dates and
registration fees. To identify which class or classes a student plans to
attend, we added to the name and address line another field that holds
a set of colon-separated numbers. These numbers identify which
seminar the student will attend.

For example, if Robin Denton has signed up for classes 1 and 3,
the name entry looks like this:

```
Robin~Denton~Tech Inc~444 Fourth St~Denver~CO~80203~1:3
```

To extract the courses Robin wants to attend, after extracting the field on the line with `IFS` set to a tilde, we would set `IFS` to a colon and then set `$8` (to process the last (eighth) field of the name-list file entry. To handle this additional information, we added the code word `~CLASSES`. By processing the address line with two different shell scripts, we can print both a registration letter and an invoice.

Summary

This mail merge application shows how to UNIX tools and shell scripts can be combined to solve everyday problems. Once you implement a solution, don't be surprised if you can use the same approach to automate other tasks as well.

21

Creating Your Own Tools

$\mathbf{T}$he UNIX System contains several tools that perform similar functions but take input and/or send output to different devices. An obvious example is `sed` and `vi`. `sed` is an editor that works as a filter, and `vi` is an editor that works with a terminal. Another example is `nroff` and `troff`, where the main distinction is output device. The same can be said for `cat` and `more` or `pg`.

Locating a Passage in a File

One useful tool that has no visual counterpart is the `grep` filter. The `grep` command often comes in handy within a pipeline or a shell script. As an interactive command, though, it leaves much to be desired.

The problem is that it prints only the line that contains the specified pattern. This makes it difficult to identify where the line that contains a matching pattern appears. Within a pipeline, file location is unnecessary. However, when you need to locate a passage in a file, it would be nice to see more than just the line containing the pattern.

For example, `mail` messages that have been read but not held or deleted usually are stored in the file `mbox` in your home directory. Suppose you need to locate the text of a message that was sent to you but currently resides in `mbox`. Since you know the sender's name, `grep` can find the line containing the name, but can't display more of the associated message. Here is where a "context" `grep` would come in handy. Such a command would locate the matching line and then show that line's context (for example, a few lines above and below the one that matches).

This problem has a straightforward solution, thanks to how two UNIX filters work. You can't print a context unless you know where the context is supposed to be. The `grep` finds the line and, if you use the `-n` option, will also print the line number.

```
$ grep -n Smith mbox
24:From: Jan Smith
294:From: Jan Smith
```

Once you know the line number, you can use `sed`'s capability to print lines by number to show the line's context. A problem presented by `sed` is also solved by its `-n` option, although it does something entirely different from `grep`'s `-n`. Because `sed` is a filter that copies input to output, it prints every line it reads, regardless of whether any editing is done to that line. The `-n` option tells `sed` not to print a line unless specifically instructed to by the `p` command.

Thus, to print a ten-line context for line 24, use this `sed` command:

```
$ sed -n '19,29 p' mbox
Yours Truly,

Billy Jones

To: Ray Swartz
From: Jan Smith

Thank you for your recent e-mail message.

I would be interested in talking with you further about
your proposal. Please give me a call next week to discuss
```

Before you start, you must decide what is a suitable context range for a line. In the previous example, I chose ten lines, five before and five after the matched text. Let's use that as the default. The script, which we'll call `cgrep`, should enable you to set the context size through a command-line option.

The command `grep -n` reports the matched line's number, a colon, and then the line. Because you want the line number only, you must extract it from `grep`'s output. This can be done using `cut`.

To separate the number from the line, notice that `grep` inserted a colon between them. If you specify the field delimiter for `cut` to be a colon, the line number is the first field. To print the line number, use this pipeline:

```
$ grep -n Smith mbox | cut -d':' -f1
24
294
```

Assume the variable named `nbr` holds the matching line number. Then `expr $nbr - 5` can calculate the top of the context segment, and the bottom of the segment is `expr $nbr + 5`.

```
begin=`expr $nbr - 5`
end=`expr $nbr + 5`
```

The following `sed` command

```
sed -n "$begin,$end p" file
```

prints the matched line's context. Note the double quotes around `sed`'s edit command argument. The double quotes are necessary so the shell interprets the `$begin` and `$end` variables but still treats the resulting command as a single argument, which is required for the `sed` command to work properly.

There is a problem with the following approach:

```
begin=`expr $nbr - 5`
end=`expr $nbr + 5`
sed -n "$begin,$end p" file
```

If `nbr` is less than 5, `sed` is passed a negative number and will fail. Instead, the shell should test `begin` for being less than 1 and then set it to 1 if this is the case. In the same way, `end` should never be larger than the number of lines in the file. Although this doesn't directly cause an error in `sed`, it is bad style (and will get in the way later).

Finding the Number of Lines in a File

You can find the number of lines in a file with `wc -l`. The `wc -l` command prints the number of lines in the file and the file name. To get rid of the file name, you can use set to assign wc's output to the command-line parameters. You can verify begin and end with these commands:

```
begin=`expr $nbr - 5`
if [ $begin -le 0 ]
then
     begin=1
fi
end=`expr $nbr + 5`
set `wc -l file`
len=$1    # len (not $1) used to help document code
if [ "$end" -gt "$len" ]
then
     end="$len"
fi
```

Now the line's context can be printed with

```
sed -n "$begin,$end p" search file
```

The foregoing commands assume that nbr holds the line number of the matched line. However, the grep -n command may find several lines. To handle several matched lines, you can use a for loop that uses the grep ¦ cut pipeline as the argument list.

```
for nbr in `grep -n "pattern" file ¦ cut -d':' -f1`
```

To draw a distinction between the context of one line and that of another, you can clear the screen between contexts with tput clear. Also, you should ask the user to "press return to continue" at the end of each iteration of the for loop, so the screen doesn't clear while the user is trying to read it.

```
set `wc -l file`
len=$1    # len (not $1) used to help document code
for nbr in `grep -n "pattern" file ¦ cut -d':' -f1`
do
     tput clear
     begin=`expr $nbr - 5`
     if [ $begin -le 0 ]
     then
          begin=1
```

```
      fi
      end=`expr $nbr + 5`
      if [ "$end" -gt "$len" ]
      then
          end="$len"
      fi
      sed -n "$begin,$end p" file
      echo "\nPress return to continue\c"
      read junk
done
```

Before you can produce the first draft of cgrep, you have to handle a few administrative details. Because cgrep needs two arguments, a search pattern and a file name, you need to test that the script command was invoked properly. Further, because set is used to extract file size out of the wc command, you will have to save the actual command-line arguments in variables. The specified pattern will be stored in pattern, and the search file's name will be stored in file.

```
case $# in
    2) pattern="$1"
       file="$2" ;;
    *) echo "Usage: $0 pattern file"
       exit 1 ;;
esac
```

When assembled, the first draft of cgrep, cgrep1, looks like this:

```
$ cat cgrep1
case $# in
    2) pattern="$1"
       file="$2" ;;
    *) echo "Usage: $0 pattern file"
       exit 1 ;;
esac
clear=`tput clear`
set `wc -l $file`
len=$1    # len (not $1) used to help document code
for nbr in `grep -n "$pattern" $file ¦ cut -d':' -f1`
do
    echo $clear
    begin=`expr $nbr - 5`
```

```
        if [ $begin -le 0 ]
        then
                begin=1
        fi
        end=`expr $nbr + 5`
        if [ "$end" -gt "$len" ]
        then
                end="$len"
        fi
        sed -n "$begin,$end p" $file
        echo "\nPress return to continue\c"
        read junk
done
```

Developing Enhancements

Although `cgrep1` works, some enhancements would be useful. The script should tell the user what part of the file is being displayed and which line matched the pattern.

Further, `cgrep1` prints no output if the search pattern isn't found in the file; the command should tell the user that the pattern wasn't found because it's designed to be interactive. Last, the context range is set at ten lines; the user should be able to change this value with an argument.

To tell the user what part of the file is being listed, let's title each segment with the file's name, the numbers of the lines being listed, and the number of the matched line.

The "title" of each segment can be printed with

```
echo $file: Lines $begin to $end (Match: Line $nbr)
```

In addition to titling each segment, you should also number the lines so the user can easily identify which one contains the match, without having to actually count the lines.

Two filters number lines. One, `pr`, was covered in Chapter 10. The other, named `nl`, is mentioned here for the first time. Incidentally, it is not unusual to find "new" UNIX commands when you have a specific task to perform.

The problem with using `pr` is that it cannot be told where to start counting, it can only begin counting at 1. To number lines with `pr` would require that the input to `sed` be run through `pr` first to number the lines. This takes far too long. A better approach is to use `nl`, which was just designed to number lines.

The `nl` command is designed to number lines in several different ways.

To number the lines in a text segment, we can use `nl`'s `-v` option. The `-v` option takes an additional parameter that tells `nl` where to start numbering the lines. Thus, `nl -v$begin` will number the lines read from the standard input, starting at whatever is stored in `begin`. To number lines, simply pipe `sed`'s output to `nl`.

```
sed -n "$begin,$end p" $file ¦ nl -v$begin
```

By default, `nl` separates the line number from the text with a tab. Since this may force long lines to wraparound on the computer screen, `nl` recognizes the `-s` option, which can be used to specify the character that separates the number from the input line.

Like `-v`, `-s` takes an additional parameter, which is the character separator. To count the lines from `begin` using a colon as the separator, use

```
sed -n "$begin,$end p" $file ¦ nl -v$begin -s:
```

The `nl` command recognizes several other options. Check your system's documentation for a complete listing.

At present, `cgrep1` prints no output if the pattern isn't matched in the file.

```
$ cgrep1 lkasdlk mbox
$
```

This can be confusing to users. Although suppressing extraneous information is appropriate for a noninteractive command, an interactive command should provide user feedback. A better idea is to have the command print a brief message, *pattern* `not found in the` *filename* `file`.

You can determine whether a pattern is located in a file by examining `grep`'s exit status. However, the exit status of a pipeline is the last command in the pipeline. In this pipeline

```
grep -n "$pattern" $file ¦ cut -d':' -f1
```

`cut`'s exit status will be reported by `$?`. Even if the `grep` command sends it no output, the `cut` command still succeeds. Thus, to identify those patterns that aren't found, you must split this pipeline into two separate commands.

```
if grep -n "$pattern" $file  /tmp/cgrep.$$
then
    for nbr in `cut -d':' -f1 /tmp/cgrep.$$`
    do
        context printing commands
    done
else
    echo "$pattern not found in $file"
fi
```

Recall that $$ is a shell metacharacter for the current process ID number. Because a process ID number is unique, adding $$ to a filename creates a unique temporary filename. To gain access to grep's exit status, you've had to introduce a temporary file, /tmp/cgrep.$$. To clean up, you will have to remove it at the end of the script.

```
rm /tmp/cgrep.$$
```

Deleting Temporary Files

To guarantee that the file is deleted under all circumstances, you should trap the three interrupt signals 1, 2, and 3 and delete the temporary file if they are caught.

```
trap 'rm /tmp/cgrep.$$ 2> /dev/null; exit 1' 1 2 3
```

Note that we discarded the standard error of the rm command to prevent the printing of meaningless error messages if the interrupt occurs before the temporary file is created (and, therefore, cannot be deleted).

Also, by specifying signal 0, termination of the child process, you can use trap to remove the temporary file at the end of the script.

```
trap 'rm /tmp/cgrep.$$ 2> /dev/null; exit' 0 1 2 3
```

A second version of cgrep, cgrep2, prints a message if the pattern isn't found.

```
trap 'rm /tmp/cgrep.$$ 2> /dev/null; exit 1' 0 1 2 3
case $# in
    2)  pattern="$1"
        file="$2" ;;
    *)  echo "Usage: $0 pattern file"
        exit 1 ;;
esac
clear=`tput clear`
if grep -n "$pattern" $file > /tmp/cgrep.$$
then
    for nbr in `cut -d':' -f1 /tmp/cgrep.$$`
    do
        echo $clear
        begin=`expr $nbr - 5`
        if [ $begin -le 0 ]
        then
            begin=1
        fi
        end=`expr $nbr + 5`
        set `wc -l $file`
        len=$1     # len (not $1) used to help document code
        if [ "$end" -gt "$len" ]
        then
            end="$len"
        fi
        echo "$file: Lines $begin to $end (Match: Line $nbr)"
        echo
        sed -n "$begin,$end p" $file | nl -v$begin  -s:
        echo "\nPress return to continue\c"
        read junk
    done
else
    echo "$pattern not found in $file"
fi
```

Let's run cgrep2 to illustrate its new output.

$ **cgrep2 set cgrep2**

screen clears

cgrep2: Lines 14 to 24 (Match: Line 19)

```
14:          if [ $begin -le 0 ]
15:          then
16:               begin=1
17:          fi
18:          end=`expr $nbr + 5`
19:          set `wc -l $file`
20:          len=$1    # len (not $1) used to help document code
21:          if [ "$end" -gt "$len" ]
22:          then
23:               end="$len"
24:          fi
```

```
Press return to continue
```

The `cgrep2` script sets the context segment size to 10 lines (11 if you count the matched line), 5 before and 5 after the line containing the pattern. This value is hardcoded in the script with the constant 5. A more flexible design is to have the default context size be 10 lines but to let the user change it with an argument.

Let's extend `cgrep2` to recognize the `-c` option. The `-c` option tells `cgrep` to set the context segment size to its argument. Thus, `-c 10` says to print a 20-line context around each matched line (10 above and 10 below it).

In command lines for UNIX tools, options precede non-option arguments. `cgrep` will be no different and will require that `-c` be placed before the pattern argument. This not only provides some consistency but also simplifies the script.

Because the `-c` must appear first on the command line, there are two possible correct invocations of `cgrep`: one with two arguments (the pattern and filename) and one with four (`-c`, a number, the pattern, and the filename). Note that the four-argument case is equivalent to the one with two arguments, with the addition of a `-c` and a number.

If a `-c` is found, a double `shift` will reset the positional parameters to the two-argument state by removing the first two arguments, leaving only the pattern and file name.

To handle `-c`, simply test at the beginning of the script whether there are four arguments. If there are, test whether the first argument is `-c`. If `-c` is found, store the second argument in the variable `csize`, which is initialized to 5. If there are four arguments but `-c` isn't the first one or if there aren't four arguments, pass control on to the existing script.

```
csize=5
if [ $# -eq 4 ]
then
    if [ "$1" = '-c' ]
    then
        csize=$2
        shift ; shift
    fi
fi
```

A usage message is displayed if there are four arguments and the first one is not -c or there are other than two arguments when not specifying -c csize.

You need to make only one other change: substitute the variable csize for the constant 5. The final script is named cgrep3:

```
$ cat cgrep3
trap 'rm /tmp/cgrep.$$ 2> /dev/null; exit 1' 0 1 2 3
csize=5
if [ $# -eq 4 ]
then
    if [ "$1" = '-c' ]
    then
        csize=$2
        shift; shift
    fi
fi
case $# in
    2) pattern="$1"
       file="$2" ;;
    *) echo "Usage: $0 [-c ##] pattern file"
       exit 1 ;;
esac
clear=`tput clear`
if grep -n "$pattern" $file > /tmp/cgrep.$$
then
    for nbr in `cut -d':' -f1 /tmp/cgrep.$$`
    do
        echo $clear
        begin=`expr $nbr - $csize`
        if [ $begin -le 0 ]
        then
            begin=1
```

```
                fi
                end='expr $nbr + $csize'
                set 'wc -l $file'
                len=$1    # len (not $1) used to help document code
                if [ "$end" -gt "$len" ]
                then
                     end="$len"
                fi
                echo "$file: Lines $begin to $end (Match: Line $nbr)"
                echo
                sed -n "$begin,$end p" $file ¦ nl -v$begin  -s:
                echo "\nPress return to continue\c"
                read junk
        done
else
     echo "$pattern not found in $file"
fi
```

Summary

Although the UNIX System offers many tools and utility programs, the time inevitably comes when there is no command that does what you need. As this chapter has demonstrated, you can write your own tools and enhance them whenever you want. This flexibility is one of the strengths of the UNIX System.

An Accounts Receivable System

One of the most important jobs a business has is getting paid by the people who owe it money. Since the accepted practice in business is to extend credit terms to good customers, it is necessary to make sure that you get paid in a timely fashion. After all, you can't pay your rent with an IOU from Joe down the street.

To stay on top of a business, you have to keep records of what comes in, what goes out, and what is stored in the back room. Large companies use custom-written or off-the-shelf accounting packages. Not every business needs the expense, either human or computer, of accounting software. Instead, you can create your own business applications using UNIX tools and shell programming. This chapter demonstrates how to write an accounts receivable system using features provided by the UNIX System.

Setting Up Data Files

Accounts receivable (A/R), like many business applications, can be implemented with just two data files: a *code* file to hold the available categories and a *transaction* file to track the records of interest.

The Customer File

In an accounts receivable system, the code file contains customer information, with a unique code for each customer. The code, or customer, file contains line entries consisting of tilde-separated fields. In this system, the code file contains a customer code, the company name, and its address.

Other information specific to your business and customers can also be stored in the customer file, such as credit limit, product codes, and date of last order. In this A/R system, the customer file is stored in the file `cust.ar`.

To save space in this book, only two customers are in `cust.ar`:

```
$ cat cust.ar
acme~Acme Computers~803 Pine St.~Santa Cruz~CA~95062
primo~Primo Computer Systems~111 First St.~San Jose~CA~95131
```

The Transaction File

The transaction file holds the unpaid invoices. Each invoice is written to a single customer, and, thus, each entry in the transaction file is assigned a customer code. The purpose of the customer code is to associate the invoice with a customer.

An accounts receivable transaction occurs when you issue an invoice, receive a payment, or generate a debit or credit memo. A second file, `trans.ar`, holds the A/R transactions. It stores the customer code, transaction date, type, amount, and number. Additional information necessary to your business, such as purchase order number, delivery instructions, and shipping method, could be added to tailor this system to your needs. Each transaction is associated with the customer it involves through the customer code.

```
$ cat trans.ar
acme~90/01/03~i~20.00~1144
acme~90/01/13~d~23.32~1144
acme~90/02/03~c~3.32~1144
primo~90/02/03~i~223.32~1145
acme~90/03/03~i~523.32~1146
acme~90/03/08~p~40.00~1144
acme~90/03/14~p~523.32~1146
```

Note that the date is listed in year/month/day order. This ensures that the transactions will sort properly by date. Also, the code `i` represents an invoice; `p` is a payment; `c` is a credit memo; and `d` is a debit memo.

Support Scripts

Adding Entries

The A/R system needs the support of a number of shell scripts. One of them is the `add.cust` script, which adds customer entries to the `cust.ar` file. Because transactions are keyed by customer codes, these codes must be unique to prevent the wrong customer from being charged on an invoice. The `add.cust` script doesn't allow the user to enter an existing customer code and makes sure that added data is in the proper format.

```
$ cat add.cust
trap "rm /tmp/$$ 2> /dev/null; exit" 0 1 2 3
while true
do
    echo "Enter Customer code (Enter stop to quit): \c"
    read code
    if [ "$code" = 'stop' ]
    then
        exit
    fi
    if grep "^$code~" cust.ar > /tmp/$$
    then
        echo "\ncode $code already assigned to\n"
        tr '~' ' '
        \012' < /tmp/$$
        echo
        continue
    fi
    echo "Enter Customer Name: \c"
    read name
    echo "Enter Customer Street Address: \c"
    read ad
    echo "Enter Customer City: \c"
    read city
    echo "Enter Customer State: \c"
    read st
    echo "Enter Customer ZIP code: \c"
    read zip
    echo $code~$name~$ad~$city~$st~$zip >> cust.ar
    echo
done
```

If the user enters an existing code, the shell displays the entry matching that code.

```
$ add.cust
Enter Customer code (Enter stop to quit): acme

code acme already assigned to

acme
Acme Computers
803 Pine St
Santa Cruz
CA
95062

Enter Customer code (Enter stop to quit): stop
```

Note that `add.cust` doesn't ask the user whether the entry is correct or enable the user to correct mistakes. These features have been omitted to save space.

Entering Transaction Dates

One vital piece of information in an accounting system is the transaction date. The `get.date` script makes entering a date and verifying that it is valid easy. `get.date` is sent a prompt, which it prints on the terminal. `get.date` then reads a date in MM/DD/YY format from the standard input, verifies it, and, if valid, converts it to YY/MM/DD format and sends it to the standard output. If an entered date is invalid, `get.date` loops and reprompts until the user enters a valid date.

Since it is likely that the date for the current transaction is the day it is entered, `get.date` offers the user a default choice, the current date. If the user presses return at the prompt, `get.date` accepts the default value. Note that the default value is enclosed in brackets in the prompt.

`get.date` is designed to be used within an assignment. For example, the command `today=`get.date "Enter Today's Date"`` prompts the user to enter the current date and verifies it. Then the shell stores the entered date (in YY/MM/DD format) in `today`. Because `get.date` will be used inside backquotes, `get.date`'s standard output has been assigned to the variable. As a result, all the `echo` statements destined for the interactive user are redirected to the controlling terminal of the user, `/dev/tty`.

Note that get.date prefixes zero (0) to any single-digit day or month numbers. This ensures that months and days sort properly because 1 and 01 sort differently within the date format.

```
$ cat get.date
prompt="$*"    # save command-line arguments
default=`date "+%D`
while true
do
     echo "\n$prompt [$default]: \c" > /dev/tty
     read date
     if [ -z "$date" ]  # accept the default
     then
         date=$default
     fi
     #
     # Break entered date into arguments
     #
     oldifs="$IFS"
     IFS='/'
     set $date
     IFS="$oldifs"
     if [ $# -ne 3 ]
     then
         echo "Date format is MM/DD/YY" > /dev/tty
         continue
     else
         #
         # Validate date
         #
         month=$1
         day=$2
         year=$3
         #
         # For consistency, put a zero in front of
         # single digit days and months.
         #
         if echo $day ¦ grep '^[1-9]$' > /dev/null; then
             day=0$day
         fi
         if echo $month ¦ grep '^[1-9]$' > /dev/null; then
             month=0$month
```

```
fi
#
# Is month valid?
#
case $month in
        0[1-9]) ;;
        1[0-2]) ;;
        *) echo "Invalid date" > /dev/tty
           continue ;;
esac
#
# Is it leap year?
#
if expr $year % 4 = 0 > /dev/null
then
        maxfeb=29
else
        maxfeb=28
fi
#
# Do the days match the month?
#
case $month in
    11|04|06|09) if [ $day -gt 30 ]
                 then
                         echo "Invalid date" > /dev/tty
                         continue
                 fi ;;
    02) if [ $day -gt $maxfeb ]
        then
            echo "Invalid date" > /dev/tty
            continue
        fi ;;
    *) if [ $day -gt 31 ]
       then
           echo "Invalid date" > /dev/tty
           continue
       fi ;;
esac
fi
#
# Valid date, echo it out in YY/MM/DD format
#
```

```
        echo $year/$month/$day
        exit 0
done
```

Writing Transaction Scripts

Now that you have the data files set up, you need to write the script that gets the A/R transactions. In addition to reading in the transaction information, `get.ar.trans` must ensure that the entered customer code is valid. It does this by searching the `cust.ar` file for the entered customer code. If the shell finds the code, the customer name associated with it will be displayed so the user can check whether the customer code identifies the correct customer.

The commands that enter and verify the customer code are the following:

```
echo "Enter Customer code (Enter stop to quit): \c"
read code
if [ "$code" = 'stop' ]   # check for exit code
then
    exit
fi
#
# Verify code by searching the cust.ar file
#
if grep "^$code~" cust.ar > /tmp/$$
then
    echo "\nCustomer: \c"
    cut -f2 -d'~' /tmp/$$   # print out customer name
else
    echo "\007\nCustomer code: $code not found\n"
    continue
fi
rest of transaction entry script
```

The `cut` command prints only the customer's name. The value `\007`, in the `echo` command statement that prints the code that wasn't found, beeps the terminal's bell.

The `get.ar.inv` script reads the customer code, transaction date, amount due, and transaction number. As listed, `get.ar.inv` doesn't ask the user whether the entered data is correct or enable the user to change the data if an error is made. These features are omitted here to save space, although in a real application they should be included.

```
$ cat get.ar.inv
trap "rm /tmp/$$.temp 2> /dev/null; exit" 0 1 2 3
while true
do
    echo "Enter Customer code (Enter stop to quit): \c"
    read code
    if [ "$code" = 'stop' ]  # check for exit code
    then
        exit
    fi
    #
    # Verify code by searching the cust.ar file
    #
    if grep "^$code~" cust.ar > /tmp/$$
    then
        echo "\nCustomer: \c"
        cut -f2 -d'~' /tmp/$$  # print out customer name
    else
        echo "\007\nCustomer code: $code not found\n"
        continue
    fi
    date=`get.date "Enter transaction date (MM/DD/YY)"`
    echo "\nEnter transaction amount: \c"
    read amt
    echo "\nEnter transaction number: \c"
    read nbr
    # you should verify that the data are correct
    echo "$code~$date~i~$amt~$nbr" >> trans.ar
done
```

Note that get.ar.inv only gets invoices. Debit memos, credit memos, and payments are a bit more complicated and will be covered later in the chapter.

Retrieving Information

You now have the rudiments of an accounts receivable system: a customer list and a way to enter invoices. Getting information out of the A/R system is a straightforward task. For example, to print a list of customer codes and names, simply `cut` the first two fields from the `cust.ar` file and convert the separating tildes into tabs.

```
$ cut -d'~' -f1,2 cust.ar ¦ tr '~' '<tab>'
acme        Acme Computers
primo       Primo Computer Systems
```

By using different field numbers, you can print other combinations of data from the customer list.

Finding Transactions for a Single Customer

Another example of an A/R application is finding all the A/R transactions for a single customer, that is, a customer code. You simply search the `trans.ar` file for the transactions that start with the specified customer code.

```
$ cat print.ar.inv
trap "rm /tmp/$$ 2>/dev/null; exit" 0 1 2 3
if [ $# -eq 0 ]
then
    echo "List transactions for what customer code? \c"
    read codelist
else
    codelist="$*"
fi
for code in $codelist
do
    if grep "^$code~" trans.ar > /tmp/$$
    then
```

```
        echo "\nInvoices for: $code"
        echo "\nDate\t\tAmount\tNumber"
        awk -F~ '{print  $2 "~" $4 "~" $3 $5 }' /tmp/$$ |
        sort -t'~' +4 | tr '~' '<tab>'  # end of pipeline
    else
        echo "No invoices found for $code"
    fi
done
```

Because the `print.ar.inv` script will be used by accounting clerks, the output is formatted into a small table and sorted by invoice number. Incidentally, the number field is a combination of a transaction's type and number; thus `i1144` is the invoice for transaction numbered 1144.

```
$ print.ar.inv
List invoices for what customer code? acme

Invoices for: acme

Date            Amount    Number
90/01/03        20.00     i1144
90/01/13        23.32     d1144
90/02/03        3.32      c1144
90/03/08        40.00     p1144
90/03/03        523.32    i1146
90/03/14        523.32    p1146
```

Note that `print.ar.inv` prompts for a customer code if one is not on the command line. There are several similar scripts that you can write to extract other information from the A/R files.

Establishing a User Interface

Before you begin writing more sophisticated A/R scripts, you must deal with an essential problem of all shell scripts: The shell lacks an easy-to-understand user interface.

An integral part of any accounting system is how it interacts with the user. A good interface can minimize data entry errors and improve productivity. A poorly designed interface simply gets in the way, making things worse.

Let's begin by designing the interface that the A/R scripts will use. First, because the system is based on the use of customer codes, a script should always verify that the system "knows" an entered code, that is, the code has been assigned to a known customer. Also, when the user enters a code, the script should display the data it represents as a visual check for the user.

Often the data required by an accounting application can be "preset" in the form of default entries. An example is the transaction date. Odds are that it's today's date. To make the system easier to use, it should present defaults whenever reasonable ones are available.

A third aspect of our accounting interface is the verification of data. The program must test for obvious errors in any information that the user enters. Most important, the user must certify that all data is correct before it is stored in a file. Remember, you are depending on these scripts to keep track of the lifeblood of your business.

Aside from actually getting paid, the most important function of an accounts receivable system is keeping the information on invoices current. You must post payments and record any invoice adjustments through the use of debit and credit memos. Incidentally, you use a credit memo to decrease and a debit memo to increase the amount of an invoice. A credit memo is issued when someone returns an item they were billed for on the invoice. A credit memo decreases the invoice amount. A debit memo is issued to increase the invoice amount. A debit would be issued to correct an error made when the discount allowed on an item was calculated incorrectly.

Invoices enter the accounts receivable system when you enter them into the `trans.ar` file (with a program like `get.ar.trans`). From then on, anything that affects that invoice is recorded with additional transactions. In general, one of three things happens to an invoice: it gets paid (payment), adjusted downward (credit memo), or adjusted upward (debit memo). The `pay.inv` script handles all of these transactions.

An accounts receivable transaction contains five pieces of information: a customer code, transaction date, type, amount, and invoice number. The entry of these fields is a common part of any accounts receivable script. As a result, it's best to write individual data entry scripts that prompt for, test, and display each field entered into the `trans.ar` file.

The strings printed by these scripts will be stored in variables in the main data entry script. Table 22.1 lists the scripts that will handle each field in a transaction.

Table 22.1. *A/R transaction scripts.*

Type of information	Script
Customer code	`get.custcode`
Transaction date	`get.date`
Transaction type	`get.transcode`
Transaction amount	`get.amt`
Invoice number inside	`pay.inv`

The simplest script to write is `get.amt`. It is passed a single argument, the default amount, which it displays in a prompt. If the user presses Return only, the default is accepted and echoed back to the standard output; otherwise, the (default) entered value is returned.

```
$ cat get.amt
echo "\nEnter transaction amount [$1]: \c" > /dev/tty
read entry
if [ -z "$entry" ]
then  # test for default
    echo $1
else
    echo $entry
fi
```

The command that will be assigned a transaction amount to a variable is `amt=`get.amt $amt`.

Because `get.amt` is designed to be used inside back quotes, you must be careful not to print the prompts to the standard output (or else they'll be stored in the variable). Instead, the output for the user is sent to `/dev/tty`.

Getting Customer and Transaction Information

Part of getting a customer code involves verifying that the entered code is valid. Thus, `get.custcode` reads the entered code and then searches the `cust.ar` file for it. Also, the script prints the name of the customer that matches the code, so the user can see that the proper code was entered. The script loops until a valid customer code is entered. The command to enter a customer code in the main data entry script is `code=`get.custcode $code`.

```
$ cat get.custcode
trap "rm /tmp/$$ 2> /dev/null; exit" 0 1 2 3
while true  # loop until a valid code is entered
do
    echo "\nEnter Customer code [$1]: \c" > /dev/tty
    read code
    if [ -z "$code" ]  # accept default?
    then
        code=$1
    fi
    if grep "^$code~" cust.ar > /tmp/$$
    then
        echo "\nCustomer: \c" > /dev/tty
        cut -f2 -d'~' /tmp/$$ > /dev/tty
        echo $code  # code returned  by script
        exit
    else
        echo "Code: $code not found\n" > /dev/tty
        continue  # get another code
    fi
done
```

pay.inv accepts three types of transactions: payments, debit memos, and credit memos. The get.transcode script obtains a transaction code. It lists the possible transaction types; reads a response; tests it for being a p, d, or c; and prints it.

```
$ cat get.transcode
while true # loop until a valid type entered
do
    echo "\np - payment" > /dev/tty
    echo "d - debit memo" > /dev/tty
    echo "c - credit memo" > /dev/tty
    echo "\nTransaction type: [$1] \c" > /dev/tty
    read type
    if [ -z "$type" ]  # accept default?
    then
        type=$1
    fi
    case $type in
        [pdc]) echo $type # type returned
               exit ;;
```

```
        *) echo "Enter p, d, c only" > /dev/tty
    esac
done
```

Earlier the `get.date` script was shown. As you recall, the `get.date` script prompts for, reads in, and tests the transaction date. Because `get.date` takes its prompt from the command line, it is flexible enough to be used in both `get.ar.trans` and `pay.inv`. `get.date` was listed previously, so the script will not be listed here.

So far, the A/R data entry support scripts have terminated when the user entered stop at the first prompt. Thus, instead of writing a separate "get-invoice-number" script, those commands will be included directly in `pay.inv` so the loop control can be made part of that prompt.

```
echo "\n\nEnter invoice number (stop to quit): \c"
read inbr
if [ "$inbr" = 'stop' ]; then
    exit   # terminate script
fi
```

Because invoices are identified by number, `pay.inv` reads the invoice number of the transaction first. It then checks whether any transactions exist for the indicated invoice number. If not, it displays a message and the script loops, reprompting for another number, because you can't pay an invoice that hasn't been entered yet.

If the script finds transactions for an invoice, it should list them so the user can verify that this is the correct invoice number and check the outstanding balance. After displaying this information, the script asks whether this is the correct invoice number.

Displaying Transactions by Invoice Number

Displaying transactions by invoice number is another common accounts receivable task, and we will write a separate script to do it. In addition to listing the individual transactions, the script should also calculate a total.

The `inv.calc` script contains an `awk` program that lists all the transactions for a specific invoice number, accumulating a total based on the transaction type of each one: payments or credit memos are subtracted from the total while invoices and debit memos are added to it. `inv.calc` takes input in the format of transactions from the `trans.ar` file.

$ **cat inv.calc**
```
awk  -F~ ' BEGIN {printf "\n%s\t%10s\t%s\t%s\n",\
        "Code", "Date", "Type", "Amount" }
    { if ($3 == "p" || $3 == "c")
        total -= $4  # payment or credit memo
      else
        total += $4
      printf "%s\t%10s\t%s\t%8.2f\n" ,$1,$2,$3,$4
    }
    END { printf "\nTotal\t\t\t\t%8.2f\n", total }' $1
```

Because all data going into the A/R systems must be verified, you need to write the `inv.verify` script to display the information entered and to ask the user whether it is correct. One way to get the data you need verified to `inv.verify` is to pass it via command-line arguments. Another, simpler method is to export the data to the inv.verify script.

$ **cat inv.verify**
```
# assume that code, date, type, and amount are exported
while true
do
    echo "\nCode: $code"
    echo "Date: $date"
    echo "Type: $type"
    echo "Amount: $amt"
    echo "\nIs this correct? (y/n) \c"
    read answer
    case $answer in
        [Yy]*) exit 0 ;;
        [Nn]*) exit 1 ;;
    esac
done
```

Note that `inv.verify` succeeds (`exit 0`) if the user says the transaction is correct and fails (`exit 1`) otherwise.

When assembled, the `pay.inv` script gets an invoice number, lists the related transactions (if there are any), then prompts for and reads the other transaction information. The individual `get` scripts prompt for each part of a transaction. Default values for customer

code and transaction date are set before the data entry scripts are
called. Note that the default customer code is taken from the first
transaction identified by the entered invoice number with the command code=`sed -n 1p /tmp/$$ ¦ cut -d~ -f1`.

```
$ cat pay.inv
trap 'rm /tmp/$$* 2>/dev/null; exit' 0 1 2 3
amt=0
export code date type amt  # used in inv.verify
clear=`tput clear`
while true
do
    echo $clear
    echo "Enter invoice number (stop to quit): \c"
    read inbr
    if [ "$inbr" = 'stop' ]
    then
        exit   # terminate script
    fi
    #
    # Are there any transactions for this invoice number?
    #
    if grep "~$inbr$" trans.ar > /tmp/$$
    then
        #
        # Amount due is saved for later
        #
        inv.calc /tmp/$$ ¦ tee /tmp/$$.1
        #
        # Verify that this is correct invoice number
        #
        echo "\nEnter a transaction? (y/n) \c"
        read answer
        case $answer in
            [Nn]*) continue ;;
        esac
        #
        # Set up default customer code
        #
        code=`sed -n 1p /tmp/$$ ¦ cut -d~ -f1`
        while true # data entry loop
```

```
    do
        code=`get.custcode "$code"`
        date=`get.date "Enter Transaction Date"`
        type=`get.transcode "$type"`
        echo
        cat /tmp/$$.1 # display amount due
        amt=`get.amt $amt`
        if inv.verify
        then
            echo $code~$date~$type~$amt~$inbr >> trans.ar
            break  # entry loop exit
        else
            echo "\nTerminate this transaction? (y/n) \c"
            read answer
            case $answer in
                [Yy]*) break ;;
                *) continue ;;
            esac
        fi
    done
    amt=0  # reset defaults
    type=''
else
    echo "\007Invoice not found"
fi
done
```

To minimize mistakes, pay.inv lists this invoice's transactions before the user enters the amount of the current transaction. Instead of reexecuting inv.calc, pay.inv stores the output of inv.calc in a temporary file, /tmp/$$.1, and simply prints its contents. Another temporary file, /tmp/$$, is used to store all the transactions found matching the invoice number so that trans.ar doesn't have to be searched twice (once by grep and once by inv.calc).

Here is the output of pay.inv as invoice number 1145 is paid:

$ **pay.inv**

screen clears

Enter invoice number (stop to quit): **1145**

```
Code           Date        Type      Amount
primo       90/02/03        i          223.32


Total                                  223.32


Enter a transaction? (y/n) y


Enter Customer code [primo]: <Return>


Customer: Primo Computer Systems


Enter Transaction Date [90/03/02]: <Return>


p - payment
d - debit memo
c - credit memo


Transaction type: [] p


Code           Date        Type      Amount
primo       90/02/03        i          223.32


Total                                  223.32


Enter transaction amount [0]: 223.32


Code: primo
Date: 90/03/02
Type: p
Amount: 223.32


Is this correct? (y/n) y


screen clears


Enter invoice number (stop to quit): stop
```

Printing Customer Account Summary Statements

One important feature of an accounts receivable system is the capability to print statements that summarize a customer's account information. Not only do customers expect monthly statements, but businesses also often use statements as their payment record. Account statements are also a good management tool. One of the easiest ways to go broke is to give too much credit to the wrong companies.

Designing the Format

The first step in creating customer account statements is designing their format. One approach is to use a preprinted form supplied by a stationery store. However, one of the most time-consuming tasks in business programming is trying to write programs to match the format of a preprinted business form. A better idea is to design your own statement and then write a script to print the data in that format.

The customer statement should be simple to create and understand. Ours will list the company's name, the statement date, and, in separate sections, the current transactions. The debits and credits will be listed together, followed by the invoices, and then the payments. Here is what the statement for Acme Computers would look like:

```
Statement for Acme Computers
Statement date: 3/31/90

Debit and Credit memos

  2/ 3/90      c-1144              3.32
  1/13/90      d-1144             23.32

Invoices

  1/ 3/90      1144               20.00
  3/ 3/90      1146              523.32

Payments

  3/ 8/90      1144               40.00
  3/14/88      1146              523.32

Total Due                         0.00
```

A statement shows only the account data for a single customer. Thus, you want to process only a single customer's data when preparing a statement. Instead of looking through the entire `trans.ar` file for the customer's code, use `grep` to locate all transaction file entries starting with that customer's code.

A customer's transactions do not appear in `trans.ar` in any particular order. However, the customer statement prints information by credits and debits, invoices, and then payments. Note that this is the order a customer's entries will be in when the transaction file is sorted by the contents of field 3!

Thus, after `grep` finds all of a customer's transactions, you pipe them into `sort` to put them in statement order. In addition to sorting by transaction code, you should generate a secondary sort for dates to list them in date order within each statement category.

The transaction date is a problem. The date is stored in YY/MM/DD format to ensure proper sorting. However, it is better to use the conventional MM/DD/YY format on the statement. You can convert the date format by pipelining `sort`'s output into a `while` loop that sends the date through a one-line `awk` program to rearrange it. For example, the following code is stored in the file `trans.test`:

```
$ cat trans.test
oldifs="$IFS"
grep "^acme~" trans.ar ¦ sort -t~ +2 -3 +1 -2   ¦
while read line
do
    IFS='~'
    set $line
    IFS="$oldifs"
    date=`echo $2 ¦ awk -F/ '{print $2 "/" $3 "/" $1 }'`
    echo $1~$date~$3~$4~$5
done
$ trans.test
acme~02/03/90~c~3.32~1144
acme~01/13/90~d~23.32~1144
acme~01/03/90~i~20.00~1144
acme~03/03/90~i~523.32~1146
acme~03/08/90~p~40.00~1144
acme~03/14/90~p~523.32~1146
```

Printing the Statement

Once the transactions are sorted, an `awk` program can be written to print the statement. Because the transactions are sorted by transaction code, a new section is identified when the transaction code changes.

When the shell finds the first entry in each section (debits and credits, invoices, payments), `awk` has to print a heading. The rest of the `awk` program keeps track of totals and prints entries. The `build.stmt` script is an `awk` program that creates our A/R statement.

```
$ cat build.stmt
    awk -F~ ' {
        #
        # Check for credit or debit memos
        #
        if ( $3 == "c" || $3 == "d" ) {
            if (cflag != 1) {   # first entry?
                cflag = 1
                printf "Debit and Credit memos\n\n"
            }
            #
            # total up credit/debit memos
            #
            if ( $3 == "c")
                dctotal -= $4
            else
                dctotal += $4
            #
            # print credit/debit entry
            #
            printf "%s        %s%s        %8.2f\n",\
                    $2, $3, $5, $4
        }
        #
        # Check for invoice entries
        #
        else if ($3 == "i") {
            if (iflag != 1) {   # first entry?
                iflag = 1
                printf "\n\nInvoices\n\n"
            }
            itotal+= $4
```

```
            printf "%s          %s          %8.2f\n", $2, $5, $4
    }
    #
    # Check for payments
    #
    else {
        if (pflag != 1) {
            pflag = 1
            printf "\n\nPayments\n\n"
        }
        ptotal += $4
        printf "%s          %s          %8.2f\n", $2, $5, $4
    }
}
#
# When done with transactions, print total
#
END { printf "\nTotal Due                      %8.2f\n",\
            dctotal + itotal - ptotal
```

Remember that `awk` supports both numeric and character variables. The context of the variable's usage is what determines how `awk` evaluates a variable. This can be a problem when comparing something to a string constant. If you do not quote the constant, say in the expression $3 == i, `awk` will assume it is a variable (which is unassigned), and the expression will have a meaningless result. Instead, you must quote string constants with double quotes. Thus, the correct expression is $3 == "i".

The `build.stmt` script reads the transactions, already selected and sorted, as input and sends the resulting statement to the standard output.

A script to drive `build.stmt` should provide a useful interface for the statement-printing application. The driver script, called `mk.stmt`, prompts for, reads, and tests the customer code; gets the customer name for this listed code; prints the first two lines of the statement (customer name and today's date); and then runs the pipeline that prints this customer's statement. This script will loop until the user enters `stop` as the customer code.

```
$ cat mk.stmt
oldifs="$IFS"
clear=`tput clear`
```

```
oldifs="$IFS"
while true
do
    echo "$clear\n\n\n" > /dev/tty
    echo "Customer code (stop to quit): \c" > /dev/tty
    read code
    if [ "$code" = "stop" ]
    then
        exit
    elif customer=`grep "^$code~" cust.ar`
    then
        IFS='~'
        set $customer
        IFS="$oldifs"
        echo "Statement for $2"
        echo "Statement date: `date +%D`\n"
        grep "^$code~" trans.ar | sort -t~ +2 -3 +1 -2 |
        while read line
        do
            IFS='~'
            set $line
            IFS="$oldifs"
            date=`echo $2 | awk -F/ '{print $2 "/" $3 "/" $1 }'`
            echo $1~$date~$3~$4~$5
        done |
        build.stmt     # end of pipeline
    else
        echo "\007Code: $code not found" > /dev/tty
    fi
    echo "\nPress return to continue: \c" > /dev/tty
    read junk
    echo '\014\c'  # \014 is formfeed character
done
```

To get the customer's name, the shell searches the cust.ar file for the entered code. It then separates the located entry at the tildes with set, and the second positional parameter contains the customer name. After it tests the customer code and retrieves the name, the pipeline searches for and sorts this customer's transactions and then prints the resulting statement.

mk.stmt is written so that the statement printed by build.stmt is sent to the standard output of mk.stmt. This design enables a user to print statements to a file, the terminal, to the printer, or into a pipeline. This increases the script's flexibility. To separate statements, the `mk.stmt` prints a formfeed (`echo '\014\c'`) after each statement.

Removing Invoices

Once `awk` prints a customer statement, you should remove from the `trans.ar` file the invoices that have been paid in full. The approach for removing lines from a file is to create a `sed` command file that lists the lines to be deleted and then runs `sed` to perform the deletions in one pass through the file.

To implement the `del.inv` script, `awk` is again called on to process the transaction file. This time, `awk` determines the total due for each unique invoice number in the file. A deleting entry is written to a `sed` command file for those invoices whose total due is 0.

To determine the total of transaction numbers, `awk` first sorts the `trans.ar` file by transaction number. Then it calculates the transaction's total due by adding the invoices and debit memos and subtracting the payments and credit memos. If the total is 0 (or the floating point equivalent), all the transactions with this number should be deleted.

`awk`'s input is the transaction list in numeric order. By simply keeping track of the last entry's number, `awk` can determine when all the transactions for a specific number have been totaled. This is done by testing whether the number of the current transaction (in `$5`) is the same as the number of the previous transaction (in `invnbr`). If the following test

```
if (invnbr == $5)
```

is true, the transaction total is augmented by this transaction's amount. If the test is false, there are no more transactions for this number and you must test whether the total is 0. If it is, format a delete command for all of this number's transactions.

Note that the total being kept by `awk` is a floating point value. It is possible that rounding errors might affect the direct comparison to 0. Thus, the following test will be used to check whether an invoice has been paid in full:

```
if (total > -.01 && total < .01)
```

One last point about this awk program. For the first transaction, the awk variable invnbr is not set. Thus, the first transaction will fail the test

```
if (invnbr == $5)
```

causing it to print out a bogus delete entry. To correct for this boundary condition, awk expands the logical test to check whether the record number (NR) is 1.

```
if (invnbr == $5 || NR == 1)
```

A similar problem exists for the last invoice. The only place awk can perform a test for the last invoice's total is in an END action. This test has been added to the awk program.

```
sort -t~ +4 trans.ar |
awk -F~ '{
    if (invnbr == $5 || NR == 1) {
        if ( $3 == "c" || $3 == "p" )
            total -= $4
        else
            total += $4
    }
    else { # first transaction of new invoice
        if (total > -.01 && total < .01)
            printf "/~%d$/d\n", invnbr
        invnbr = $5
        total = 0
    }
}
END {
    if (total > -.01 && total < .01)
        printf "/~%d$/d\n", invnbr
}'
```

After the awk program, the script must check whether any invoices are to be deleted (which depends on whether there was any output from the awk command). If so, sed does the job, and the result is stored in a temporary file and then moved over to the new trans.ar file.

If no invoices are to be deleted, the script says so. The final script is named del.inv.

```
$ cat del.inv
trap "rm /tmp/$$ 2>/dev/null; exit" 0 1 2 3
sort -t~ +4 trans.ar |
awk -F~ '{
    if (invnbr == $5 || NR == 1) {
        if ( $3 == "c" || $3 == "p" )
            total -= $4
        else
            total += $4
    }
    else { # first transaction of new invoice
        if (total > -.01 && total < .01)
            printf "/~%d$/d\n", invnbr
        invnbr = $5
        total = 0
    }
}
END {
    if (total > -.01 && total < .01)
        printf "/~%d$/d\n", invnbr
}' > /tmp/$$
#
# Any to delete?
#
if [ -s /tmp/$$ ]; then
    trap '' 1 2 3   # so interrupts won't terminate
    sed -f /tmp/$$ trans.ar > /tmp/$$.1
    mv /tmp/$$.1 trans.ar
    rm /tmp/$$ 2> /dev/null
else
    echo "No invoices to delete"
fi
```

Expanding the A/R System

Taken as a whole, these scripts provide a minimal accounts receivable tracking system. Where to go from here? There are several choices.

At minimum, you should add a menu interface for the scripts so that accounting clerks can use them without having to interact with UNIX too much.

The A/R system could be expanded to include other A/R functions such as editing the transaction and code data files, generating the invoices, printing payment reminder notices, and tracking customer credit limits. The A/R script even can be recoded into a compiled programming language, like C or COBOL, which will speed it up and provide expanded capabilities.

Summary

Whether used as is or expanded to handle your business needs, the A/R scripts provide a good example of how to write real applications with shell scripts. Unless an application is clearly outside the scope of the UNIX tools due to huge data requirements or specialized programming or interface requirements, always consider implementing the first draft of an application with UNIX tools. Shell scripts not only enable you to get the application up and running quickly, but they also help you refine your design.

APPENDIXES

Bourne Shell Quick Reference

File-Matching Metacharacters

Metacharacter	Meaning
[...]	Range of characters
[!...]	Characters not matching the listed range
?	Any single character
*	Zero or more of any character

Redirection Metacharacters

Metacharacter	Meaning
>	Overwriting output redirection
>>	Appending output redirection
<	Input redirection
<<	In-line input redirection
2>	Overwriting output redirection for standard error
2>>	Appending output redirection for standard error

Process Execution Metacharacters

Metacharacter	Meaning
$a \mid b$	Send the output of a to the input of b
a &	Run a in the background
$a ; b$	Execute a; when finished, execute b
$a \mid\mid b$	Execute a; if it fails, execute b
a && b	Execute a; if it succeeds, execute b
(a)	Execute a in a subshell
{ a }	Execute a in the current shell

Quoting Metacharacters

Metacharacter	Meaning
' . . . '	Ignore all characters inside quotes
" . . . "	Interpret $, `, and \ (in front of $ and `), ignore all others
`a`	Execute a and replace the ` . . . ` with its standard output
\	Ignore the single character that follows the backslash

Preset Shell Variables

Variable	Meaning
$$	The current process ID
$#	The number of positional parameters
$?	The exit status of the last (nonbackground) command executed
$!	Process ID of last background process executed
$-	Current shell's command-line arguments
$*	All the positional parameters

`"$@"`	All the positional parameters individually quoted
`$0`	Program name for this process
`$n`	Where *n* is 1 to 9, the first nine positional parameters

Special Environment Variables

Variable	Meaning
`CDPATH`	Search path for the `cd` command
`HOME`	Pathname of home directory
`IFS`	Characters used by the shell to separate arguments
`MAIL`	Pathname to your mail file
`MAILCHECK`	How often, in seconds, to check for mail
`PATH`	Command search path
`PS1`	The shell's primary prompt
`PS2`	The shell's secondary prompt
`SHELL`	Pathname of the shell to use

Variable Evaluation Options

Variable	Meaning
`$var`	The value stored in *var*
`${var}`	The value stored in *var*
`${var:-str}`	The value of *var* if it is set and not empty, *str* otherwise
`${var:=str}`	The value of *var* if it is set and not empty, otherwise *var* set to *str*
`${var:?str}`	The value of *var* if set and not empty, otherwise print *str* and exit
`$(var:+str}`	The value of *str* if *var* is set and not empty, nothing otherwise

test Arguments

String Tests

Test	Meaning
a	Is *a* nonempty?
a = *b*	Does *a* match *b*?
a != *b*	Does *a* not match *b*?
-n *a*	Does *a* contain characters?
-z *a*	Is *a* empty?

Numeric (Integer) Tests

Test	Meaning
a -eq *b*	Is *a* equal to *b*?
a -ne *b*	Is *a* not equal to *b*?
a -lt *b*	Is *a* less than *b*?
a -le *b*	Is *a* less than or equal to *b*?
a -gt *b*	Is *a* greater than *b*?
a -ge *b*	Is *a* greater than or equal to *b*?

File Tests

Test	Meaning
-b *filename*	Is *filename* a block special file?
-c *filename*	Is *filename* a character special file?
-d *filename*	Is *filename* a directory?
-f *filename*	Does *filename* exist?
-g *filename*	Does *filename* have set-group-id set?
-k *filename*	Does *filename* have sticky bit set?
-p *filename*	Is *filename* a named pipe?

-r *filename*	Is *filename* readable by this process?
-s *filename*	Does *filename* have a nonzero length?
-t *fd*	Is file descriptor *fd* associated with a terminal?
-u *filename*	Does *filename* have set-user-id set?
-w *filename*	Is *filename* writable by this process?
-x *filename*	Is *filename* executable by this process?

Shell Invocation Options

Option	Meaning
--	Do not view following arguments as shell options
-a	Automatically export any variable that is modified or created
-c *str*	Take commands from *str*
-e	Exit immediately if a command fails (has a nonzero exit status)
-f	Disable file-matching metacharacters
-h	Locate the commands inside a function definition when a function is defined (normally the commands aren't located until the function is executed)
-i	The shell is interactive; ignore *interrupts*
-k	Let variables assigned anywhere on a command line be passed to a new process, not just those assigned before the command name
-n	Read commands but do not execute them (good for checking syntax)
-r	Start a restricted shell
-s	Read commands from the standard input; treat command-line arguments as positional parameters to the shell
-t	Exit after reading and executing one command
-u	Make evaluating an unset variable an error
-v	Print input as the shell reads it
-x	Print command lines as they are executed (good for debugging)

Other Characters Recognized by the Shell

Character	Meaning
:	Execute no command, successful exit
#	Text following is a comment
. *file*	Execute commands in *file* in the current shell

Shell Programming Keywords

Keyword	Meaning
break	Terminate a loop
break *n*	Terminate *n* enclosing loops
continue	Restart loop
continue *n*	Restart *n*th enclosing loop
exit	Terminate this process
exit *n*	Terminate this process with exit status *n*
export	Show list of exported variables
export *var*	Make *var* an environmental variable
return	Exit function (uses exit status of last command executed)
return *n*	Exit function with exit status *n*
shift	Move positional parameters "down one"
shift *n*	Move positional parameters "down *n*"
trap *args signal*	Perform listed commands if listed signals occur
wait	Wait for all the child processes to terminate

Built-In Shell Commands

Command	Meaning
cd *dir*	Change to directory *dir*
echo *str*	Send *str* to the standard output
eval *cmd*	Execute *cmd* after processing it with the shell
exec *cmd*	Replace current process with *cmd*

newgrp *grp*	Change current group-ID to *grp*
pwd	Print the pathname of the current directory
read *x*	Read a line from the standard input and store it in *x*
type *cmd*	Print what is executed if cmd is entered as a command
ulimit	Print the maximum number of (512-byte size) file blocks that this process can write
umask	Default file creation mask

B

Regular Expressions Quick Reference

In the following tables, *a*, *b*, and *re* represent any regular expression and *c* represents a character.

Characters

Character	Meaning
c	The character *c*, if *c* is a nonregular expression character
c	The character *c*, if *c* is a regular expression character

Wildcard Matches

Wildcard	Meaning
[. . .]	Match any one of the characters inside the brackets
[^ . . .]	Match any of the characters not listed inside the brackets
.	Any single character
re*	Zero or more of *re*

Positional Matching

Character	Meaning
^	Start of the line
$	End of the line

Bracketed Regular Expressions

Expression	Meaning
re\ { *min, max*\ }	At least *min* and at most *max* matches of *re*
\ (*re*\ )	Put the characters matching *re* into the next register
\ *num*	The contents of register *num* (1-9 available)

Extended Regular Expressions

Expression	Meaning
re+	One or more matches to *re*
re?	Zero or one match of *re*
a⎮*b*	A match of either *a* or *b*
(. . .)	Treat whatever is inside parentheses as a single regular expression

C

Bibliography

The common reference I used was the UNIX System V manual. In additon, I was constantly looking up information in a variety of books. Here is a list of the books that always seemed to be stacked up by my terminal.

Arthur, Lowell Jay. *UNIX Shell Programming*. New York, NY: John Wiley and Sons, 1986.

Bach, Maurice J. *The Design of the UNIX Operating System*. Englewood Cliffs, NJ: Prentice-Hall, 1986.

Bourne, S.R. *The UNIX System*. Reading, MA: Addison-Wesley, 1983.

Dougherty, Dale, and Tim O'Reilly. *UNIX Text Processing*. Indianapolis, IN: Howard W. Sams, 1987.

Haviland, Keith, and Ben Salama. *UNIX System Programming*. Reading, MA: Addison-Wesley, 1987.

Kernighan, Brian W., and Rob Pike. *The UNIX Programming Environment*. Englewood Cliffs, NJ: Prentice-Hall, 1984.

Kochan, Steve, and Patrick Wood. *UNIX Shell Programming*. Hasbrouck Heights, NJ: Hayden Book Company, 1985.

Lapin, J.E. *Portable C and UNIX System Programming*. Englewood Cliffs, NJ: Prentice-Hall, 1987.

Libes, Don, and Sandy Ressler. *Life with UNIX*. Englewood Cliffs, NJ: Prentice-Hall, 1989.

McGilton, Henry, and Rachel Morgan. *Introducing the UNIX System*. New York, NY: McGraw-Hill, 1983.

Sage, Russell. *Tricks of the UNIX Masters*. Indianapolis, IN: Howard W. Sams & Co., 1987.

Thomas, Rebecca, and Rik Farrow. *UNIX Administration Guide for System V*. Englewood Cliffs, NJ: Prentice-Hall, 1989.

D

Answers to Hands-on Exercises

Chapter 2

2.1   Because you used >, the output overwrites the file and only the current time is stored in `login.time`.

2.2   The error redirection applies to the process running `cat`. However, it is the shell that encounters the error since it can't connect `badfile` to the process's standard input, because `badfile` doesn't exist. Thus, the error is sent to the shell's standard error, which in this case is the terminal. Note that `errfile` does not get created because the input redirection error occurs before the shell gets to the `2>`. Further, the `cat` command is not executed.

2.3   The first command, `who > junk`, overwrites whatever was stored in the file `junk` with the current user list. The second command, `cat`, reads its standard input, which was set to the file `junk` when the subshell was created, and prints the output of `who`, which was just deposited in `junk`. The third command overwrites `junk` with the current date. The fourth command, `cat`, sends what's currently in `junk` to its standard output (the terminal), which prints the current date. Note that if the file `junk` doesn't exist when the command is executed, the entire command terminates without starting because a nonexistent file cannot be an input stream.

2.4a   The `cat msgs` command is put in the background and will probably fail (this depends on what files are in the current directory) and print `cat: cannot open msgs`. The part of the file name after the `&` is a legal UNIX command that runs `mail` and sends the output to the file `tom`.

2.4b   The `cat` command will probably fail and print `cat: cannot open ideas`. The shell views the rest of the file name (after the `;`) as a command, but first must check whether the file name matches the pattern. Any file that matches `ch.[1-3]` is executed; otherwise, the shell tries to execute `ch.[1-3]`. Any command that is executed should fail either because no file matches (error message: `ch.[1-3]: not found`) or the file name matched does not have executable permission (error message: *filename*`: execute permission denied`).

2.4c   The shell generates an error without executing any part of this command and prints the error message `syntax error: '(' unexpected`. The error is caused by not having a command terminator before the `(`.

2.5a   `ls file*`

2.5b   `ls file\*`
         `ls 'file*'`
         `ls file[*]`

2.5c   `ls file[\-13]`
         `ls file['-13']`

2.5d   `ls xx???`

2.5e   `ls xx[\&\'\]]yy`

2.6   The file name pattern used by the shell is `xx`, followed by `[[` (a `[` inside `[]`), followed by `]yy`. Although no file is named `xx[]yy`, the shell passes along the entered pattern, which `ls` can't find.

Chapter 4

4.1   Every phone number has a - as the second character so
         `$ grep 4- phone.list`
         also works.

4.2   Use the `-v` option:
         `$ grep -v '<tab>4' phone.list ¦ grep 6`

4.3   `(grep ', T' phone.list ; grep ', S' phone.list) > temp`
         `grep '<tab>5' temp ; grep 8 temp`

Chapter 5

5.1   grep ', ...<tab>' phone.list
      Note that the pattern is a comma, a space, three dots, and a tab.

5.2   grep '8.$' phone.list
      or
      grep '8[0-9]$' phone.list

5.3   grep '<tab>[2-5]' phone.list
      or
      grep '[2-5]-' phone.list

5.4   grep ', [C-R]' phone.list

5.5   grep '[2-5]-...[567]$' phone.list

5.6   grep '[^567]$' phone.list

5.7   grep '^[J-Z].*[2368]$' phone.list

5.8   grep '[789]\{2,4\}' phone.list

5.9   grep '^....., .\{3,4\} <tab>' phone.list
      or
      grep '^[A-Za-z]\{5\}, [A-Za-z]\{3,4\} <tab>' phone.list

5.10 grep ', T.* <tab>[^46]' phone.list
      or
      grep ', T.*[^46]-' phone.list

5.11 grep ', [A-Z].*[A-Z].*\2<tab>' phone.list

5.12 grep '\([0-9]\).*\1' phone.list

Chapter 6

6.1   sed 's/Brown/Browne/' phone.list
      sed '4/s/Brown/Browne/' phone.list
      sed '/Brown/s//Browne/' phone.list

6.2   It changes only a 2 at the end of a line into a 3 in lines 2 through 4.
      Note that the phone number for Chris Stair remains unchanged
      because it is in line 5.

6.3   sed 's/[0-9]-/X/' phone.list

6.4   sed 's/, .*<tab>/<tab>/' phone.list

6.5   sed 's/<tab>/<tab>Phone: /' phone.list

6.6   `sed 's/^\(.\).*, /\1/' phone.list`

6.7   `sed 's/^\(.\).*, \(.\).*<tab>/\1 \2         /' phone.list`

6.8   `sed 's/<tab>\(.\)\(.*\)/<tab>\1\2 (Bldg \1)/' phone.list`

6.9   `sed '/[237]-/d' phone.list`
    or
    `grep -v '[237]-' phone.list`

Chapter 7

7.1   `awk '{print $1, $2 "<tab>phone:", $3}' phone.list`

7.2   `awk '/<tab>[456]/{print $1, "(" $2 ")<tab>" $3}' phone.list`

7.3   `awk '$3 ~ /^5/ ¦¦ $3 ~ /5$/' phone.list`

7.4   `awk '$1 ~ /...../ && $2 ~ /..../' phone.list`

7.5   `sed 's/, \(.\).*/ \1./' phone.list ¦`
    `awk '{print "_____", $2, $1}'`

7.6   `awk ' /[45]-/{print $2, $1 "<tab>73" $3}' phone.list ¦`
    `sed 's/,//'`

Chapter 8

8.1   `sort +2.3 phone.list`

8.2   `sort +2.7 -3 membership`
    or
    `sort -t- +1 membership`

8.3   `sort +2 -2.4 membership`

8.4   `sort +2 -2.4 +1 membership`

Chapter 9

9.1   `ls -s ¦ sed 1d ¦ sort -r +4`

9.2   `ls -l ¦ sort +4`

9.3   `ls -l ¦ sort +4 -5 +8`

9.4   `ls -l ¦ awk '$5 > 10000'`

9.5   `grep ', [a-zA-Z.]* [a-zA-Z. ]*<tab>' phone.list.2`

9.6   `sort -t'<tab>' +3 name.list`

9.7   `grep '<tab>San Jose<tab>[^<tab>]*<tab>[^<tab>]*$' name.list`

9.8   `awk -F'<tab>' '$4 ~ /[Cc][Aa]/' name.list`

9.9   `grep '<tab>CA<tab>[^<tab>]*$' name.list ¦`
       `sort -t'<tab> +5 ¦ awk -F'<tab>' '{ print $1`
       `print $2`
       `print $3`
       `print $4 ",", $5, $6`
       `print "\n\n" }'`

9.10   `sed 's/ \([^<tab> ]*\)<tab>/<tab>\1<tab>/' name.list > new.name.list`

9.11   `awk -F'<tab>' '{print $6 "<tab>" $1 "<tab>" $2 "<tab>" $3 \`
       `"<tab>" $4" <tab>" $5}' name.list > /tmp/name.tmp`
       `mv /tmp/name.tmp name.list`

Chapter 10

10.1   `cut -d, -f1 phone.list.tab`

10.2   `ls -l ¦ sed 1d ¦ cut -c2-4,15-23,55-`

10.3   `who ¦ cut -c12-24`

10.4   `sed 's/^.*<tab>//' name.list ¦ sort ¦ uniq -c`

10.5   `who ¦ awk '{print $1}' ¦ sort ¦ uniq`

10.6   `sed 's/<tab>/<tab>Phone  /' phone.list ¦ sort > /tmp/phone.list.s`
        `sed 's/<tab>/<tab>Office Number  /' room.list ¦ sort > /tmp/room.list.s`
        `join -t'<tab>' /tmp/phone.list.s /tmp/room.list.s`

10.7   `who ¦ cut -d' ' -f1 ¦ sed 's/$/:/' > /tmp/temp`
        `sort /etc/passwd ¦`
        `join -t: -o 2.1 1.7 - /tmp/temp`

10.8   `tr -d ',-' < phone.list ¦ tr '<space> <tab>' '[~*]'`

Chapter 11

11.1   `There are 1 command line arguments`
        `The file executed is show.args`

```
        The first argument is arg1 arg2
        The second argument is
        The third argument is
        All of the arguments are arg1 arg2
```

11.2   `grep "\$$1" price.list`

11.3   The arguments are passed to `grep` individually, which is the same
problem that occurred earlier in the chapter when $1 was left
unquoted and the user sent in `'Adams, Tom'`.

Chapter 12

12.1   The period is a regular expression character that matches "any
single character." As a result, `phone.list` matches the word
`phone`, followed by any single character, followed by the word `list`.

12.2a   The word `help` spelled with any combination of upper- and
lowercase characters.

12.2b   Any string that begins with an uppercase alphabetic character.

12.2c   The word `stop`, `exit`, or `quit`.

12.2d   The exact string that is listed, only. Remember that a $ is a regular
expression character, not a shell file-matching metacharacter.

12.3
```
    case $# in
        0) echo "Usage: $0 pattern"
           echo "pattern is what to look for in the phone list" ;;
        1) grep "$1" phone.list ;;
        2) grep "$*" phone.list ;;
        *) echo "Too many patterns - only one allowed" ;;
    esac
```

12.4
```
    case $# in
        0) echo "Usage: $0 pattern"
           echo "pattern is what to look for in the phone list" ;;
        1) case $1 in
           -a) cat phone.list ;;
            *) grep "$1" phone.list ;;
           esac ;;
        *) echo "Too many patterns - only one allowed" ;;
    esac
```

12.5
```
    case $# in
        0) echo "Usage: $0 pattern"
```

```
        echo "pattern is what to look for in the phone list"  ;;
    1) grep "$1" phone.list ;;
    2) case $1 in
        -f) grep ", $2<tab>" phone.list ;;
        -p) grep "<tab>$2" phone.list ;;
        *)  echo "Too many patterns -- only one allowed" ;;
        esac ;;
    *) echo "Too many patterns - only one allowed" ;;
esac
```

Chapter 13

13.1   `ls` fails when an incorrect option is chosen, when the directory can't be read, or when the file can't be found.

13.2
```
case $# in
    0) echo "Usage $0: login-name" ;;
    1) $ cat ison.2
       ( who | grep "^$1" > /dev/null &&
       echo "$1 is currently logged on" ) ||
       ( echo "$1 is not logged in"; exit 1 )
    *) echo "Too many arguments -- only one allowed" ;;
esac
```

13.3
```
( who | grep "<space>.*$1.*<space>" > /dev/null &&
echo "$1 is currently in use" ) ||
echo "$1 is not in use"
```

13.4
```
case $# in
    0) echo "Usage: $0 filename" ;;
    1) ( ls | grep "^$1$" && cat "$1" ) ||
       echo "$1 not found" ;;
    *) echo "Too many arguments -- only one allowed" ;;
esac
```

13.5
```
case $# in
    0) echo "Usage: $0 pattern"
       echo "pattern is what to look for in the phone list"
       exit 1 ;;
    1) grep "$1" phone.list ||
       ( echo "$1 not found in list" ; exit 1 ) ;;
    *) echo "Too many patterns - only one allowed"
       exit 1 ;;
esac
exit 0
```

Chapter 14

14.1
```
phonefile=/usr/data/phone.list
case $# in
    0) echo "Usage: $0 pattern"
       echo "pattern is what to look for in the phone list" ;;
    1) grep "$1" phone.list 2> /dev/null ||
       grep "$1" $phonefile 2> /dev/null ||
       echo "$1 not found in list" ;;
    *) echo "Too many patterns - only one allowed" ;;
esac
```

14.2
```
echo "Pattern to search for: \c"
read pattern
grep "$pattern" $phonefile ||
echo "$pattern not found in the list"
```

14.3
```
echo "Which phone list to use:
echo "1) One in current directory"
echo "2) System phone list"
echo "\nEnter choice: \c"
read choice
case $choice in
    1) phonefile=phone.list ;;
    2) phonefile=/usr/data/phone.list ;;
    *) echo "Invalid entry"
       exit 1 ;;
esac
echo "Pattern to search for: \c"
read pattern
grep "$pattern" $phonefile ||
echo "$pattern not found in the list"
```

14.4
```
case $# in
    0) echo "Usage: $0 filename" ;;
    1) ( test -f "$1" && cat "$1" ) ||
       echo "$1 not found" ;;
    *) echo "Too many arguments -- only one allowed" ;;
esac
```

14.5
```
case $# in
    0) echo "Usage: $0 filename" ;;
    1) test -r "$1" ||
       ( echo "You don't have read permission on $1"; exit 1 )
       ( ls | grep "^$1$" && cat "$1" ) ||
```

```
            echo "$1 not found" ;;
       *) echo "Too many arguments -- only one allowed" ;;
    esac
```

14.6a `test -r "$file" -a -x "$file"`

14.6b `test -z "$response" -o "$response" = QUIT -o "$response" = quit`

14.7
```
phonefile=phone.list
test -f "$phonefile" ¦¦ phonefile="/usr/data/phone.list"
case $# in
    0) echo "Pattern to search for: \c"
       read pattern
       grep "$pattern" $phonefile ¦¦
       echo "$pattern not found in the list" ;;
    1) grep "$1" $phonefile ¦¦ echo "$1 not found in list" ;;
    *) echo "Too many patterns - only one allowed" ;;
esac
```

14.8a `expr "$str" : "[A-Z][a-z][a-z]*"`

14.8b `expr "$str" : "[A-Za-z][A-Za-z][A-Za-z][A-Za-z]"`

14.8c `expr "$str" : "[Yy][Ee][Ss]"`

Chapter 15

15.1
```
phonefile=/usr/data/phone.list
 case $# in
     0) echo "Usage: $0 pattern"
        echo "pattern is what to look for in the phone list" ;;
     1) grep "$1" $phonefile ¦¦ echo "$1 not found in list" ;;
     *) count=1
        for pattern in $*
        do
            echo "\nThe result of search number $count\n"
            grep "$pattern" $phonefile ¦¦
            echo "$pattern not found in list"
            count=`expr $count + 1`
        done ;;
esac
```

15.2
```
phonefile=/usr/data/phone.list
case $# in
    2) sed "s/$1/$2/" $phonefile > /tmp/chg.tmp
```

```
              mv /tmp/chg.tmp $phonefile ;;
       *) echo "Usage: $0 old new"
          echo "$0 substitutes new for old in the phone list" ;;
     esac
```

15.3
```
     total=0
     for nbr in $*
     do
         total=`expr $total + $nbr`
     done
     echo "Total is $total"
```

Chapter 16

16.1
```
     phonefile=/usr/data/phone.list
     echo "\nFirst Name: \c"
     read fname
     echo "Last Name: \c"
     read lname
     echo  "$fname $lname's phone extension: \c"
     read phnbr
     case $phnbr in
         [0-9]-[0-9][0-9][0-9][0-9]) ;; # empty case option
         *) echo "Phone extension's format is #-####"
            exit 1 ;;
     esac
     echo "$lname, $fname <tab> $phnbr" >> $phonefile
```

16.2
```
     looptest=y
     phonefile=/usr/data/phone.list
     while [ $looptest = y ]
     do
         echo "Pattern to find: \c"
         read pattern ¦¦ exit
         test -z "$pattern" && exit  # terminate if no pattern
         grep "$pattern" $phonefile ¦¦
             echo "$pattern not found in the list"
         echo "\nEnter another pattern? (y/n) \c"
         read answer
         case $answer in
             [Yy]*) looptest=y ;;
```

```
                [Nn]*) looptest=n ;;
          esac
     done

16.3   outerlooptest=y    # controls the list selection loop
       while [ $outerlooptest = y ]
       do
             looptest=y          # controls the data entry loop
             echo "\n1) Search Business List"
             echo "2) Search Personal List"
             echo "\nQ) Quit"
             echo "\nEnter choice: \c"
             read choice
             case $choice in
                 1) phonefile=/usr/data/bus.list ;;
                 2) phonefile=/usr/data/phone.list ;;
                 [Qq]) outerlooptest=n
                       looptest=n;;
                 *) echo "Invalid entry"
                    looptest=n ;;   # skips data entry loop
             esac
             while [ $looptest = y ]
             do
                 echo "\nFirst Name: \c"
                 read fname
                 echo "Last Name: \c"
                 read lname
                 echo  "$fname $lname's phone extension: \c"
                 read phnbr
                 echo "$lname, $fname<tab>$phnbr" >> $phonefile
                 echo "\nEnter another name? (y/n) \c"
                 read answer
                 case $answer in
                     [Yy]*) looptest=y ;;
                     [Nn]*) looptest=n ;;
                 esac
             done
       done


16.4   phonefile=/usr/data/phone.list
       while true
       do
             echo "\nFirst Name (stop to exit): \c"
```

```
        read fname
        case $fname in
            [Ss][Tt][Oo][Pp]) exit ;;
        esac
        echo "Last Name: \c"
        read lname
        echo  "$fname $lname's phone extension: \c"
            read phnbr
        correct=n
        until [ $correct = y ]
        do
            echo "\n1. $fname"
            echo "2. $lname"
            echo "3. $phnbr"
            echo "\nIs this correct? (y/n) \c"
            read answer
            case $answer in
                [Yy]*) correct=y ;;   # loop exit condition
                *) echo "\nNumber to correct (0 to stop): \c"
                   read nbr
                   case $nbr in
                       0) correct=y ;;   # terminate corrections
                       1) echo "First Name: \c"
                          read fname ;;
                       2) echo "Last Name: \c"
                          read lname ;;
                       3) echo "Phone Number: \c"
                          read phnbr ;;
                       *) echo "Invalid entry" ;;
                   esac ;;
            esac
        done  # end of until loop
        echo "$lname, $fname<tab>$phnbr" >> $phonefile
    done  # end of while loop

16.5   phonefile=/usr/data/phone.list
       until false
       do
           echo "\nFirst Name (stop to exit): \c"
           read fname
           case $fname in
               [Ss][Tt][Oo][Pp]) exit ;;
           esac
```

```
    echo "Last Name: \c"
    read lname
    echo  "$fname $lname's phone extension: \c"
    read phnbr
    correct=n
    while [ $correct = n ]
    do
        echo "\n1. $fname"
        echo "2. $lname"
        echo "3. $phnbr"
        echo "\nIs this correct? (y/n) \c"
        read answer
        case $answer in
            [Yy]*) correct=y ;;  # loop exit condition
            *) echo "\nNumber to correct: \c"
               read nbr
               case $nbr in
                   1) echo "First Name: \c"
                      read fname ;;
                   2) echo "Last Name: \c"
                      read lname ;;
                   3) echo "Phone Number: \c"
                      read phnbr ;;
               esac ;;
        esac
    done  # end of while loop
    echo "$lname, $fname<tab>$phnbr" >> $phonefile
done  # end of until loop
```

16.6
```
phonefile=/usr/data/phone.list
while true
do
    echo "\nFirst Name (stop to exit): \c"
    read fname
    case $fname in
        [Ss][Tt][Oo][Pp]) break ;;
    esac
    echo "Last Name (XX to restart): \c"
    read lname
    case $lname in
        XX) continue ;;  # skip rest of loop
    esac
    echo "$fname $lname's phone extension: (XX to restart) \\c"
```

```
                read phnbr
                case $phnbr in
                    XX) continue ;; # skip rest of loop
                esac
                correct=n
                until false
                do
                    echo "\n1. $fname"
                    echo "2. $lname"
                    echo "3. $phnbr"
                    echo "\nIs this correct? (y/n) \c"
                    read answer
                    case $answer in
                        [Yy]*) break ;;  # loop exit condition
                        *) echo "\nNumber to correct: \c"
                           read nbr
                           case $nbr in
                               1) echo "First Name: \c"
                                  read fname ;;
                               2) echo "Last Name: \c"
                                  read lname ;;
                               3) echo "Phone Number: \c"
                                  read phnbr ;;
                           esac ;;
                    esac
            done  # end of until loop
            echo "$lname, $fname<tab>$phnbr" >> $phonefile
        done  # end of while loop
```

16.7
```
    phonefile=/usr/data/phone.list
    while true
    do
        echo "\nFirst Name (stop to exit): \c"
        read fname
        case $fname in
            [Ss][Tt][Oo][Pp]) break ;;
        esac
        echo "Last Name: (XX to restart) \c"
        read lname
        case $lname in
            XX) continue ;;  # skip rest of loop
        esac
        echo "$fname $lname's phone extension: (XX to restart) \c"
```

```
    read phnbr
    case $phnbr in
        XX) continue ;; # skip rest of loop
    esac
    if egrep "$lname, $fname<tab>¦<tab>$phnbr" $phonefile
    then
        echo "\nDuplicates were found in the list"
        while true
        do
            echo "\nCancel this entry? (y/n) \c"
            read answer
            case "$answer" in
                [Yy]*) continue 2 ;;
                [Nn]*) break ;;
                *) echo "\nEnter Y or N only\n" ;;
            esac
        done
    fi
    correct=n
    until [ $correct = y ]
    do
        echo "\n1. $fname"
        echo "2. $lname"
        echo "3. $phnbr"
        echo "\nIs this correct? (y/n) \c"
        read answer
        case $answer in
            [Yy]*) correct=y ;;  # loop exit condition
            [Nn]*) echo "\nNumber to correct: \c"
                    read nbr
                    case $nbr in
                        1) echo "First Name: \c"
                            read fname ;;
                        2) echo "Last Name: \c"
                            read lname ;;
                        3) echo "Phone Number: \c"
                            read phnbr ;;
                    esac ;;
                *) echo "Invalid entry" ;;
        esac
    done  # end of until loop
    echo "$lname, $fname<tab>$phnbr" >> $phonefile
done  # end of while loop
```

16.8
```
phonefile=/usr/data/phone.list
while true
do
    echo "\nFirst Name (stop to exit): \c"
    read fname
    case $fname in
        [Ss][Tt][Oo][Pp]) break ;;
    esac
    echo "Last Name (XX to restart): \c"
    read lname
    case $lname in
        XX) continue ;;  # skip rest of loop
    esac
    if grep "$lname, $fname<tab>" $phonefile
    then
        echo "\n$fname $lname is already in the list"
        echo "\nCancel this entry? (y/n) \c"
        read answer
        case $answer in
            [Yy]*) continue ;;
        esac
    fi
    echo "$fname $lname's phone extension: (XX to restart) \c"
    read phnbr
    case $phnbr in
        XX) continue ;; # skip rest of loop
    esac
    if grep "<tab> $phnbr" $phonefile
    then
        echo "\n$phnbr is already in the list"
        echo "\nCancel this entry? (y/n) \c"
        read answer
        case $answer in
            [Yy]*) continue ;;
        esac
    fi
    correct=n
    until [ $correct = y ]
    do
        echo "\n1. $fname"
        echo "2. $lname"
        echo "3. $phnbr"
        echo "\nIs this correct? (y/n) \c"
```

```
        read answer
        case $answer in
            [Yy]*) correct=y ;;  # loop exit condition
            *) echo "\nNumber to correct: \c"
                read nbr
                case $nbr in
                    1) echo "First Name: \c"
                        read fname ;;
                    2) echo "Last Name: \c"
                        read lname ;;
                    3) echo "Phone Number: \c"
                        read phnbr ;;
                esac ;;
        esac
    done  # end of until loop
    echo "$lname, $fname<tab>$phnbr" >> $phonefile
done  # end of while loop
```

16.9
```
phonefile=/usr/data/phone.list
while true
do
    echo "\nFirst Name (stop to exit): \c"
    read fname
    case $fname in
        [Ss][Tt][Oo][Pp]) break ;;
    esac
    echo "Last Name (XX to restart): \c"
    read lname
    case $lname in
        XX) continue ;;  # skip rest of loop
    esac
    echo "$fname $lname's phone extension: (XX to restart) \c"
    read phnbr
    case $phnbr in
        XX) continue ;; # skip rest of loop
    esac
    correct=n
    until [ $correct = y ]
    do
        #
        # Duplicate checking here to do it all in one place
        #
        if egrep "$lname, $fname<tab>¦<tab>$phnbr" $phonefile
```

```
                then
                        echo "\nDuplicates were found in the list"
                        while true
                        do
                                echo "\nCancel this entry? (y/n) \c"
                                read answer
                                case "$answer" in
                                    [Yy]*) continue 2 ;;
                                    [Nn]*) break ;;
                                    *) echo "\nEnter Y or N only\n" ;;
                                esac
                        done
                fi
                echo "\n1. $fname"
                echo "2. $lname"
                echo "3. $phnbr"
                echo "\nIs this correct? (y/n) \c"
                read answer
                case $answer in
                    [Yy]*) correct=y ;;   # loop exit condition
                    *) echo "\nNumber to correct: \c"
                        read nbr
                        case $nbr in
                            1) echo "First Name: \c"
                               read fname ;;
                            2) echo "Last Name: \c"
                               read lname ;;
                            3) echo "Phone Number: \c"
                               read phnbr ;;
                        esac ;;
                esac
            done # end of until loop
            echo "$lname, $fname<tab>$phnbr" >> $phonefile
        done # end of while loop

16.10   phonefile=/usr/data/phone.list
        while true
        do
                echo "\nFirst Name (stop to exit, ? to show list): \c"
                read fname
                case $fname in
                    [Ss][Tt][Oo][Pp]) break ;;
                    \?) pg $phonefile
```

```
                continued ;;
esac
echo "Last Name (XX to restart, ? to show list): \c"
read lname
case $lname in
    XX) continue ;;  # skip rest of loop
    \?) pg $phonefile
        continue ;;
esac
echo "(XX to restart, ? to show list)"
echo "$fname $lname's phone extension: \c"
read phnbr
case $phnbr in
    XX) continue ;; # skip rest of loop
    \?) pg $phonefile
        continue ;;
esac
if egrep "$lname, $fname<tab>¦<tab>$phnbr" $phonefile
then
    echo "\nDuplicates were found in the list"
    while true
    do
        echo "\nCancel this entry? (y/n) \c"
        read answer
        case "$answer" in
            [Yy]*) continue 2 ;;
            [Nn]*) break ;;
            *) echo "\nEnter Y or N only\n" ;;
        esac
    done
fi
correct=n
until [ $correct = y ]
do
    echo "\n1. $fname"
    echo "2. $lname"
    echo "3. $phnbr"
    echo "\nIs this correct? (y/n) \c"
    read answer
    case $answer in
        [Yy]*) correct=y ;;  # loop exit condition
        [Nn]*) echo "\nNumber to correct: \c"
```

```
                        read nbr
                        case $nbr in
                            1) echo "First Name: \c"
                                read fname ;;
                            2) echo "Last Name: \c"
                                read lname ;;
                            3) echo "Phone Number: \c"
                                read phnbr ;;
                        esac ;;
                    *) echo "Invalid entry" ;;
            esac
        done  # end of until loop
        echo "$lname, $fname<tab>$phnbr" >> $phonefile
    done  # end of while loop
```

Chapter 17

17.1
```
phonefile=/usr/data/phone.list
looptest=y
while [ "$looptest" = y ]
do
    echo "\n\n"
    echo "A - Add a name to the Phone List"
    echo "L - Look for 1 pattern in Phone List"
    echo "M - Look for many patterns in the Phone List"
    echo "P - Print the Phone List"
    echo "S - Sort the Phone List by Last Name"
    echo "\nQ - Quit the menu"
    echo "\nEnter choice and press <RETURN> \c"
    read choice ¦¦ continue
    case $choice in
        [Aa]) phone.add ;;
        [Pp]) cat $phonefile ;;
        [Ll]) echo "\nSearch pattern? \c"
            read pattern ¦¦ continue
            phone.find "$pattern" ;;
        [Mm]) while true
            do
                echo "\nSearch pattern? (stop to quit) \c"
                read pattern ¦¦ continue
                case $pattern in
```

```
                       [Ss][Tt][Oo][Pp]) break ;;
                          *) phone.find "$pattern" ;;
                    esac
                done ;;
          [Ss]) sort $phonefile -o $phonefile ;;
          [Qq]) looptest=n ;;
          *) echo "Invalid Entry" ;;
      esac
  done
```

17.2
```
phonefile=/usr/data/phone.list
looptest=y
while [ "$looptest" = y ]
do
    echo "\n\n"
    echo "A - Add a name to the Phone List"
    echo "L - Look for 1 pattern in Phone List"
    echo "M - Look for many patterns in the Phone List"
    echo "P - Print the Phone List"
    echo "S - Sort the Phone List by Last Name"
    echo "\nQ - Quit the menu"
    echo "\nEnter choice and press <RETURN> \c"
    read choice || continue
    case $choice in
        [Aa]) phone.add ;;
        [Pp]) echo "\nPrint phone list to\n"
            echo "1) Terminal"
            echo "2) Printer"
            echo "3) A file"
            echo "\nEnter choice: \c"
            read choice || exit
            case $choice in
                1) cat $phonefile > /dev/tty ;;
                2) lp $phonefile ;;
                3) echo "\nName of file: \c"
                   read fname || continue
                   if [ -z "$fname" ]
                   then
                       echo "Empty filenames are not allowed"
                   elif [ -f $fname ]
                   then
                       echo "$fname exists; overwrite? (y/n) \c"
```

```
                                read answer ¦¦ continue
                                case $answer in
                                    [Yy]) cat $phonefile > $fname ;;
                                    [Nn]) echo "Phone list not written"
                                            continue ;;
                                    *) echo "Invalid input"
                                      continue ;;
                                esac
                            else
                                cat $phonefile > $fname
                            fi ;;
                    esac ;;  # ends the [Pp] option
            [Ll]) echo "\nSearch pattern? \c"
                  read pattern
                  phone.find "$pattern" ;;
            [Mm]) while true
                  do
                        echo "\nSearch pattern? (Enter stop to quit) \c"
                        read pattern ¦¦ continue
                        case $pattern in
                            [Ss][Tt][Oo][Pp]) break ;;
                            *) phone.find "$pattern" ;;
                        esac
                  done ;;
            [Ss]) sort $phonefile -o $phonefile ;;
            [Qq]) looptest=n ;;
            *) echo "Invalid Entry" ;;
        esac
    done

17.3  echo "\n\n"
      echo "P - Personal phone list"
      echo "C - Company phone list"
      echo "\nEnter letter of phone list to use: \c"
      read list ¦¦ exit
      case "$list" in
          [Pp]) PHONEFILE=/usr/data/$LOGNAME.list ;;
          [Cc]) PHONEFILE=/usr/data/phone.list ;;
          *) echo "Invalid entry"  # assign a default?
             exit ;;
      esac
      export PHONEFILE
      phonefile=$PHONEFILE
```

```
      looptest=y
      while [ "$looptest" = y ]
      do
           echo "\n\n"
           echo "A - Add a name to the Phone List"
           echo "L - Look for information in Phone List"
           echo "P - Print the Phone List"
           echo "S - Sort the Phone List by Last Name"
           echo "\nQ - Quit the menu"
           echo "\nEnter letter of choice and press <RETURN> \c"
           read choice ¦¦ continue
           case $choice in
               [Aa]) phone.add ;;
               [Pp]) cat $phonefile ;;
               [Ll]) echo "\nSearch pattern? \c"
                     read pattern  ¦¦ continue
                     phone.find "$pattern" ;;
               [Ss]) sort $phonefile -o $phonefile ;;
               [Qq]) looptest=n ;;
               *) echo "Invalid Entry" ;;
           esac
      done
```

17.4
```
      trap 'rm $tempfile 2> /dev/null;
      echo "Original phone list restored" ;
      exit ' 1 2 3 15
      phonefile=${PHONEFILE:-/usr/data/phone.list}
      cp $phonefile /tmp/phoneno.$$   # use PID to make unique
      tempfile=/tmp/phoneno.$$
      while true
      do

           read fname
           case $fname in
               [Ss][Tt][Oo][Pp]) break ;;
           esac
           echo "Last Name: (XX to restart) \c"
           read lname
           case $lname in
               XX) continue ;;  # skip rest of loop
           esac
           echo "$fname $lname's phone extension: (XX to restart) \c"
           read phnbr
```

```
    case $phnbr in
        XX) continue ;; # skip rest of loop
    esac
    if egrep "$lname, $fname tab ¦ tab $phnbr" $tempfile
    then
        echo "\nDuplicates were found in the list"
        while true
        do
            echo "\nCancel this entry? (y/n) \c"
            read answer
            case "$answer" in
                [Yy]*) continue 2 ;;
                [Nn]*) break ;;
                *) echo "\nEnter Y or N only\n" ;;
            esac
        done
    fi
    correct=n
    until [ $correct = y ]
    do
        echo "\n1. $fname"
        echo "2. $lname"
        echo "3. $phnbr"
        echo "\nIs this correct? (y/n) \c"
        read answer
        case $answer in
            [Yy]*) correct=y ;;  # loop exit condition
            *) echo "\nNumber to correct: \c"
                read nbr
                case $nbr in
                    1) echo "First Name: \c"
                        read fname ;;
                    2) echo "Last Name: \c"
                        read lname ;;
                    3) echo "Phone Number: \c"
                        read phnbr ;;
                esac ;;
        esac
    done  # end of until loop
    echo "$lname, $fname tab $phnbr" >> $tempfile
done  # end of while loop
```

Chapter 18

18.1   ```
mkscript ()
{
    vi $1
    chmod +x $1
}
```

18.2    ```
ncd ()
{
case "$#" in
    0) cd ;;
    *) if grep "$1" $HOME/dirs > /tmp/dir.$$
       then
            amt=`wc -l /tmp/dir.$$ ¦ awk '{ print $1 }'
            if [ $amt = 1 ]
            then
                cd `cat /tmp/dir.$$`
            else
                pr -n -t /tmp/dir.$$
                echo "\nDirectory wanted: \c"
                read answer
                cd `sed -n "$answer p" /tmp/dir.$$`
            fi
       else
            cd
       fi
       rm /tmp/dir.$$ ;;
esac
}
```

18.3   ```
mkdir ()
{
case $# in
    0) /bin/mkdir ;;   # prints usage message
    *) if /bin/mkdir $1
       then
            (cd $1; pwd) >> $HOME/dirs
       fi ;;
esac
}
```
```

18.4
```
rmdir()
{
    case $# in
        0) /bin/rmdir ;;   # prints usage message
        *) pathname=`(cd $1; pwd)` # cd done in sub-shell
           if /bin/rmdir $pathname
           then
               grep -v "\^$pathname$" $HOME/dirs > /tmp/$$
               mv /tmp/$$ $HOME/dirs
           fi ;;
    esac
}
```

18.5
```
IFS=' ()-'
```

18.6
```
monthdays="31 28 31 30 31 30 31 31 30 31 30 31"
echo "Enter date: \c"
read date
oldifs="$IFS"
IFS='/'
set $date
IFS="$oldifs"
month=$1
day=$2
year=$3
if [ "$month" -lt 1 -o "$month" -gt 12 ]
then
    echo "Invalid month number"
    exit 1
fi
maxdate=`echo $monthdays | cut -d' ' -f$month`
if expr "$year" % 4 = 0 \& "$month" = 2 > /dev/null
then
    maxdate=29
fi
if [ "$day" -lt 0 -o "$day" -gt "$maxdate" ]
then
    echo "Invalid day number"
    exit 1
fi
echo "Valid date"
```

Index